THE MAKING OF IRAQ, 1900–1963

SUNY Series in the Social and Economic History
of the Middle East
Donald Quataert, editor

Issa Khalaf, *Politics in Palestine: Arab Factionalism and Social Disintegration, 1939–1948*.

Rifa'at 'Ali Abou-El-Haj, *Formation of the Modern State: The Ottoman Empire, Sixteenth to Eighteenth Centuries*.

M. Fuad Köprülü, *The Origins of the Ottoman Empire*, translated and edited by Gary Leiser.

Guilian Denoeux, *Urban Unrest in the Middle East: A Comparative Study of Informal Networks in Egypt, Iran, and Lebanon*.

Zachary Lockman, ed., *Workers and Working Classes in the Middle East: Struggles, Histories, Historiographies*.

Palmira Brummett, *Ottoman Seapower and Levantine Diplomacy in the Age of Discovery*.

Ali Abdullatif Ahmida, *The Making of Modern Libya: State Formation, Colonization, and Resistance, 1830–1932*.

Ayşe Buğra, *State and Business in Modern Turkey: A Comparative Study*.

Donald Quataert, ed., *Manufacturing in the Ottoman Empire and Turkey, 1500–1950*.

Hala Fattah, *The Politics of Regional Trade in Iraq, Arabia, and the Gulf, 1745–1900*.

Samira Haj, *The Making of Iraq, 1900–1963: Capital, Power, and Ideology*.

THE MAKING OF IRAQ, 1900–1963
Capital, Power, and Ideology

Samira Haj

State University of New York Press

Published by
State University of New York Press, Albany

© 1997 State University of New York

Printed in the United States of America

For information, address State University of New York Press, State University Plaza, Albany, NY 12246

Production by Christine Lynch
Marketing by Nancy Farrell

Library of Congress Cataloging-in-Publication Data

Haj, Samira, 1945–
    The making of Iraq, 1900–1963 : capital, power, and ideology / Samira Haj.
        p.   cm. — (SUNY series in the social and economic history of the Middle East)
    Includes bibliographical references and index.
    ISBN 0-7914-3241-6 (alk. paper). — ISBN 0-7914-3242-4 (pbk. : alk. paper)
    1. Iraq—History—1921–1958.   2. Iraq—History—1958–   I. Title. II. Series.
DS79.H27   1997
956.704—dc20   96-7618
                                                                       CIP

10 9 8 7 6 5 4 3 2 1

For Nadeem

CONTENTS

Acknowledgments   viii

Introduction   1

PART I. THE FORMATION OF CAPITAL

Chapter 1.   Land, Power, and Commercialization   9
Chapter 2.   Peasant Economy and Merchant Capital   41
Chapter 3.   Industry   55

PART II. THE NATION-STATE: POLITICS AND REVOLUTION

Chapter 4.   State Crisis and the End of the Oligarchic Monarchy   79
Chapter 5.   The Revolution of 1958 and Its Defeat   111

PART III. EPILOGUE

Epilogue   143

Notes   151

Glossary   197

Bibliography   199

Index   211

ACKNOWLEDGMENTS

Funding for the initial research on this project was provided by a Social Science Research Council pre-doctoral grant in 1983.

In preparing the book itself, I have benefitted enormously from the close criticism and advice of both Johanna Brenner and Norman Finkelstein. I must also express my thanks to Peter Gran, Talal Asad, Henry Bernstein, Charles Hirschkind, Afaf Marsot, Robert Brenner, and Perry Anderson for commenting on several parts of this book. A special thanks to Taysier al-Shoosh for his help with the Arabic transliteration.

INTRODUCTION

This book explores several major developmental problems as they manifested themselves in Iraq. The case of Iraq, with its amazingly rapid growth and sharp contradictions, underscores problems which exist, albeit in an attenuated form, in most developing countries. Because of the world's desperate dependence on oil, the oil-producing countries have become the object of close scholarly attention. However, these countries are largely seen as sui generis, and their social structures are analyzed only as a function of their oil-producing capacities. A study of modern Iraq indicates that agrarianism, not oil, is the crucial variable. Just as with Egypt and India, the researcher who seeks to explain what happened in Iraq is forced to examine the situation at the village level.

The 1958 revolution and the pervasive violence of Iraqi national politics are best understood by the land tenure system and the social conflicts attending the evolution of new agrarian structures. In particular, the collapse of the old economy in Ottoman "Iraq" following its partial integration into the world market in the latter part of the nineteenth century resulted in two strikingly different agrarian structures: commercial non-capitalist (*hacienda* or *izba*-type) agriculture on the one hand, and nascent capitalist agriculture on the other. This development precipitated two fundamental social conflicts. First, there was a conflict between rising capitalist interests (in both agriculture and industry) and the tribal oligarchy. Second, there was the conflict between the tribal oligarchy and its peasant sharecroppers. Within this context, oil revenues were spent largely to promote the interests of the tribal oligarchy and to reproduce non-capitalist agriculture, rather than on social and economic prosperity for the majority of the population. These dynamics hastened the arrival of the 1958 national revolution.

The book focuses on the formation of capital in modern Iraq and addresses four theoretical categories. First, I examine the nature of domestic economic change in the context of global capitalism. Using Iraq as an example, I look at the limitations of both modernization theory and its critique by dependency/world system theorists. The notion that social and economic changes in modern Middle Eastern societies like Iraq are Western-induced is shared by proponents of modernization theory (Khadduri, Issawi, Marr) and opposition scholars alike (Salman Hasan, al-Jawahiri). By ascribing social

1

change to external forces, both modernization theory and its critics overlook the importance of internal forces in shaping domestic development. I show, for example, that the dominant socioeconomic structures, embedded in a tribal society and economy, blocked the development of a modern capitalist sector in agriculture in lower Iraq. The emergence of huge tribal estates was not an inevitable result of the encroachment of the capitalist world market, and commercialization of agriculture did not itself create this agrarian system. Rather, this system was the outcome of the successful effort by powerful tribal groups to take advantage of the new political (Ottoman centralization) and market opportunities (international market) opened to them in the late nineteenth and early twentieth centuries. Once in place, the new class of tribal landowners pursued income-maximizing policies which undermined long-term agricultural growth.

Second, I address the history of elites and the "modern"/"traditional" dichotomy by questioning the role in national revolutions of individuals and elites on the one hand, and the struggle between "modern" and "traditional" forces on the other. Majid Khadduri has explained the 1958 revolution as the result of an ideological "conflict between an elite adhering to the old patterns—status quo—and the new, who press for modernization and progress, [which] is perhaps inevitable and often takes a violent form."[1] In a more recent work, Phebe Marr recapitulates, in a more subtle way, the modern/traditional dichotomy by arguing that the events of 1958 were the result of the contradictions created by the "unraveling" of traditional society under the impact of modernization and the emergence of a new generation of educated urbanites who were "shaped by intellectual and cultural influences different from and inimical to those of the established regime."[2] I do not deny that elite groups and individuals figure prominently in history. History, however, is not about isolated individuals or elites acting in a vacuum. To understand historical change in any society, an analysis of the particular institutions and social forces at work is needed. The reason is quite simply that individuals and collective agents act within the constraints and possibilities of specific historical structures.

Third, I address the nature of the conflict in the contemporary period. It is often argued that ethnic, religious, and tribal divisions rooted in a primordial culture are the source of conflict in the modern Middle East, and Iraq in particular. Again, without wanting to diminish the importance of religious, ethnic, tribal, and other factors in shaping modern conflicts, I suggest that these divisions must be considered within specific historical contexts.

For instance, a "primordial" Sunni-Shi'i schism is often invoked in analysis of sociopolitical struggle in contemporary Iraq. To explain the turbulence of the post-revolutionary period, Uriel Dann, for example, argues that the Shi'a of southern Iraq "form a distinctive unit . . . by virtue of their sectarianism. . . . Beset by a persecution complex," the Shi³a came to be "the revolutionaries of Iraq par excellence . . . in rebellion against the state, its stability and its progress." Social conflicts are understood as irrational acts of violence rooted in a primordial culture. Dann insists that "violence is part of the political scene in Iraq. . . . It is an undercurrent which pervades the vast substrata of the people outside the sphere of power politics. Hundreds of souls can be easily mobilized on the flimsiest pretext. They constitute a permanently restive element ready to break into riots which more than once in recent years resulted in butchery."³ A different (secularized) variation of this Shi³a-Sunni schism is to be found in Samir al-Khalil's more recent work, *Republic of Fear*, in which he argues that "Iraqi Sunnism and Shi³ism do not find their raison d'etre in doctrinal difference. Both creeds always have been held together in a political embrace rooted in distrust and originating the question: Who am I?"⁴

The division between tribe, town, and state is another popular theme in the historiography. Writers across the political spectrum assume that tribes are intrinsically autonomous and inherently hostile social entities set apart from, and in opposition to, the urban population and the modern state. Although this notion has been rebutted as theoretically unviable and historically invalid, it is still being reproduced in the field.⁵ Robert Fernea still holds the view that pre-1958 Iraqi society was locked in a "hegemonic struggle between "tribalism" and "statism": "a struggle between two different ways of thinking and acting, the ways of the state vs. those of the tribe."⁶ Even the distinguished historian Hanna Batatu relies on this essentialist notion when analyzing the tribes. His narrative posits the dichotomy between "tribes" and sedentaries as essential to understanding the diversity of Iraqi history. He repeatedly draws on the notion of an inherent contradiction between tribal and urban lives to explain the history of modern Iraq.

These interpretations ignore the fact that specific historical reasons account for social conflicts and, more importantly, that the reasons change as historical conditions change. The fluidity in the meaning and the contestation over the title of "shaykh" among the tribes of southern Iraq, for instance, are not necessarily a characteristic feature of the "tribes" because they are "tribes," as Fernea suggests, but are more likely an expression of the sociopolitical changes and the ways in which these tribes reacted to and interacted with these changes. Similarly, violent social conflicts in modern Iraq, as elsewhere, resulted from the development of modern structures, not from the inherent qualities of certain social groups. Essentially, such conflicts (religious, tribal, or ethnic) can be rationally explained.

Fourth, I explore the issue of oil and social change. I take issue with the mainstream thesis which argues that lack of capital in developing nations accounts for their backwardness. I argue that oil (or the revenues from it) is not, in and of itself, a developmental force. It is true that the revenues from oil increased Iraq's chances to break from the plight of many underdeveloped nations, yet capital was not enough to initiate development. The barriers to social and economic progress encompassed much more than the "shortage of capital," "inefficient planning," and/or "lack of know-how," as modernization economists largely contend. The fundamental problem was structural, namely, the prevailing class and power structures then present in Iraq. Instead of transforming the economy and sustaining widespread prosperity, oil capital in the pre-revolutionary period was used to perpetuate social and economic inequalities.

There is one work on modern Iraq that represents a break with the descriptive and cursory political historiography dominant in the field—Hanna Batatu's *The Old Social Classes and the Revolutionary Movement in Iraq*. A mine of information, this work presents a brilliant reconstruction of modern Iraqi history. Batatu is one of the first scholars to introduce class analysis to the study of Iraqi history, challenge traditional historiography by shifting attention from the urban elites to a much more diverse countryside, and integrate town and countryside in the making of the modern Iraqi nation. His work is a formidable challenge to any new scholar attempting to work on modern Iraq. But as Roger Owen rightly says, "we can [either] be dazzled by it" or "we can try and use it as a basis for asking new questions" and proposing new interpretations.

It is in this spirit that I would like to address some of the problems in Batatu's work. His book, as he admits, expresses a tension between two contrary "intellectual traditions" that influenced his framework of analysis: the Marxian-Weberian on the one hand, and British empiricism on the other. Batatu's empiricist tendencies for the accumulation of a "large amounts of facts" that "pointed frequently in many different directions" often hinders his ability to uncover overarching insights. This fetish for facts has two more drawbacks implicit in the inability to generalize and systematize his findings: (1) the unintentional stressing of the "unique" in Iraqi historical experience, and (2) the absence of a theory regarding the formation of Iraqi capital and its relations to global capitalism.

My book provides a different perspective on the development of modern structures in Iraq by situating its development within the theories of the transition to capitalism and the scholarly debates over the nature of nationalism and the nation-state.

To establish the origins of the 1958 revolution, the first three chapters examine the socioeconomic transformation of Iraq following its integration into the world market. The first two chapters discuss how the disintegration of a regional transit-trade economy under the pressure of integration triggered the development of commercial agriculture and the rise of new class relations in the countryside. The agrarian structures that evolved, however, were uneven. In the tribal regions, a highly exploitative, non-capitalist agrarian system based on large estates and shaikh-tenant relations evolved. In the areas where a peasant economy prevailed, an intensive and a relatively more efficient form of agriculture emerged. Questioning both the neo-Marxist and modernization theories of development, I attribute these changes to the particular sociopolitical conditions that influenced the development of different property relations in these regions rather than to the international market or the adoption of Western technology. The predominantly communal structures in the tribal regions favored the rise of an inefficient *iqta'* system, while the prevalence of smaller holdings and free-holds encouraged the emergence of a more intensified agriculture sponsored by an entrepreneurial class of merchant-mullak. The rise of non-capitalist agriculture on the one hand, and nascent capitalist agriculture on the other, was not without its class contradictions. The huge tribal estates, detrimental to agricultural production and the expansion of capitalist agriculture, created a conflict of interest not only between the tribal shaykhs and peasant-sharecroppers, but also between the landed class and rising capitalist interests. These contradictions and class antagonism became much more pronounced in the 1950s when oil revenues were diverted to agricultural projects that by and large benefited the oligarchic landed class, instead of modernizing agriculture and improving the conditions of the peasantry.

Besides arresting agricultural development, the tribal agrarian system came to be a formidable barrier to industrial development. The third chapter, which looks at the formation of industry, discusses the frustrated hopes of industrial capital to accumulate within the context of lax protectionist policies, a backward agricultural system dominated by *iqta'*, and an absent consumer home market. Special attention is paid to the oil industry and the impact of oil revenues on the economy in general, and rising class antagonism in particular. The issue raised by mainstream development theories of whether or not oil is in of itself a developmental force is questioned in the context of this discussion.

In contrast to the first three chapters, which concentrate on the formation of capital, the last two focus on the politics of the nation-state and nationalism. In chapter 4, I discuss how the process of state-building under British mandate rule in the 1920s and 1930s laid the foundation for the development of indigenous interests and social classes that became aligned with the new state and the preservation of the Iraqi nation, as it created the conditions for those who opposed it. From 1940 to 1958, the national question and national independence became the fundamental political rallying point for the various oppositional groups, despite their ideological diversity and conflicting class interests. The chapter also describes how the government, which was dominated by the monarchy and the landed oligarchy allied to the British, used both co-optation and repression to contain political opposition and rising social unrest. But once the state apparatus became less dependent on the domestic economy for its revenues (due to the dramatic rise in oil revenues after 1952), the government became more tyrannical and less responsive to the demands of the opposition, leading to the further radicalization of the opposition.

Tracing the socioeconomic and political developments in Iraq in the first half of the twentieth century, I discuss in the first four chapters how the 1958 revolution was inevitable. In the final chapter, I analyze why the revolution was bound to fail. Whereas the 1958 revolution succeeded in destroying the old political structures, it was too fragile to carry out the second stage of the revolution. Once the oligarchic monarchy was overthrown, the unified national front that brought about the revolution collapsed. Its breakdown can be attributed to conflicting class interests which were articulated over two primary issues. First, unification with the United Arab Republic, which split the coalition between those who supported pan-Arabism and those who supported Iraqi nationalism, and second, land reform, which led to the split between the nationalists backed by the revolutionary government and the Iraqi communists.

The book (particularly the last two chapters) implicitly incorporates a critique of mainstream Western nationalist thought. In the epilogue, I elaborate and make explicit this critique. The epilogue also takes into account the more recent theoretical writings on the nation-state and post-colonial nationalism to complement, revise, and expand on some of the ideas discussed in the text.

I

THE FORMATION OF CAPITAL

1

Land, Power, and Commercialization

Agrarian studies on modern Iraq generally fall into one of two economically oriented schools of thought: "modernization" or "political economy." The modernization school attributes social and economic change to the expansion of European capitalism through trade and capital investment. For example, prominent economist Charles Issawi sees Iraq as experiencing dramatic changes as trade with Europe increased following the establishment of steam navigation between Bombay and Basra in the 1860s and especially since the opening of the Suez Canal in the 1870s. Iraq, Issawi writes, "gained immensely as its sea route to western Europe was reduced from 14,000 miles to under 10,000, putting it within reach of the steamers of that time. Its sea trade multiplied several fold, and its agriculture was profoundly affected by the expanding demand for its produce."[1] According to Issawi, trade expansion also helped precipitate the rationalization of the economy and the secularization of society.[2]

This linear prognosis of modernization theory has been questioned by Marxist writers who assert that the impact of the world market on local economies was regressive, not progressive in nature. The Iraqi economist Muhammad Salman Hasan argues that European penetration, rather than carrying out its capitalist mission, generated a precapitalist *iqta*[3] system founded on the exploitation of the peasantry by a feudal class composed of tribal chieftains, town merchants, and government officials.[3] Samir Amin, while agreeing with Salman Hasan et al.[4] that the expansion of the capitalist market did not lead to capitalist development in Iraq, argues that the underdevelopment resulted from an "unequal exchange" between the advanced capitalist countries and the periphery. The outcome of increased trade with Europe was the growth, not of a feudal class, but a dependent agrarian bourgeoisie who produced for the world market by using precapitalist methods of production and abundant cheap labor.[5]

Although their criticisms of the modernization theory are well taken, Marxist writers like Salman Hasan and Samir Amin do not question modernization's fundamental notion—that the expansion of the European capitalist market determined the course of economic development in Iraq. In ascribing societal changes to external forces, these writers, like the

9

modernization theorists, fail to take into account the internal social and economic conditions that shape historical development. As Robert Brenner, the most notable critic of this line of Marxist writing, argues, by displacing class relations from the center of their analysis, these writers end up constructing an alternative theory of capitalist development that is "the mirror image of the 'progressist' thesis they wish to surpass."[6]

No one can deny that the advent of the international market signaled a new era in the evolution of rural social and economic structures in Iraq. Whereas transit trade, the dominant form of trade in the premodern era, provided little incentive for the development of commercial agriculture, Iraq's incorporation into the world capitalist market encouraged the development of market-oriented agriculture. However, unlike the early modern European agricultural system where a radical change in the social division of labor (including proleterianization) and intensification of production through greater use of technology led to a decline in labor force, under *iqta'* capital achieved control over production without undertaking its immediate organization and/or dispossessing the direct producers. Thus, paternalistic kinship relations and traditional forms of production, such as extensive expansion of land and sharecropping, continued to be practiced. However, to attribute the rise of the *iqta'* system and shaykh-sharecropper relation of exploitation to commercialization itself is, in my view, questionable. In explaining *iqta'*, one must consider instead the particular social, political, and economic conditions that discouraged the development of the productive forces in agriculture despite the increasing opportunities offered by international trade. As I argue in this chapter, the emergence of commercial *iqta'* lies in the constitution of power structures and the particular character of property relations among the tribal communities.

Moreover, as I will demonstrate in chapter 2, the similar sets of circumstances produced by commercialization did not precipitate the same type of agrarian system throughout modern Iraq. While *iqta'* was typical among the tribal communities in the south and the Kurdish north; a more intensive and a relatively more efficient agrarian system emerged among the settled peasant communities. Instead of a class of a shaykhly lords under *iqta'*, an entrepreneurial class of merchants and city mullak managed to establish control and improve productivity by modernizing production. These incongruous developments in agriculture, however, cannot be elucidated by the market forces alone. As I will illustrate, it was the different histories of these regions, with their different social, economic, and political circumstances, that shaped the character of agrarian development in Iraq.

THE CASE OF *IQTA*^ɔ IN LOWER IRAQ

Even though *iqta*ɔ was distinctive of the tribal communities in both the south and the Kurdish north, the discussion of *iqta*ɔ will be limited to the fertile irrigated zone of lower Iraq, the natural locus for agricultural expansion and where the most inimical *iqta*ɔ relations prevailed. While the northern region, including Kurdistan, will not be thoroughly addressed, I will occasionally refer to the similarities between the two regions. In considering the case of the irrigated zone of lower Iraq, I will argue in particular that the nature of property relations was crucial to the rise of the *iqta*ɔ system once the old structures, including the economy of transit trade, began to disintegrate under pressure from the world market and Ottoman centralization policies.

It is important to note in this context that the system of *iqta*ɔ, which emerged in the late nineteenth and early twentieth centuries, should not be confused with the military landholdings of the same name predominant in medieval Islamic societies. Modern *iqta*ɔ is very different in structure, content, and form.[7] Hence, I will make qualified use of the term *iqta*ɔ since it is neither "feudal" nor "medieval" but a modern agrarian system characterized by patriarchal mechanisms of labor control, such as sharecropping and tenancy on large estates, similar to the hacienda common in Latin America and the ^ʕ*izba* in Egypt.

Even though *iqta*ɔ was organized around production for a capitalist market, it did not achieve the productivity levels of advanced capitalist agriculture. Based on large estates of 100,000 to over 400,000 dunums and exploitative shaykh-sharecropper relations, this system increased output largely through extensive expansion of agricultural lands and by intensification of peasant exploitation. It was the social relations of production characteristic of this agrarian system and not "unequal exchange" or an "export-oriented economy" that blocked economic growth in agriculture. While it is true that the initial expansion of production for the market under this system moved agriculture beyond subsistence, by the 1940s agricultural production in the most fertile regions of lower Iraq had begun to deteriorate dramatically. Productivity declined and exploitation intensified, leading to the massive flight of peasants into towns.

I will discuss the development of commercial *iqta*ɔ in lower Iraq over three historical periods. The Ottoman period of 1850–1914 marked the first stage in the transition as the old social structures began to disintegrate under pressure of modernization and commercialization.[8] The paramount tribal houses, taking advantage of new political and economic opportunities promoted by Ottoman centralization policies and the international market, began to establish their control over the land. In the second period, British colonial rule from 1914 to 1932, the intensification of a market economy combined with colonial state policies accelerated the process of consolidation of huge estates and shaykh-sharecropping relations of exploitation in the countryside. Finally, the monarchic-oligarchic regime from 1932 until the national revolution of 1958 represented the last chapter in the history of *iqta*³. In this period, the tribal landowning class, braced by the monarchic state (and Britain), engaged in income-maximizing policies that were detrimental to long-term agricultural (as well as national) growth, leading to an agrarian crisis that culminated in the national revolution of 1958. Each of these periods will be traced and analyzed individually. The final section will look at the impact of the new class relations on agriculture. The decline in productivity and the consequent intensification of exploitation in the third period in particular will be the subject of discussion in this section.

THE OTTOMAN PERIOD: 1860–1914

During this time, the advent of the world capitalist market, together with the centralization policies pursued by the Ottoman Porte, triggered a transformation in the organization of the tribes occupying lower Mesopotamia. As the foundation of the old social formation eroded, the economic activities emphasized by the tribes shifted from a predominantly pastoralist economy (animal husbandry) to one based on agriculture (cultivation). At the same time, the leading tribal houses adopted a land-grabbing strategy as they came to recognize that the new regime of power was to be founded on the direct control of the land and agricultural production. Within this context, the dominant relations of production on the land began to evolve from relatively autonomous production units based on households to cultivation by dependents who were tenants and sharecroppers.

Before examining these transformations, it is important first to describe the conditions of the tribes in lower Mesopotamia on the eve of these changes. It is crucial to note in this context that contrary to the common view in mainstream historiography, the overall communal corporate character of the tribes in the premodern era was in no way incompatable with social differentiation, structures of domination, and inequality. These social inequalities were the product of differences in power and wealth, which were closely related to the varied economic activities of the tribes and the value of their economic contribution to the larger economy. This is significant because the power and wealth of the paramount tribes placed them in the best possible position to establish control over agricultural land once the older economies, based on pastoralism and long-distance trade, began to disintegrate.

Power, Tribes, and Regional Markets

Lower Mesopotamia, which includes the modern districts of Kut and ᶜAmarah on the Tigris river and the districts of Diwaniyah, Hillah, and the Muntafiq in central and lower Euphrates, was occupied mainly by tribes. Along the Euphrates, from the Qurnah district to Samawah and along the Gharraf river, lived the Muntafiq confederation, whose leading units were the Ajwad, the Bani Malik, and the Bani Saᶜid, and whose minor offshoots included the Bani Huchaim in Samawa, the Bani Khaiqan, and the Bani Asad. From Samawa to Musayyib along the Middle Euphrates lived a series of confederations and tribes, including the Zubaid confederation, which consisted of the Albu Sultan and Jhaysh tribes and occupied the area between the Tigris and the Euphrates; the Bani Hasan tribe, which settled west of Hindiyah between Karbala and Kufah; the Fatlah tribe, which lived on the Mushkhab and Shamiyah rivers and along Hindiyah; the Khazaʾil confederation, whose many tribes and clans were scattered between Kifl, Diwaniyah, and Samawah; and the ᶜAqrah and ᶜAfij tribes on Shatt-al-Dhagharah. Along the Tigris, from Qurnah to Baghdad, lived the Kaʾab under the shaykh of Muhammarah, the Albu Muhammed, the Rabiʾah, the Bani Lam, Shammar Tuqah, and part of the Zubaid confederation.[9]

It is important to stress that in the pre-world market era, the social and economic organization of the tribes was not "primordial" or "communal" as is often postulated in the literature. The historiography on the tribes of Iraq, for example, characterizes the "tribes" (reads also "bedouins" and "ashaʾir") as having a distinctive socioeconomic nature that sets them apart, from and in opposition to, settled communities and any form of organized authority. This essentialist notion of the inherent oppositional relations between "tribes"/towns, on the one hand, and "tribes"/central government on the other, was first championed by the French Orientalists. In French colonial historiography, North African societies were viewed in terms of a state/tribe dichotomy doubled by an ethnic division between Arabs and Berbers. This "Kabyle Myth," which introduced the notion of two distinctive and intrinsically opposed social structures—the tribal, egalitarian "Noble Savages" (Berbers), on the one hand, and the despotic "Ignoble Arabs," on the other—was first elaborated by the French following the colonization of Algeria.[10] The myth of Berber democracy versus Arab despotism was further refined by the French after they established a "protectorate" over Morocco. The noble savage vs. the ignoble Arab was then complemented by yet another construct—namely, the distinction between *balad al-Siba* (Tribal Independent Land) and *balad al-Makhzan* (centralized autocratic government).[11] In the work of contemporary anthropologists, the contradictions between these two societies were no longer just political, but also legal and religious. In contrast to the towns,

which upheld the shari³a and Orthodox Islam, the Berbers were said to up-
hold their customary tribal laws and local saints.¹²

This elaborate body of knowledge on the tribes helped to inform and
refine how the French exercised their power in these colonies. Through the
systematic adoption of different institutional practices directed at the tribes
and town populations, the French regulated and normalized these distinctions
between "tribes" and towns.¹³

British colonial historiography on the tribes was similar to the French.
Following British rising interest in the region in the nineteenth century, the
tribes of Mesopotamia became the subject as well as the object of knowledge.
British officers, administrators, and travelers learned the languages common
to the region (Arabic, Kurdish, and Persian) and their various dialects, then
journeyed through the unknown terrain of Mesopotamia, Kurdistan, Persia,
and Syria, exploring and collecting data on the tribal communities inhabiting
these regions. This body of knowledge recorded the names of the tribes and
recounted their lives, economies, social and customary practices, as well as
their "religions." Similar to French historiography, the discourse on the tribes
reproduced the same essentialist categories and notions that emphasized the
inherently oppositional character of the tribes to towns and central government. The tribes were described as a community that "recognize(d) no common civil authority," were feared and despised by the townspeople who
considered them both "a constant potential source of dissension and grave
public insecurity," and "uncivilized."¹⁴ Moreover, while the tribes were considered to be respectful of law, it was *"their own law only, not Turkish (Shari³a
Islamic law) or European law."*¹⁵ Reproducing the "noble savage" notion, the
tribes were represented in these texts as "egalitarian" and their political constitution as the "purest example of democracy."¹⁶ At the same time, "highway
robbery" and/or "plunder" were perceived as "not only permitted, but held to
be a right," and so was "warfare." These features were viewed as intrinsic to
the tribespeople's "love of liberty" and their aversion of "authority."¹⁷

As in the French case, this apprised body of knowledge on the tribes was
used to assist the British to occupy the region during the First World War and
inform the mandate regime that followed on the particular technologies and
effective tactics of power to discipline and normalize the tribes as "tribes."

The essentialist notion of state/tribe dichotomy (and its twin notion of
ethnic division of Kurd vs. Arab and Sunni vs. Shi³a), however, did not end
with the termination of British colonial regime. Postcolonial and nationalist
writings, though they articulated anticolonial sentiments and disputed some
of the postulations and assumptions made by European orientalist writers,
continued nonetheless to reproduce the same categories and notions regarding
the tribes.

For example, although the Iraqi historian Ghassan al-ʿAtiyyah makes a distinction between the nomadic and settled tribes, he still maintains that as "tribes" they shared communal, egalitarian, and warlike characteristics. Thus, in describing them, he says:

> War rather than peace was their natural condition. Each tribe had its own rules and norms which regulated a life based on the principle of equality of kinsfolk and of the supremacy of communal interest. . . . Traditionally, the beduin tribes had defied all kinds of authority and had constituted a permanent menace to the settled tribes and fringe towns.[18]

The same was true of the settled tribes who, according to ʿAtiyyah, "were continuously shadowed by the possibility of war with neighboring tribes or with central authorities . . . [who] continued to think of themselves as warriors. . . ."[19]

Even Hanna Batatu, whose writing marks a radical departure from "traditional" orientalist historiography, can sometimes be faulted for relying on this essentialist notion when analyzing the "tribes." His interpretation posits the dichotomy between "tribes" and sedentaries as central to understanding the diversity of Iraqi society. Thus, it is the distinctive autonomous socioeconomic character of the "tribes" which, in his view, has produced the urban-rural antagonism in modern Iraq:

> A wide schism . . . divided the main cities from the tribal country. Urban and tribal Arabs, except for the dwellers of towns situated deep in the tribal domain or tribespeople living in the neighborhood of cities, belonged to two almost separate worlds. The links between them were primarily economic. But even on this regard their relationship could scarcely be said to have been vigorous. . . . No less was the social and psychological distance between the urban and tribal Arabs.

Batatu uncritically adopts the anthropologist version of the "Kabyle Myth" when he writes:

> In many ways they were very different from each other. The life of urban Arabs was on the whole governed by Islamic and Ottoman laws, that of the tribal Arabs by Islamically tinged ancient Arab customs . . . Many of the townsmen had, in the words of the nineteenth century Iraqi historian, 'become habituated to submission and servility.' The freer of the tribespeople were by contrast irrepressible. As far as they were concerned, government was a matter of contempt.[20]

In common with mainstream Iraqi writers, Batatu repeatedly draws on this notion of an intrinsic contradiction between tribal and urban lives to explain the history of modern Iraq:

> In brief, through the whole period of 1921–1939 the monarch, centered in Baghdad, had in effect a social meaning diametrically opposed to that of the tribal shaykhs, the then still virtual rulers of much of the countryside. The shaykh represented the principle of the fragmented or multiple community (many tribes), the monarch the ideal of an integral community (one Iraqi people, one Arab nation). Or to express the relationship differently, the shaykh was the defender of the divisive tribal *urf* (customary law), the monarch the exponent of the unifying national law.[21]

The essentialist representation of "tribes" as intrinsically distinct, separate, and hostile social entities is distortive in two ways. First, it is misleading to view the twentieth-century Iraqi tribes as autonomous given their interaction throughout history with other social groups that led to their transformation and incorporation within the larger social, economic, and political structures.[22] A better approach is to contextualize the tribes—by identifying and analyzing the larger historical formation within which these tribes reproduced themselves as "tribes." Second, precisely because of their constant formation and transformation through history, tribes as units have considerable internal variations as well as differing external relations with other social groups. Therefore, there is no fixed, characteristic socioeconomic structure of tribes simply because they are "tribes."[23]

A different reading of the historical account that contextualizes rather than decontextualizes the tribes gives us a very different chronicle of the tribes in lower Iraq. Rather than the autonomous, self-contained tribes, the revised version reveals:

a.   that the tribal economy was unmistakably an integral part of the wider economy, as it was organized not only around herding, but also around agriculture and regional trade;

b.   the interdependence of towns and tribes for subsistence; and consequently

c.   a considerable variation in the internal organization, as well as in the external relations of the tribes to sedentaries and to central power.

The Arab tribes (nomadic, semi-nomadic, and settled), far from being "primordial," were highly specialized with a substantial disparity in their economic and social organization. Correspondingly, the structure and the character of the tribes differed from tribe to tribe depending on their economic and internal social organizations, as well as their location within the larger power structure.

For example, the social organization of production varied considerably between the pastoral tribes of ᶜAnaizah and Shammar and the mostly settled tribes of Bani Lam, Rabiᵓah, Fatlah, and others who occupied the middle region and engaged in agricultural production. To the nomadic mobile tribes, like Shammar Jarbah of Shammar, Ruwalah of ᶜAnaizah, and al-Saᵓdun of Muntafiq, land was solely used for grazing since it was herds and not land that constituted their principal means of production and wealth. The social organization of the tribe was therefore developed around constant movement with their herds in search of water and pasture. Among these tribes, livestock was individually owned while land was collectively appropriated, whereby animals belonged to households and pastures to all.

The tribes or clans known as *ahl al-ibl* (the people of the camel) specialized primarily in the herding of camels, even though their property in livestock comprised a mixed variety of flocks such as sheep, goats, and—the highly valued commodity—horses.[24] They took care of their camels but hired others to look after their flocks. It is important to note that this division of labor was not so much the product of tribal culture; the so-called "aristocratic" camel herders disdaining herding sheep because of the incompatibility of herding different kinds of livestock together.[25] The terrain, the knowledge, and the skills involved in breeding these various flocks were markedly different from one another. Whereas camelherding involved extensive movement throughout the year, sheepherding, for example, required much less seasonal movement and an abundance of water and grass.[26]

By comparison, the organization of production was quite different among the semi-settled groups that combined herding with agriculture. The semi-settled, like ᶜashair al-Ajwad of al-Muntafiq,[27] were mostly sheepherders *(ahl al-shawiyah)* who had permanent residence and engaged in seasonal cultivation. Because they combined herding with agriculture, their internal organization, including specialization and division of labor, tended to differ from one tribal unit to another. Within ᶜashair al-Ajwad some like ᶜashair al-Budur (known as the aristocracy of Arab al-shawiyah) engaged mostly in sheepherding. Others, like ᶜashair al-ᵓAbudah of Shatrah, were largely cultivators who specialized in the production of barley, wheat, and rice. The al-Uzairij, al-Ghazi, and other tribes combined herding with agriculture and divided their labor according to clans, whereby some members specialized in herding and others in cultivation.[28] Among the semi-settled, as among the nomadic tribes, livestock was individually owned by households. But land tenure was different. Property relations combined collective *lazma* with individual *lazma,* which gave hereditary tenancy to cultivating tribes.[29] To a degree, the differing property relations in each case depended on the economic activities of the individual tribes, clans, or households.

Variations in economic occupation and property relations were not uncommon among the settled tribes. The *ahl al-mi⁾dan* of Banu Asad were settled marsh-dwellers who had little agriculture and lived mostly by breeding buffaloes, fishing, and weaving reed mats. In fact, many of their component clans worked as seasonal laborers, either as sharecroppers on the estates of other cultivating tribes such as those in al-Gharraf, or as day laborers in the blooming date-packing industry in the south.[30] One thus assumes that the internal organization of these marsh-dwellers would be markedly different from some of ⁽ashair al-Majarrah[31] of Suq al-shuyukh or those of Shamiyah Hindiyah,[32] the settled tribes who specialized in the production of the labor-intensive crops—rice and dates. Kinship cohesion (⁽*asabiyyah), for instance, was recognized to be much stronger among the rice-producing tribes than among the migrating tribespeople or the semi-settled tribes.

Most significantly, however, since agriculture was the basic means of production for the cultivating tribes, land was central to their internal organization. Therefore, the nature of land tenure and property relations was noticeably different among the settled tribes than it was among the pastoral or semi-pastoral tribes.

Property Relations: Legal and Cutomary

Property structures prior to the 1860s were in most cases governed not by one but two different relations, the legal and the customary. The Ottoman legal system considered all lands state land while the customary deemed land the possession of the tribe by virtue of occupancy and cultivation. The practical tradition that acknowledged occupancy rights on the one hand, and the Ottoman state that formally denied it on the other, set the premise upon which inter- and intra-tribal struggle over the control of land unfolded once the old social structures began to disintegrate.

The Ottoman state, as owner of all public lands, practiced the *iltizam* (tax farming) system in lower Mesopotamia.[33] Under this system, tribal land was farmed out in the form of estates *(muqata⁾at)* to the tribal shaykhs or chieftains for an agreed amount of tax paid to the Ottoman rulers in money or in kind.[34] The practice of tax farming, however, was not steady or fixed since it varied from one region to another depending on the practiced policy of Ottoman rulers of the period.

As tax farmers, the shaykhs secured some control over the land. In general, the land was farmed out to the members of the prominent tribes and tended to devolve by inheritance along with the shaykhdom *(imirat)*. Some of these contracts *(shartnamas)* were renewed yearly or every other year (mid-Euphrates), while others were extended for a few years at a time (the Muntafiq). As tax farmers, the heads of these households received a share of the tribal holdings, and one fifth to one third of the total produce, depending on the internal organization and economic activities of the component tribes. This share covered the state tax, as well as other private and public expenses of the shaykhs.[35] Most of the ruling tribes received an income in the form of rent from their cultivators for their *tal'iyah* land—rich tracts of nontaxable land granted to them under tribal customary practice to defray their public expenses.[36] Further down the tribal hierarchy, similar privileges were granted to leading shaykhs of individual tribes.

In contrast to the legal rights, which considered all lands state land, customary rights were much more complicated and diverse. The holding rights whose nature depended on the internal organization and the economic activities of the component tribes, clans, and households, tended to vary from tribe to tribe and from one region to another.[37] Besides the acknowledged communal rights in land occupancy (communal *lazma*), there were other types of holdings that gave the cultivating tribes strong rights of possession.[38] Other than the individual lazma that provided hereditary tenancy, the strongest rights, often considered closest to freehold *(mulk)*, were *naqshah* and *ta'abah*.[39]

Naqshah was closely identified with the labor-intensive cultivation of rice. It gave the tribespeople, in addition to the common usufructuary rights, the right to inherit and to alienate the land either through sale or gift. One feature differentiating naqshah from mulk was that under tribal customary law, transfer to persons outside the tribe was forbidden. This was not the case with ta'abah. Enforceable by law, the rights of the ta'abah included the right to inherit and the right to alienate to anyone, as long as other holders or mullak during the period of contract also consented. Ta'abah was closely associated with another labor-intensive crop, dates. In addition to his labor, the ta'ab contributed the trees he planted and nurtured over the duration of a contract, which might run from ten to thirty years. By planting trees, he became entitled to own a portion of the land which, along with the trees, constituted a form of freehold under shari'a law.[40]

The reasons for such variations in landholding practices remains open to speculation: the size of the estates, variation in farming systems for rice, cereals, and dates, tribal organization, and the variegated policies of Ottoman rulers are generally given as explanations. Although all are important, none of these explanatory factors alone is satisfactory. For example, the tendency toward strong property rights was clear in rice holdings of Suq al-shuyukh and Shamiyah, but in ͨAmarah, the heartland of rice production, customary rights were weak.

Variations in property relations appear to be the product of a combination of factors including labor processes according to crops, the size of the estates, the internal cohesion of the tribe, and Ottoman land policy. What is most relevant here, however, is that the course toward consolidation by the leading tribes seems to have been closely related to the presence or absence of strong property rights among the tribespeople. We see this differentiated progress in land consolidation much more clearly when the old economies began to disintegrate under pressure from the world capitalist market and Ottoman centralization policies.

There was a multitude of customary holding rights among the tribes. Some of these rights gave the cultivators strong holding rights including, in addition to the right to occupy, the right of usufruct, the right to inherit, the right to alienate, and the right of pre-emption. Besides individual lazma, which gave hereditary tenancy, there were also stronger types, such as naqshah, tal ͗iyah, and ta ͗abah rights, with variations in names and content. The latter were the closest in form to freehold, or mulk.[41]

Due to the variations in the internal social organization of the tribes, it is rather difficult to establish a fixed, characteristic structure to the tribes by virtue of being "tribes." Even though kinship was the organizing principle among the different tribes, nomadic and settled alike, the internal organization tended to differ from tribe to tribe according to their variant economic activities, differing property relations, and their location within the regional power structure. Moreover, these variations in the internal organization of the tribes conditioned, in different ways, the social, economic, and political relations of the tribes to towns and vice versa. As the next section will demonstrate, tribes and towns were not just dependent on each other for subsistence; their relations were also not always the same, since different tribes related in different ways to towns and to the wider economy.

Tribes, Towns, and the Regional Market

The Arab tribes of lower Iraq were able to survive and reproduce themselves as tribes only within the context of the Ottoman Empire at large and the region in particular. Since the "tribal population" was integrated into the political economy of the region and the empire in very different ways, the conditions of their reproduction also varied greatly.

Of the estimated one and a quarter million people in the province of Ottoman Iraq in the nineteenth century, nearly two thirds were tribes who lived by herding, transit trade, and cultivation. The other third were towns-people who lived off handicraft industries, internal or regional market trading, and administration.[42] Considering the different economic activities of the tribes, their contribution to the larger economy varied accordingly. Thus, pastoralism was complementary to long-distance trade as the nomadic tribes, camel-herders in particular, were the ones to supply the animals (camels and horses) needed for transportation (not to mention their military use).[43] The production of semi-settled and settled tribes was as crucial to the overall economy, since they supplied the townspeople with grain and dates, meat and dairy products, raw wool, and animal skin. These items that were essential for local consumption as well as for exchange. The tribes depended on the towns for their survival as well. Towns provided them with various necessities, such as manufactured goods, weapons, and tools, as well as luxury items like tea and coffee.

The local historiography confirms that tribes not only produced for the market but were extensively involved in the marketing and trading operations themselves. As a matter of fact, the regional market played an important role in unifying town and countryside as land- and sea-trading houses brought tribal-merchants and town-merchants together in the pursuit of running a greater and safer regional market.[44]

Local historiography confirms that many of the important shaykhs of tribes in lower Mesopotamia and the Gulf were powerful merchants involved in trade of one form or another. For example, the prominent tribes of al-Muhammarah were well-known merchants who specialized in the grain and horse trade. The same was true of the shaykhly houses of Shammar and ʿAnaizah, whose pure-bred Arabian horses found markets as far away as India.[45] The early leading house of the Muntafiq confederation, al-Shabib, was known to finance resident traders and tribal merchants with loans and credits to purchase and sell goods.[46] Al-Saʾdun, the leading house in the nineteenth century, continued this tradition of financing trade to Najd and Basra along with other regional and town merchants.[47] Similarly, the formidable merchants of al-Zuhayr of Najd, whose trade center was the town of Zubayr, were well known for their extensive trading transactions in Mesopotamia as well as in the Gulf.[48]

Like al-Zuhayr, many of these powerful tribes had their own market towns, which they often controlled and administered. Dayr al-Zur was a depot for trade and the exchange of goods between tribespeople and townspeople. The tribes of ʿAnaizah and Shammar invariably used this town as their center to sell Arabian horses, camels, and sheep, and to buy manufactured goods, including tools, weaponry, and luxury goods. Among the most famous tribal market towns was Suq al-shuyukh, the trading center of the Muntafiq tribes. Named after their shaykhs, Suq al-shuyukh was central to the trade between Najd, Basra, and Baghdad.[49] It was the center of exchange of manu-factured goods such as ʿaba, agricultural products and byproducts like barley, rice, animal skins, ghee, and raw wool, as well as camels and horses.[50]

Close town-tribal relations were not limited to trading partnerships and transactions. For example, many of the wealthy tribal shaykhs owned and invested in urban property. We are told that the town of Basra, with its surrounding agricultural groves, was owned mostly by the tribal shaykhs of Kuwait, Najd, and al-Muntafiq.[51] In a similar fashion, the town merchants did not refrain from investing in profitable livestock, especially sheep, which they entrusted to local tribespeople.[52]

Tribal-town relations could not always have been those of opposition. In fact, the varying relations between town and the countryside were essential to the social reproduction of the tribes. As to how these relations contributed to the formation and transformation of the internal structures of a tribe is something that must be empirically established in each case. Different tribes related in different ways to the towns and the wider economy which, in turn, contributed to the variations in the tribe's internal structures. Therefore, it is not just that tribes and towns were dependent on each other; rather, that the social, political, and eco-nomic relations between tribes and towns were not always the same.

It is equally invalid to assume that tribes, by virtue of being "tribes," are necessarily hostile to central power. As there is no inherent contradiction between tribes and settled population, there is also no such contradiction between tribes and state. This view, of course, does not deny that opposition existed. It simply states that when there is opposition, one must identify its nature by placing it within its specific historical context. To put these con-flicts in historical perspective, it is therefore necessary to identify the forces behind, the reasons for, and the outcome of the specific conflicts.

Commercialization and Ottoman Centralization Policies: 1860–1914

As the foundation of the old social formation eroded, the economic actitivities emphasized by the tribes shifted from a predominantly pastoralist economy (animal husbandry) to one based on agriculture (cultivation). At the same time, the leading tribal houses adopted a land-grabbing strategy as they came to recognize that the new regime was to be founded on the control of land and agricultural production. It is within this context that the dominant relations of production on the land began to evolve from relatively autonomous production units, based on households, to cultivation by dependent tenants and sharecroppers.

In the first half of the nineteenth century, seaborne trade with Europe was insignificant; but from the 1850s the rapid expansion of the international market began to undermine regional markets.[53] As the value of transit trade declined, many of the nomadic and semi-nomadic tribes which occupied the countryside were willing to take up farming.[54] With the rise in sedentarization, old irrigation canals were reopened, new ones were built, and the Hindiyah dam was constructed, opening large tracts of new land for cultivation.[55] By 1913, over a million of the 1.6 million dunums of agricultural land were estimated to be in the newly sedentarized regions. This expansion in agricultural land naturally led to an increase in production: the output of dates tripled between the 1860s and 1913. The expansion of date production, like that of wheat and barley, occurred largely in response to the demands of the international market, as evidenced by the sharp rise in the export of these items.[56]

With integration into the world market, the primary economic activities of the tribes changed from pastoralism (animal husbandry) to cultivation. Out of the struggle to control land and agricultural production, new class relations evolved, with the dominant tribes emerging as the triumphant agrarian landed class. Ottoman centralization policies during this period proved critical for the consolidation of land in the hands of the dominant tribal households. Despite their original intention to break down leading tribal authority, the Ottomans were forced to retract and improvise methods, besides force, to co-opt the strong tribal houses into the new regime of power. This strategy varied from one district to another and from one tribal confederation to the other, setting in motion an intense three-way conflict between:

1.   central authority and particular tribes;

2.   tribes and their paramount shaykhs; and

3.   prominent shaykhs within the same household or across competing households.

Conflicts between these shaykhs and their tribespeople were distinctive of the areas where strong customary rights to land gave tribespeople the political and economic power to resist the alienation of their lands to their shaykhs, as in Suq al-shuyukh in Muntafiq and in Shamiyah. On the other hand, conflicts within and between prominent tribal houses were characteristic of the areas where the absence of customary rights deprived the cultivating tribespeople of the power to resist land alienation, as in ʿAmarah and

Kut. Finally, conflicts between the state and tribes were more typical in areas, such as the mid-Euphrates, where the particular geopolitical situation, combined with centralization policies, exacerbated an already existing tension between certain tribes and the state over the extraction of surplus.

The question of conflict was obviously more complicated than the binary state/tribe construction presented in the historiography. The relationship between the state and the tribes was not always one of opposition; and when it was oppositional, the conflict was not due to inherent tribal hostility to central power. As in any other social conflict, it was the product of specific historical conditions created by contradictions in interests (political, economic, and social) among the contending social groups.

The Land Code of 1858 and the Emergence of New Agrarian Relations

As part of Ottoman centralization/modernization policy, Ottoman rulers used both coercion and co-optation to try to attain dominance in the region. One strategy was to establish control over the regional market and its trade by establishing control over the major trading centers and routes, thus eradicating the economic base of independent tribal merchants.[57] Another was to try to expand commercial agriculture by encouraging or forcing the sedentarization of the pastoral tribes. A third was to replace proportional rent with a fixed rent to gain tighter control over agriculture and its returns.

The Ottoman state, seeking a more effective system of surplus extraction, attempted to centralize the collection of taxes in all of its provinces.[58] Accordingly, in 1858, the Ottomans introduced the Land Code which officially abolished the iltizam system and introduced direct taxation by salaried state officials *(muhassil)*. As in the case of French absolutism, the Ottoman state needed to limit the power of local ruling elites so as to accrue more taxes from direct producers.[59] However, this strategy proved difficult to implement in the countryside, especially in distant provinces where the state could not impose its power and was forced to either retreat or improvise new measures to ensure control.

This was the case in lower Mesopotamia. The Ottomans, unable to establish direct control, continued to practice tax farming until 1870. Although the Ottomans were able to increase their revenues in this period, the policy of auctioning off land to the highest bidder from among the dominant tribal households precipitated political confusion and economic disarray. In the distant province of Muntafiq, the shaykhdom and the land were auctioned off every three to five years. According to local sources, the Ottomans were able to nearly double their tax revenue from the Muntafiq from 1860–1866 by pitting one member of the ruling household against another.[60] In ʿAmarah, which was closer to the governor of Baghdad, the land was auctioned off yearly, resulting in great hostilities among and within the shaykhly houses. The tactic of having brothers from the Albu Muhammad household bid against each other, and sometimes against their antagonists from Bani Lam, in the annual auctions for the tax-farms, was disastrous. According to a British source, these yearly auctions encouraged the shaykhs "to bid against one another until the amounts bid reached a figure far above the value of the estate," and when the shaykh failed to pay his dues, "his lands and houses would be confiscated, and the estate would be put up afresh to auction and farmed for a still higher and more impossible rent to the rivals of the sup-planted man. Scarcely a year passes without conflict. The waterway of the Tigris would be blocked by the insurgent chiefs of the Albu Muhammed or the Bani Lam . . ."[61]

The political and economic instability in the countryside provided the new *wali* (Ottoman governor) of Baghdad, Midhat Pasha, with the pretext in 1870 to finally implement the Land Code of 1858. Under the new land code, title deeds *(tapu sanad)* were granted to individuals who proved ten years of undisputed occupancy. These deeds were expected to ratify the inalienability of usufructuary practices by giving the cultivating tribespeople legal and heritable rights to the land. The intention of the Land Code was to break down the power of the tax-farmers by registering the land in the name of the actual cultivators so that they could pay more in direct taxes to the state. This policy, as noted earlier, was far too difficult to implement in the region of lower Mesopotamia. As a result, the Ottoman rulers, including Midhat Pasha, found themselves with no other choice but to ally with, and concurrently incorporate, the leading members of the dominant tribal houses into the new state bureaucracy. Members of the leading houses of ʿAnaizah, Shammar, and Muntafiq were endowed with titles of pasha and granted the official positions of *qaʾimmaqam* (sub-governor) and *wali* of their administrative districts.[62] Soon after, these tribal families began to exercise their new official power, not just to extract taxes for the state, but also to promote their new interests in agriculture and thus establish control over the land. The annals of the Muntafiq history bear witness to the Saʾduns' combative drive to register land in their own names and the names of their relatives and associates.[63] As the new governors of Basra, the family of Saʾdun used the Ottoman army to extract their *mulkiya* (a 40 percent rent) from the cultivating tribes and to evict those who refused.[64] Although tapu officially came to an end following a new Ottoman ordinance in 1881, a large proportion of the land had already been legally transferred into the hands of those who had power and wealth.[65]

In the mid-Euphrates, the land of the Khazaʾil tribes, the situation was more complicated thus making it more difficult for Midhat Pasha to implement his plans. Natural alterations in the flow of the Euphrates in the 1850s and the diversion of the river from its original bed in Shatt al-Hindiyah and into the Hindiyah canal diminished the fertility of land, exacerbating the conflict between certain tribal shaykhs and the state over the control of the dwindling surplus.[66] In 1869, Midhat Pasha decided to close the Dhagharah canal as a preliminary step to defeat and disperse the rebellious Khaza'il tribes in the region. The Ottoman governors who followed Midhat Pasha used tapu deeds as instruments to reward or punish local tribes in order to establish control over taxation. The Fatla tribe, for example, was given priority over lands of the Mushkhab in the mid-Euphrates, despite the fact that this land had been already occupied by the Shibil and Ibrahim clans of the Khaza'il confederation. As a result of this policy, the history of this region continued to be characterized by strife between tribes competing over rights way beyond the Ottoman days.[67] As for the district of ʿAmarah on the Tigris, the Ottomans never introduced the tapu system and continued to practice iltizam since these lands were considered part of the saniyah (royal) domains.[68]

The emerging internal tribal struggle—a crucial dimension of class struggle—over the control of agricultural land during the transition was largely influenced by the variations in land-policy practices during the Ottoman period. It was mostly in areas like ʿAmarah and Kut, for instance, where cultivating tribes could not secure any usufructuary rights to the land, that the most unmediated type of iqtaʾ emerged. Political and economic instability, combined with the frequent redistribution of the estates, prevented cultivators from securing any form of tenure. The constant mobility of these cultivating tribes made it virtually impossible for tribespeople to establish customary rights that would have given them the means to resist the authority of their shaykhs as landholders. In contrast, in areas such as Suq al-shuyukh, Shatrah, and Gharraf, different conditions allowed some of these cultivating tribes to establish strong customary rights to the land. This in turn made it possible for them to challenge the authority of new landholders once they tried to establish control over the land.

It is important to note in this context the common practice of sharecropping on these estates. Whether cultivators had strong customary rights as in the Muntafiq, Shamiyah, and Hindiyah, or had none, as in ʿAmarah, all cultivating tribes tilled the land against a share in the crop. The practice continued despite the introduction of commercial agriculture and cash-crop production. However, under the new agrarian system, sharecropping was recast and redefined, representing new relations of exploitation.

During much of the nineteenth century, cultivating tribes and their household units functioned independently of the tax-farmer. Production was primarily for use with a varying share of the crop owed to the landholder. The determination of a cultivator's share appears to have been decided through negotiation between the tax-farmer and the sub-shaykh *(sirqal)*, representing all the cultivating households of the tribe. In contrast, under the *iqta*ʾ system, direct control over land and the production process by the new landholders mandated the development of new methods of control. To ensure direct control, for example, the new system required the individual cultivators to enter into contracts with landlords or their agents who not only assigned the land to be planted, seeds to be sown, and the timetable of ploughing, watering and harvesting, but also were able to keep the cultivator *(fellah)* on the land (in bondage) as long as the latter was indebted to him. Particularly where cultivators had no access to (or rights in) land, they became in practice laborers working not for a fixed wage but for a share of the crop. The share retained by the fellah under the new system varied widely, depending on whether the sharecropper had access to land under customary right or did not. Accordingly, the portion varied from as high as 60 percent, as in Suq al-shuyukh, to less than 30 percent, as in ʿAmarah where the landholder provided the seeds and the tools, and sometimes charged interest on advances he made to cultivators.

This modern system of sharecropping, like *iqta*ʾ itself, was not so clearly defined or consolidated in this period. Although the trajectory for the emergence of *iqta*ʾ was set during the Ottoman period, it was in the following period, under British mandate rule, that the huge tribal estates and shaykh/sharecropper relations were finally implanted. The collapse of the Ottoman Empire after the First World War marked the end of this first phase of the transition and the beginning of the second.

THE BRITISH PERIOD: 1914–1932

Prior to the late nineteenth and early twentieth centuries, British influence in the three Ottoman provinces of Basra, Baghdad, and Mosul was confined to commercial activities and political representation. The advance of Russia and the appearance of Germany as serious imperial contenders in Mesopotamia, Arabia, and the Gulf region in the late nineteenth and early twentieth centuries, however, changed British priorities. It realized that "to safeguard the routes to India," Britain must assume "political control, direct or indirect . . . over territories through which lay actual and potential highways to her indispensible Eastern possession."[69] With the outbreak of the war in 1914, Britain made sure "to secure, once and for all, by the establishment of political control, the Mesopotamia portion of the land route to India."[70]

Following their military occupation, the British in 1921 created Iraq out of the three provinces, installed a monarchy, and set up their own mandate rule over it.

Under the mandate system, commoditization and integration into the world market moved at a much faster pace, hastening the implantation of *iqta*ᵓ relations in lower Iraq. British rule, despite its ambiguities, proved to be crucial to the emergence of the dominant tribes as the triumphant agrarian landed class in lower Iraq. Like the Ottomans before them, the British came to realize that their domination of lower Iraq was not possible without the support of powerful members of the leading tribal houses, who themselves were looking for a political power to safeguard their interest in agriculture.

The consolidation of *iqta*ᵓ relations under British land policy generated different kinds of resistance by tribal members and cultivators. Conflict between tribal shaykhs and their tribespeople characterized those areas where strong customary rights to land allowed direct producers to challenge the claims of the paramount houses effectively, as in the case of Suq al-shuyukh. In these areas, the consolidation of *iqta*ᵓ took longer and was less thorough. On the other hand, conflict between chiefly houses was more typical of those areas like ᶜAmarah and Kut, where direct producers were unable to establish usufructuary rights to the land. It is these areas that witnessed the most thorough implantation of *iqta*ᵓ relations.

Initially, Britain's land tenure program for Iraq was neither clear nor consistent. In fact, in the early years of rule, the colonial administration was seriously divided over the issue of land policy. Colonel Stephen Longrigg, among others, wanted the mandate regime to back small cultivators' claims to land, arguing that they were morally and legally legitimate. Moreover, he and his followers considered that modernization required breaking down the traditional authority of tribal shaykhs, "liberating" small cultivators from the unjust burdens of "servitude." Others, led by Henry Dobbs, contended that the issue was not one of morality or "rights" but of political expediency. They argued that it would be impossible to maintain British rule without the support of powerful members of the leading tribal houses, particularly in the regions designated as "tribal."

The British pursued different strategies in different areas. In the Muntafiq, for example, the British administrative officer, indignant at the claims of tribal landlords, disclosed that the province was undergoing a "miniature French revolution," a "revolt of the serf population against a landed class . . . the aristocrats of the land and the absentee landlords of the worst type."[71] In the initial years of its occupation, the British administration did not attempt to interfere in Suq al-shuyukh and Nasiriyah even on the issue of government tax, and accepted one tenth of the produce as rent, when given. In 1918, the British colonial government tried to raise its share to 20 percent and to endorse the tapu holders' right to mulkiya (another 20 percent in land rent), but retracted its demands in response to resistance from the individual tribes.

In a negotiated settlement with the rebellious tribes, the British lowered the exaction to 30 percent (instead of the original 40), to be divided between the government and the tapu holder equally. And to avoid further conflict between the government and cultivators, the British political officers in charge assumed the responsibility for collecting both the government's and tapu holder's shares of 30 percent and to pay the legal owner his share of 15 percent.[72]

In contrast to the Muntafiq, in ᶜAmarah and Kut, where state land and the iltizam system prevailed, the British followed a policy of political expediency. They farmed out large estates to "loyal" tribal chiefs and members of their ruling houses.[73] ᶜAmarah, for example, was divided into twenty-eight large estates *(muqataᵓah)*. Each was leased for five years to the highest bidder from among the loyal shaykhs. They backed up the authority of the tribal shaykhs by introduced the *Tribal Civil Dispute Regulation Act* of 1919 that institutionalized tribal and customary law. In addition to creating a system of jurisdiction specifically for the tribes, the Tribal Regulation Act, in practice, authorized and enforced new relations of exploitation in agriculture by sanctioning the shaykhs power over their tribespeople. Under the act, the British designated "suitable" tribal leaders as "government shaykhs" and gave them the power to settle all disputes, including land disputes, as well as levy taxes on behalf of the government.[74]

The 1920 revolt against British rule, spearheaded by the Shiᵓa leaders of Najaf and fostered by the clans, decisively affirmed the judiciousness of Dobbs' expediency policy in lower Iraq. Many of the larger tribal shaykhs refused to participate in the revolt, although some were pressured to join once it was declared. Other large landholders, who knew where their economic and political interests lay, campaigned against the revolt, forcibly preventing their own clans from joining. Such was the case with Shaykh Abdallah al-Yasin, whose power was feared throughout the districts of Kut (south) and Gharraf, and whose influence, money, and power prevented the spread of the revolt to clans of Kut. His role was especially appreciated in preventing the takeover of the Kut-Baghdad railroad by rebel forces, which would have cut off all supplies to the British army in the region. Crucial support for the British came also from Shaykh Muhammad al-Sayhud, the paramount emir of Rabiᵓah, who stopped his clans in northern Kut (ᶜAmarah province) from joining the rebellion, and who was also credited by the British for obstructing the spread of the rebellion northward to ᶜAmarah. A third powerful shaykh renowned for his support to the British was Khayyun al-Ubaid, the head of al-Ajwad and the qaimmaqam of Shatra. In cooperation with the British political officer of the district, Khayyun and his supporters built a human wall which prevented communication between the rebellious tribes of al-Gharraf and al-Furat

(Euphrates tribes). He was thus decisive in halting the spread of the revolt to Shatt al-Hai in Gharraf.[75] The British colonial records provide ample evidence of the many tribal shaykhs who, like those previously named, saw support for the colonial power and opposition to their own tribespeople to be in their best interest.[76]

After the revolt was crushed, the alliance between the tribal shaykhs and the mandate state was well cemented. The advocate of this alliance, Henry Dobbs (now High Commissioner), wrote two documents (in 1926 and 1928) on land policy, indicating that political order required the backing of the tribal ruling houses in Iraq. Criticizing Stephen Longrigg's "Note on Land and Revenue Policy" of 1926, Dobbs reaffirmed his opposition to direct dealings with individual cultivators in the tribal regions on the grounds that the government lacked the means "to go through the population of Iraq with a fine tooth comb," since "the machinery of the Iraq Government would be hopelessly inadequate to undertake a policy . . . of extreme tribal disintegration. . . heading for dealing direct with the individual cultivator." For "the convenience of administration and preservation of social order," he suggested the "bigger men (shaykhs) should be on top," and be recognized as "the owners with responsibility for the payment of land revenue."[77]

From this point on, colonial officers took systematic measures to legitimize the power of the shaykhly class and their claims to the land. In addition to granting them land, money, and tax exemptions, the government bolstered the shaykhs' power by incorporating the *Tribal Criminal and Civil Disputes Act* into the Iraqi constitution of 1925. They were also awarded seats in the first parliament to be introduced in 1924—34 percent of the seats were given to the shaykhs who came out in support of the British during the revolt.[78]

In supporting the claims of the shaykhs, the state did not refrain from using force to bring the cultivating clans to submission. One striking case was the conflict between the ruling house of al-Manaʾ, the tapu holders of agricultural lands in Masbah (south of Shatra), and al-Hatim, the cultivators and original holders of the land. In 1927, al-Hatim refused to pay rent and threatened to take action against their landlords. The British, acknowledging that al-Hatim's lands were acquired dubiously by the Manaʾ shaykhs, nonetheless sent in the air force to destroy two of al-Hatim's villages, disperse their leadership, and force the tribe into submission.[79]

Force was also used in the rebellious regions of the Muntafiq, but with little success. The persistence of Suq al-shuyukh tribes in their struggle against their tribal shaykhs forced the British (by 1929) to renegotiate and give new concessions to the tribes, including lowering the rent to 7.25 percent, instead of the earlier 15 percent arrangement.[80] As in Suq al-shuyukh, in other areas where cultivators held strong customary rights to the land, smaller holdings were archetypal. In the rice and date plantations of Dhagharah, Jarbawiyah below Hillah, and in Shamiyah and Abu Sukhair, a small holding class of peasant proprietors emerged to challenge tribal rulers.[81]

In sharp contrast to these areas, the authority of the tribal landholders in ⁽Amarah and Kut was rarely contested by their tribespeople. Conflict was largely characterized by intra-tribal disputes between the leading shaykhs.[82] The absence of struggle between shaykhs and tribespeople among the Tigris tribes, combined with the backing of the mandate state, prepared the ground for the emergence in the 1930s of huge estates of between 50,000 to over 100,000 dunums each.

British policy of supporting large landholders in lower Iraq was incompatible with another of their aims—to accelerate commercialization through intensification and improvement of the productive forces. The British agricultural development plan continued Ottoman policies of opening old and new canals, strengthening river embankments, and constructing new dams. By 1930, they had either "extensively repaired or entirely reconstructed the Hindiyya dam," (re)opened the Saqlawiyah, Yusifiyah, Iskandariyah canals among others, built new embankments on the Euphrates and the Tigris, and erected various devices to regulate the water level on the river Hai and Gharraf.[83] The Department of Agriculture also attempted to introduce new and improved seed strains (for barley and wheat), new industrial crops (like cotton and flax), and modern machinery.

International Trade Under the Mandate

Iraq's exports to the world market, while expanded under British rule, consisted of traditional crops. Dates continued to be Iraq's most important export, increasing by over a 100 percent from the prewar period, and Iraq became the supplier of over 80 percent of the world's supply (see Table 1).

Table 1. Date Export

Year	Tonnage (1,000)	Value (Sterling:1,000)	Dates as % of total exports (by value)
1912	70.0	252	18
1922–23	123.4	n.a.	n.a.
1924–25	148.4	1,185	51
1925–26	144.9	1,538	41
1927–28	151.1	1,376	30
1929–30	135.0	1,410	33

Source: Great Britain, Colonial Office, *1931: 216–17*

Although the export of grain (barley and wheat) increased in volume, attempts to introduce new and better varieties were not that successful, and quality remained largely poor. Classified as "Gulf grain," along with Persian produce, it was sold for animal feed in United Kingdom markets. Moreover, although Iraqi grain production increased in volume, exports continued to fluctuate dramatically from one year to another depending on climatic conditions in Iraq, as well as changing market prices.[84]

Other exports included raw wool and animal hides and skins, but in general these items became less significant as the tribes became more sedenterized and gave up animal herding for agriculture. British attempts to commoditize livestock also faced difficulties and were largely unsuccessful.

Like the Ottomans before them, the British had modernization goals that often conflicted with their politically expedient strategies. Their plans to "modernize" agriculture were frequently incompatible with their policy of maintaining the traditional structures of authority based on kinship and shaykh-sharecropper relations of exploitation. This was best exposed in their failed attempts to introduce cash crops and modern technology into a system where sharecropping prevailed.

Ultimately, however, the disastrous consequences of *iqta*' relations on agriculture were felt much more deeply in the third phase, namely, under the monarchic-oligarchic regime of 1932 to 1958. It is in this period that *iqta*' proved to be not only an impediment to the development of agriculture but a deterrent to national growth. In tracing the developments in this period, two issues will be considered: first, how tribal landholders used their positions of power within the state apparatus to legitimate and expand their control over land, and second, how they pursued policies that increased their wealth through the extensive expansion of agriculture at the expense of long-term agricultural growth.

THE MONARCHIC OLIGARCHY AND THE AGRARIAN CRISIS: 1932–1958

Once the monarchic oligarchy was established and the social groups sympathetic to the British were firmly in power, British mandate rule was no longer necessary. In 1932, British rule was officially terminated, and under the Iraq-British Treaty, Iraq was internationally recognized as sovereign. But the terms of the treaty and the events following 1932 made it clear that Iraq was far from independent. The British, through the monarchic oligarchy, continued to exert immense power and to command tremendous authority in the affairs of Iraq. The treaty, dictated by the British and backed by the monarchy and the shaykhly landed class packing the parliament, ensured British control. The treaty granted the British the right to keep their military air bases intact. It also dictated that Iraq must consult closely with Britain in all matters of foreign policy, and must extend to the British in times of war or a "threat of war" all available facilities and assistance.

The monarchic-oligarchic regime inherited the political parliamentary system installed by British imperialism. This parliamentary system was strikingly different from its supposed Western model. Under Iraqi parliamentary government, not only were political freedoms and individual rights virtually nonexistent, so also were all other forms of "mass representation" associated with Western parliamentary democracy. The elected members of the two houses of the Iraqi parliament were chosen primarily through indirect balloting, instead of by direct election. As noted earlier, the first parliament introduced under British mandate rule in 1924 set the precedent for future elections. The British packed the parliament with tribal shaykhs and town politicians who were sympathetic to them during the 1920 revolt. Following this precedent, in consecutive elections most members were chosen "unopposed" by proxy. Even though indirect elections ended formally in 1952, the royal parliaments continued to be selected rather than elected.

As part of the ruling class, the tribal shaykhs in this period had the power to legislate and enforce policies to legalize their control over agriculture and its resources. One of the first legislative measures passed by the national parliament was the Law of the Settlement of Land Rights.[85] The settlement, and its various amendments introduced in subsequent years, conclusively legitimated, as well as expanded, the authority of the tribal shaykhs in the countryside.[86] The law, combined with the power exerted by the shaykhs, made it possible for the various *taswiya* (settlement) courts to favor the influential and powerful over the producers. As succinctly summarized by Hasan M. ᶜAli, the president of the Department of Land Settlement, the taswiya courts made it possible for:

> influential people and chieftains to obtain control over vast areas of cultivable lands. The introduction of lazma tenure to recognise prescriptive rights to tribal land opened the way towards such an end. With inexperienced land settlement officers, and with the doubtful integrity of the administration, influential people and shaykhs were able to get such grants by presenting even more tenuous evidence as proof of their prescriptive claims. The 1933 law also made it legal for the government to rent the miri-sirf land for a period of no more than six years. Again the landlords and the chieftains had control over these lands, and since the tribal members could not afford to pay the rent, they had to be satisfied with their role as share-croppers.[87]

The policy of renting out miri-sirf land to landowners, provided under the new law, was just the first step toward alienating state lands to influential tribal shaykhs. Parliament passed a series of laws under which reclaimed arable lands were turned into freehold tenures either by auctioning them on the open market, or else through the "productive clause," which automatically made these lands eligible for ownership under the law of 1932. Of the 2 million plus dunums (2,126,589) miri-sirf lands reclaimed following the construction of the Kut barrage and the completion of the Dujaila canal, only 232,960 dunums were distributed to small farmers in the years 1952 to 1954, while the rest went to the big landholders in the region.[88]

The outcome was of a formidable concentration of land holdings. By 1958, two-thirds of the total agricultural land in Iraq was held by only 2 percent of the landowning class. This concentration was most striking in ᶜAmarah and Kut, where conflict over land control was initially least evident. By 1958, four of the largest and wealthiest landowners in Iraq were from the district of Kut.[89] ᶜAmarah was known to have the highest concentration of *iqta*ᵓ in the entire country. Three shaykhs and the sons of four others held 54 percent of the total land in ᶜAmarah, while ten others held an additional 19 percent of the total.[90]

In comparison to these two regions (and in spite of such blatant cases as Shaykh Muhsin Khairalah of Nasiriyya district), in other areas of the Muntafiq, concentration of this form of *iqta*ᵓ was less marked.[91] In Suq al-shuyukh, where resistance against consolidation was most intense, smaller-sized holdings under the control of sub-shaykhs (heads of clans) or sirkals (agents) were more typical. Such was the case of the al-Hasan tribe near Suq al-shuyukh. At one time they had no more than a single sirkal for each of their two major sections, but by 1930 they had increased to 10,000 in number.[92] Apparently the land that had previously been managed by two sirkals was divided into smaller plots among the various clans and households.[93]

Even when compared to other Middle Eastern countries, where concentration of landholding was also prevalent, Iraq stood out in terms of the concentration of land held by large landowners. In Egypt and Syria, for instance, the large landed classes before the land reforms of 1952 and 1958 controlled about half as much of the total agricultural land as was held by the Iraqi landholding class (35 percent in Egypt and 36 percent in Syria, compared to 65 percent in Iraq).[94] This striking feature of Iraq may be attributed to the tribal nature of land accumulation there, which facilitated the expropriation of the lands of the direct producers. In Egypt and Syria, mostly non-tribal landownership forms existed.

Highly concentrated landholdings and a huge inequality in land distribution were not the only effects of *iqta*ᵓ. The system had a negative effect on agricultural productivity. Despite the initial increase in output, the *iqta*ᵓ system led to a crisis in agriculture marked by a decline in crop yields, land abandonment, and peasant flight.

Although output under *iqta*[3] increased in response to the demands of the market, this increase largely occurred through the expansion of cultivated areas and the intensification of peasant exploitation. Instead of maximizing production through capital investment to improve the productive level of both labor and land, the tribal landed class tended to increase production by opening new lands to sharecropping cultivation. According to government reports, the cultivated area increased from 9 million dunums in 1943, to 13.7 million dunums between 1952 and 1953, to 16 million dunums by 1957–1958.[95]

The expansion of cultivated areas led to an increase in the production of barley and wheat, marked by a rise in their exportation. In comparison to 1930, when Iraq exported 146,492 tons of grain, its exports increased to 267,700 tons between 1935 and 1936. The expansion of these winter subsistence crops was due primarily to the extensive expansion of agricultural land. In the 1940s, for example, the land used for other crops was converted to cereal production because of high gains in wartime markets. Yields, however, remained the same. Between 1940 and 1944, wheat prices increased six fold and barley seven to eight fold. Yet, it was the landowners and speculators who profited, not the cultivators who had no access to markets and were forced to sell their share at a fixed price to the landlord.

The tribal landowners were thus able to increase production and income without making substantial capital investments. Although modernization theorists often blame inefficient methods of production on the backwardness of the peasantry, in this case the landholders' influence over the state apparatus and their ability to manipulate kinship relations (as a means of control) contributed to the retardation of capitalist development in agriculture.[96]

The landed classes' influence on state policies in agriculture is evident in one of the most controversial policies of the 1950s: the publicly funded irrigation projects. These projects addressed more than the technical problem of flood control and water storage; they ensured the continuous colonization of new lands for cultivation. Although many local and foreign advisors acknowledged the need for public expenditure on flood control, most questioned the soundness of further expenditure to open new lands for cultivation. Improving the methods of production, these advisors suggested, would be more effective "to build dams for the purpose of river control is one thing, and to build those dams to provide stored water for irrigation is another. This is so because while flood control is essential, bringing new land under cultivation may not be economically justifiable if a different system of utilization of the land already under cultivation can be devised."[97]

The same conclusions were reached by the International Bank for Reconstruction and Development (IBRD), which in 1952 had advised against further land colonization. In spite of these conclusions, the regime, pressured by tribal landowning interests, continued to finance irrigation projects which reclaimed new land.

The state-funded projects, including land reclamation, cost the landholders practically nothing. Although agriculture was the largest sector of the economy, it was lightly taxed and thus contributed very little to state revenues compared to other sources, particularly indirect taxation.[98] It was not until the 1950s, when oil became the major source of state revenues, that the poorer classes, and especially the peasantry, were relieved from partially subsidizing these projects from which they themselves had gained little. Following the new oil agreement reached in 1952 by the Iraqi government and the Iraq Petroleum Company, spending on irrigation projects grew immensely after the sharp rise in oil revenues.[99] Agriculture, and in particular irrigation projects, claimed the lion's share of the government's capital expenditures.[100]

In spite of the enormous capital investment on agriculture, by the 1950s lower Iraq was facing a serious economic and social crisis. Declining productivity led to an intensification in exploitation and to peasant rebellions.[101] Land reclamation allowed landowners to rely on inefficient and wasteful methods of production, such as the traditional system of leaving half or more of the land fallow.[102] The tribal shaykhs who controlled hundreds or even thousands of dunums could afford to leave half or more of it fallow. To utilize land more intensively would have required the landowner to put part of his capital back into the land, to introduce crop rotation, fertilization, modern tools, and machinery. So long as he could expand land cultivation and extract surplus from his tenants through other methods, both legal and customary, landowners had little incentive to undertake such initiatives.[103]

The most detrimental effect was the increased salinity of the soil, rendering many of the newly reclaimed lands useless. The major cause of salination, reported a member of the Development Advisory Board, was the wasteful use of irrigated water. According to the IBRD, over 60 percent of the land in the irrigated areas was seriously affected by salinity. While as much as 30 percent of available land had been abandoned by 1952, the remaining land experienced a 20 to 50 percent decline in yield.[104]

Salinity also affected the kinds of crops being produced. Irrigated areas were turned over to the production of barley since it has more tolerance for salty soil than other crops such as wheat and rice. Barley, in spite of its poor quality, became the principal crop, ranking above dates as Iraq's most important export. Wheat, more sensitive to saline soil, was now being mainly produced in the northern and mid-regions of Iraq. Poor-quality rice continued to be grown in the marshes of lower Iraq but its production declined and was now limited to local consumption (see Table 2).

Table 2. Principal Exports of Iraq, 1949–1957 (in metric tons)

Exports	1949	1950	1951	1954	1955	1956	1957
Barley	325.9	461.9	438.7	489.8	320.8	289.5	203.5
Dates	140.8	211.9	330.1	217.9	249.6	264.5	228.1
Wheat	6.8	58.6	43.5	28.9	70.2	0.0	0.0
Wool	3.7	5.8	4.9	4.8	5.7	7.6	6.2

Sources: Simmonds, *1953: 17, 37–38;* United Nations Yearbook, *1958: 297–98.*

In response to deteriorating conditions in agriculture, the IBRD emphasized the importance of improving the methods of production rather than further expanding land usage. They recommended that drainage should be given priority over other irrigation projects. Aware of the high cost to the state of building drainage systems, the IBRD suggested that landlords as the primary beneficiaries should be required to cover some of the cost.[105]

It was not possible to impose levies or to legislate policies without the support of the landowning class. A bill providing that the cost of drainage be paid in installments by the landowners was immediately thrown out of the parliament.[106] The landed class had no reason to support investment in drainage since it had the option of abandoning exhausted saline lands for newer and more productive acreage reclaimed at public expense. The virtually inexhaustible supply of rich irrigated lands, combined with the low ratio of labor to land, provided a very strong rationalization for the policy of land reclamation. In addition to drainage, the IBRD stressed the importance of mechanization in improving productivity levels.[107] Yet very little was done in this area. Conditions continued to deteriorate in lower Iraq, most strikingly in areas such as ᶜAmarah and Kut where *iqtaᵓ* relations were strongest.[108] In these areas, productivity decline resulted in harsher exploitation and an escalation in violence. By the 1950s, many of the sharecroppers who lived on the land received no more than 15 to 20 percent of their annual crop, after paying their rent for land and tools, interest on accumulated debt, and other imposed fees of one kind or another.[109]

When faced with resistance, landowners used different forms of pressure to extract the necessary surplus. In one case, for example, the tribal landowner al-ᶜUraibi, involved in a dispute with his sub-lessee, opted to deprive him of access to 10,000 dunums of his land by refusing to rent it out that year.[110] Since ᶜUraibi controlled over 100,000 dunums in ᶜAmarah, leaving one estate in fallow for one year was a minimal cost to him but a significant hardship for his sharecroppers. In addition to economic pressure, landowners used their armed guards to crush peasant resistance, as was the case in the al Uzairij revolts of 1951 and 1952 in ᶜAmarah.[111]

The ⁽Amarah peasant uprising of 1952 was triggered by a new law passed by parliament, the "Law for Granting Lazma Rights in Miri-Sirf Land in ⁽Amarah Liwa," which would have guaranteed the transfer of most of the miri-sirf land in the province to the tribal shaykhs and their relatives.[112] Even though this law was canceled under emergency decree due to persistent peasant pressure, the new law that replaced it in 1955 was never carried out.[113]

Another manifestation of deteriorating conditions under *iqta*⁾ was the peasants' flight to towns. According to government census reports, rural population in Iraq declined from 70 percent of the total population in the 1930s to 58 percent in the 1950s. Eighty-four percent of rural-urban migration came from the central and southern regions. Of the southern regions, the highest rate of migration came from ⁽Amarah.[114]

In striking contrast to ⁽Amarah, a new law was passed in 1952, the "Law for the Settlement of the Disputes of State Land Held by Tapu in the Muntafiq Province," which recognized the full rights of possession by cultivators of the land. Under the law, tapu holders who failed to establish control over their land were promised compensation by the government, either in the form of cash or state land elsewhere.[115]

CONCLUSION

The dominant class structure was responsible for blocking the development of capitalist agriculture in lower Iraq. The development of an agrarian economy based on large estates worked by peasant sharecroppers was not the inevitable result of the encroachment of the capitalist world market; rather, the response to changing market conditions was determined by the existing socioeconomic organization of the region, which was embedded in a tribal (or kinship) social structure and economy. The emergence of *iqta*⁾ can be understood as a result of the successful effort by tribal ruling groups to take advantage of the new political and market opportunities. Out of the struggle for control of land and agricultural production, the dominant tribes, who had both power and wealth, emerged as the triumphant agrarian landed class in lower Iraq. However, the transition to *iqta*⁾ was uneven, more thorough in some areas than others, and generated different forms of class conflict. Conflicts between shaykhs and tribespeople characterized the areas where strong customary rights to the land gave tribespeople the power to resist the claims of the dominant houses effectively. In these areas, a weaker form of *iqta*⁾ relations emerged. In contrast, conflict between shaykhly houses was typical in the areas where cultivating tribes had no access or rights to the land. These areas witnessed the emergence of the strongest and most exploitative forms of *iqta*⁾.

Once in power, the new class of tribal landowners pursued income-maximizing policies that undermined long-term agricultural growth. As long as members of this class had access to state power and could increase their wealth through the extention of cultivation subsidized by the state, they had little incentive to improve productivity, especially since that would have involved putting part of their assets back into the land.

2

Peasant Economy and Merchant Capital

As argued earlier, the integration of the Ottoman provinces of Baghdad, Basra, and Mosul into the world market, combined with the centralization policies pursued by the Ottoman Porte, precipitated the disintegration of the old transit economy and the rise of commercial agriculture as the main source of power, wealth, and social conflict. The preceding described how the commercialization of agriculture in the tribal regions of southern Iraq led to the rise of an inefficient *iqta'* system based on exploitative landlord-tenant relations. In this chapter, I will consider the regions where household peasant agriculture prevailed. I will argue that, in contrast to the south, commercialization here encouraged the emergence of a more efficient and more productive agrarian system. The prevalence of smaller-size holdings and the prominence of free-holdings *(mulk)*, as well as proximity to urban centers and commercial capital, checked the development of *iqta'* and fostered the development of a more efficient agrarian system. Just as the "tribal" regions saw the emergence of a tribal oligarchic class, the other areas witnessed the rise of an entrepreneurial class with interests quite distinct from those of the shaykhly landholders. But, as it will become clear, the aspirations of this entrepreneurial class were to be restricted by the political predominance of the tribal oligarchy. The regime (the oligarchic monarchy), heavily swayed by tribal landed interests, pursued measures that continued to create the social conditions necessary for the reproduction of *iqta'* relations, thus obstructing the growth and the generalization of capitalist agriculture.

Peasant commercial agriculture developed over three periods. First, during the late Ottoman period (1870–1914) merchant capital moved in to wrest ownership from peasant proprietors. Commoditization, however, was primarily confined to the sphere of circulation, in particular to trade, usury, and leasehold. Second, the British mandate period (1914–1932) was marked by an intensification of a market economy which drove mercantile capital to exert control, not only through the domain of circulation (trade, usury), but by directly entering into production. Third, in the oligarchic monarchy period (1932–1958), mercantile capital finally secured its claim to the agricultural land and embarked on the mechanization of production. However, the power of entrepreneurial capital in agriculture remained limited and insignificant in comparison to the tribal oligarchy and its further expansion was impeded by the dominance of *iqta'* relations.

THE LATE OTTOMAN PERIOD

Prior to the emergence of a world market, peasant agriculture flourished mainly in the areas surrounding the towns where availability of water and urban markets encouraged the evolution of permanent agriculture and village life. It was in the areas surrounding Basra (Shatt al-Arab region), around Baghdad, Karbala, and parts of al-Hillah in the irrigated zone, as well as a narrow belt in the rain-fed zone extending from Mosul through Arbil to the Diyalah river, that small holdings and peasant household economy prevailed. Peasant cultivators were either free-holders with individual lazma rights or leaseholders of rented land from town merchants and elites and sometimes from the mosques, as in the case of *waqf* land.[1]

Even though many of the small holders with established lazma rights had little difficulty claiming tapu rights after the introduction of the Ottoman Land Code in 1870, widespread peasant control of land never fully took hold.[2] By 1913, many of these peasants had lost their right of occupancy either to urban merchants or to Ottoman officials and local elites (*sayyids*). Many of the sources on land tenure in the late Ottoman period point to the dwindling number of petty peasant producers in the rain-fed zone in the years following commercialization. Although Gertrude Bell might have exaggerated the conditions in order to show the benefits of British rule, she did aptly describe the heavy loss of land by small peasants:

> There are indications that the bulk of the land . . . was originally in the hands of peasant proprietors; but at present most of the land has passed into the hands of large proprietors, who are generally inhabitants of Mosul. They hold by right of *tapu* sanads. Complaints as to how this process was effected are frequent. It is said, for instance, that a peasant would be offered for his land 25 percent of its value, and on his refusal to sell, he would be cast into prison on trumped up charges of murder to remain there for years unless he changed his mind.[3]

As in the north, in the irrigated zone of Hindiyah, Shamiyah, and Karbala, little of the original land alienated in tapu form to small holders survived. By 1914, most of the tapu holders in these areas were city merchants, sayyids, or government officials.[4]

The exception to this trend was some areas in the northern plains, especially the villages of ʿAqrah and ʿAmadiyah, where, according to Dowson's land tenure report of 1930, more than 90 percent of peasant land remained in the hands of its original holders. Protected by their patriarchs, bishops, and churches, the great majority of the Christian peasantry was able to keep its land out of the reach of mercantile capital.[5]

Even with the scant evidence at hand, the loss of land is clearly related to the endemic indebtedness of the peasantry to merchant capital, which forced many of the peasants to abandon their legitimate rights of occupancy to town merchants. Of course, peasant indebtedness per se is not peculiar to commercial capital and/or the penetration of capital, since it was a phenomenon which predated both. The difference is that during this period debt served to hasten the expropriation of lands from their legitimate holders. While the change from relative subsistence to commercial agriculture opened new opportunities for merchant urban capital to accumulate vast amount of wealth through investments in agriculture, it pushed the peasants into greater debt.

With the change to commercial agriculture, the peasants, producing largely for exchange, became more and more dependent on the market for subsistence. The market, however, was both unpredictable and highly unstable due to the constant fluctuation in price, which was largely determined by the law of supply and demand. An unstable market combined with an increasing need for cash often forced the peasants to part with their produce at very low prices and/or sell in advance. Explaining the mechanics of this transaction of selling in advance, known in Iraqi dialect as *al-bay*ʾ *ʿala-al-akhdar* (selling green) Batatu observed:

> Before the maturing of their crops, cultivators, in particular, the small peasant proprietors that abounded in the mid-Euphrates, were often forced to rely on the merchants for ready money, which was not advanced to them unless they made out forward contracts to the effect that they would surrender so many tons of grain or all the produce at such and such a rate, which was almost always the market rate at the time of the harvest.[6]

Their dependency on the market, in general, and their subservience to mercantile capital, in particular, is best put by economist Salman Hasan:

> It was men of (small) capital like the chalabis and tujjar al-jumlah (merchants and whole-sale-traders) who, as wusataʾ (intermediaries) in the latter part of the nineteenth century, were able to monopolize the grain market and, as a result, accumulate massive amount of wealth by exploiting the price differentials (of buying cheap and selling high).[7]

Looking at the important families that came to represent large wealth in agriculture (as well as industry) in twentieth-century Iraq, one finds that most seemed to have been the product of this period of commercialization. The vast fortunes of the Sabunji family, for example, are largely credited to

Muhammad Chalabi al-Sabunji, a nineteenth-century merchant who managed in the latter part of the century to bring several of the villages around Mosul under his control. According to Batatu, Sabunji's wealth came mostly from marketing cash crops he "received in his capacity as owner or part owner of the numerous villages that he wrested . . . from the defenseless peasants. . . ."[8] There were also others, like al-Shallash, Chalabi, Fattah, the Khudairi, Asfar, al-Pachachi, and Jamil, who, as urban merchants or notables and sayyids, were able to accumulate a vast amount of wealth by securing control over agriculture and its trade.[9]

In the late Ottoman period, however, penetration and accumulation of capital was limited to the sphere of circulation. Though commercialization in the late nineteenth century might appear to have at first encouraged the expansion of antidiluvian capital—i.e., usury, trade, and investment in leasehold— following the turn of the century we see not the preservation of the old forms of mercantile capitalism, but the transition from old to new forms of relations between commercial capital and agriculture. With the intensification of commodity relations under British mandate rule, merchants with capital entered into production attempting to reorganize the labor process in order to raise productivity.

The British Mandate Period: 1914–1932

As noted earlier, British agricultural policies were not necessarily consistent. While maintaining traditional structures of authority in the tribal regions, the mandate rule at the same time introduced new measures to accelerate commercialization through intensification and improvement of the productive forces. Under the Agricultural Development Plan, for example, the British continued Ottoman policies of (re)opening old and new canals, strengthening river embankments, and constructing new dams. By 1930, they had entirely reconstructed the Hindiyah dam, reopened the Saqlawiyah, Yusifiyah, Iskanariyah canals among others, built new embankments on the Euphrates and the Tigris, and constructed various devices to regulate the water level on the river Hay and Garraf.[10]

The department began to also experiment with and introduce new and different strains of wheat and barley to improve and increase their yield. High-yield varieties of wheat and barley (Punjab 17 and California) were first issued to cultivators in 1923, followed with a more improved strain of wheat called the ʿAjiba. The latter became popular with the cultivators because of its high yield and its excellent quality, which was suitable for both local consumption and export.[11]

The British tried to diversify agriculture as well by introducing new industrial crops, like cotton, flax, and sericulture. The most interesting and promising of these experiments was the attempt to commercialize the production of cotton. The British developed a special interest in cotton production for the potential of turning Iraq into another Egypt, that is, a large cotton estate.[12] To launch this ambitious plan, the British Cotton Growers Association set up experimental farms to test the type of cotton best suited to Iraqi soil. The initial success of these experiments encouraged the mandate government to promote cotton cultivation on a large scale, offering tax breaks and land concessions to local investors interested in cotton production. The only takers were urban entrepreneurs and town mullak who were motivated by the potential for high returns on their investments.

The first government concession was given in 1923 to three prominent entrepreneurs, Najib al-Asfar, Hamdi al-Pachachi, and Thabit ʿAbd al-Nur, to form two companies: Eastern Irrigation, Ltd. and the Diyalah Cotton Plantation Co. The offer included a study of irrigation projects (the Habaniyah Reservoir and the Fallujah Barrage) especially planned for large-scale production of cotton in these areas. Although the concession embraced other agricultural activities, cotton was one of the key cash crops on which the hopes of these concessionaires were pinned.[13] Similar offers were given to Mosul Farms Limited—an agricultural development company particularly interested in the promotion and expansion of cotton cultivation in the north. The company, whose capital was entirely subscribed locally, obtained a very generous concession from the government: "a thirty year lease of the Saniya (state) lands of Jurf and Dhibaniya, between Nimrud and the mouth of the Zab, for which they are to pay, including both land tax and rent, the equivalent of one tenth of the value of their crop, assessed every five years."[14]

Interest in cotton cultivation was not limited to group or company endeavors. It included individual entrepreneurs from among the town mullak, especially those who owned tracts of land in the mid-region of Diyalah, Saqlawiyah, and al-Hillah. Fakhri Jamil Zadah, a wealthy Baghdadi landowner of urban and agricultural lands, leased his Haroniyah lands in Diyalah to a British firm, Wolfra Syndicate, to create a cotton plantation after their successful joint venture to cultivate cotton on his other farms in Dabaniyah along the Tigris. As on all experimental farms, the British firm used modern machinery as well as wage labor.[15] As a result of these initiatives, cotton production more than tripled in one year—from 300 bales in 1922 to 1,100 bales in 1923, increasing to 3,500 bales by 1926. Its cultivation continued to rise despite the slump in prices due to the flooding of the market with American cotton. In 1928, according to British sources, 5,200 bales produced that year were exported.[16]

Despite these initial successful investments by private urban capital, cultivation of cotton did not reach the scale originally intended. One major reason was the dominance of *iqta*[3], especially in those areas where extensive cotton production would have been most feasible—the irrigated zone in lower Iraq. The tribal shaykhs who controlled the larger part of these lands were generally not interested in any kind of capital investment, let alone in a risky crop like cotton. The different responses of urban entrepreneurs and land-holding shaykhs to commercial opportunity expressed the structural differences between private urban capital, which is always looking for profitable ventures, and a landed class whose power came from the control of rent and taxes.

The share system of cultivation also constrained the expansion of cotton production. Cotton, as an industrial crop, was unpopular among sharecroppers for two reasons: first, it simply did not feed them as grain crops did, and second, cotton cultivation brought longer hours and intensified labor, for sharecroppers would be expected to farm cotton in the summer in addition to harvesting their regular winter crops of barley and wheat.

Although sharecroppers resisted cotton cultivation, urban entrepreneurs and town mullak continued to use sharecroppers rather than moving to hire wage labor.[17] It appears that production costs lay at the heart of the problem. In order for Iraqi cotton to be competitive on the world market, it had to be produced cheaply. One way of lowering the cost of production was to use sharecroppers who were cheaper than hired labor.[18] Wage labor was initially used on several of the private estates, but was soon abandoned for sharecropping. Such was the case with the Wolfra Syndicate, the British company managing the estates of Fakhri Jamil. Within one year the Syndicate was forced to reintroduce sharecropping and abandon the use of mechanical cultivators while retaining only their ginning plants.

Agricultural labor was too expensive to use on these farms for the following reasons: first, the relative scarcity of population in relation to the available land for cultivation, and second, the evolution of property relations in agriculture as described in chapter 1. Until the land settlement of 1932, most of the cultivators had in some form or another a legal (customary) entitlement that gave them access to land, their basic source of subsistence.[19] These property rights, of course, varied greatly. Some cultivators had stronger rights, as in the case of naqsha. Others held land under lazma (the communal and the individual) which nonetheless gave them the right of occupancy and therefore the right to stay on the land. As a result, the proportion of the agricultural population which was landless peasants was relatively small. Labor was accordingly relatively expensive:

> [T]he demand for labor has often exceeded the available supply and employers were competing to obtain workmen by raising the advances which they were

offering. The cultivators have profited from this demand by moving from holding to holding in pursuit of higher advances. In some instances, the advances offered have been as high as Rs.300 per man.[20]

Nonetheless, it was the crash of 1929 that provided the last blow to the cotton venture. The dramatic slump in the purchasing power of the world market shattered any prospect of its extensive cultivation in this period. As disclosed by a British officer in charge:

> The world economic crisis struck a sad blow to Iraq's hopes of becoming one of the great cotton growing countries of the world. The profits accruing to farmers from the crop are now so low (if indeed they exist) that its cultivation has largely been abandoned.[21]

Although it is true that many abandoned cotton during this period, its cultivation picked up again in the 1930s after the land settlements, and especially in the 1940s during the Second World War, when imports of all foreign goods sharply declined. Once the land settlements guaranteed private capital more control over the land and its labor, and in response to the demands of the home market, cotton cultivation was seriously undertaken by private enterprise, especially in the north (al-Jazira) and in the mid-region surrounding Baghdad.[22] As in the 1920s, 1930s, and 1940s, in the 1950s cotton cultivation was again largely taken up by an entrepreneurial class of urban merchants and town mullak seeking the highest returns on investment.

The British regime was more successful in its efforts to encourage the use of machinery than in attempting to diversify agriculture. The "Law for the Encouragement of Cultivators to Use Pumps," introduced in 1926, was intended for land reclamation through the use of a more efficient method of irrigation—mechanical pumps—instead of the traditional water wheels. But since the cultivators themselves lacked the capital to invest in pumps, the government sought to encourage private capital to enter into this venture by offering investors tax breaks along with tapu rights to unclaimed state lands. The law also encouraged investment in pumps on already-claimed lands, allowing private capital to receive 15 to 30 percent of the crops produced by peasant proprietors in return for their investment. As in the case of cotton, the law on the whole attracted urban merchants, and very few large landholders, to invest in pump installation. A pump owner, as described by British officials, "was usually an enterprising capitalist townsman, lacking land and anxious to develop a portion of the Domains (miri land) already subject to occupation."[23]

In fact, irrigation pumps made a marked impression in the mid-region due to the investments made by urban capital. In a period of ten years, power pumps increased numerically from 21 to 2,047 in 1929 and 2,500 in 1930, opening over a million acres of new lands to cultivation. Nearly 60 percent of the installations, according to British reports, were in the province of Baghdad, and about 13 percent in Diyalah, and 11 percent in the Diwaniyah province.[24]

The installation of mechanical pumps not only extended agriculture, it also changed the nature of property relations in the region. As the main contributor to pump irrigation, mercantile capital was able to complete its subjugation of agriculture by claiming full rights of ownership to both land and labor. The world economic crisis of 1929 helped to accelerate this process by pushing the cultivators in the pump regions to the edge of bankruptcy. With the contraction of the world market, Iraqi exports fell by more than 40 percent in value, putting pressure particularly on those cultivators who could not come up with the pump owners' share of the payment.[25] As described by a British official, peasant indebtedness was the harshest in the newly claimed lands:

> The fellah's indebtedness was most severe in the pump areas where extensive areas of land brought under cultivation during the last three years by means of pumps are chiefly made up of state domain lands. The greatest difficulty confronting the department is to maintain the balance between the existing occupier and the incoming townsman pump owner. The former, by reason of long continuous occupation, is the virtual owner, though not actually recorded in the land registry as such; the latter expects the government to give him rights in land in return for pioneering enterprise and capital sunk in the land . . . he is thus anxious to have the greater control over both land and labor which the position of landowner would give him. The severe setback which cultivation by pump suffered during 1929 has made the pump owners more anxious than ever to stabilize their position.[26]

In response to the crisis, the mandatory government set up a committee to inquire into the different claims, as well as regulate the various rights of landownership. Despite the conclusions reached by the author of the report, Ernest Dowson, who defended equally the claims of the cultivator and the pump owners, the land settlement that followed gave the pump owners greater control over both land and labor by guaranteeing them full rights of ownership. The land settlement of 1932, implemented under the oligarchic monarchy, legitimated the claims of private capital in the pump region by granting it full rights of ownership not only over newly reclaimed miri lands, but also over lands whose cultivators had defaulted.

International Trade Under the Mandate

Iraq's exports to the world market, while expanded under British rule, consisted of traditional crops. Dates continued to be Iraq's most important export, increasing by over 100 percent from the prewar period, and Iraq became the supplier of over 80 percent of the world's supply (see Table 2).

Although the export of grain (barley and wheat) increased in volume, attempts to introduce new and better varieties were not that successful, and quality remained generally poor. Moreover, although Iraqi grain production increased in volume, exports continued to fluctuate dramatically from one year to another depending on climatic conditions in Iraq, as well as changing market prices.[27] Other exports included raw wool and animal hides and skins, but in general these items became less significant as the tribes became more sedenterized and gave up animal-herding for agriculture. British attempts to commoditize livestock also faced difficulties and were largely unsuccessful.

So, even though British rule accelerated the commercialization of agriculture and its integration into the world market, its plans to "modernize" agriculture were not as successful. Like the Ottomans before them, British modernization goals often conflicted with their politically expedient strategies. The political arrangement of maintaining the traditional structures of authority based on kinship and shaykh-sharecropper relations of exploitation was incompatible with their modernization project. This was best exposed in their failed attempts to introduce cash crops and modern technology into a system where the old modes of sharecropping were left intact.

The struggle between these two systems of agriculture continued under the oligarchic monarchy. Even though private capital was able to gain some victories, as in the land settlement of 1932 and its various amendments, which encouraged it to initiate mechanization as a way to improve productivity in agriculture. Private capital, nonetheless, continued to face major obstacles in the way of its expansion due to the dominance of the *iqta*[3] system and its powerful backer, the oligarchic class.

THE OLIGARCHIC MONARCHY: 1932–1958

The Land Settlement of 1932 based on Dowson's study (*An Inquiry into Land Tenure and Related Questions*) was passed by the new regime to regulate land tenure in light of the class/power relations present in the countryside. It was the first in a series of property settlements which institutionalized commercial property relations by recognizing and defining the rights of the various interests involved, from tribal chiefs and tribespeople, to pump owners and cultivators. Under the three types of classification—miri tapu, miri lazma, and miri sirf— many lands fell into the hands of tribal shaykhs as well as urban mullak. "Lazma Law Number 51" (part of the 1932 settlement), in particular, addressed the needs and interests of the pump owners, anxious to establish control over the land.

Under this law, the pump owners were granted full property rights in case of default by the cultivators. The pump owners were accordingly recognized as the legitimate lazma holders of most of the miri lands recently reclaimed by pump irrigation. A revised version of this law, the 1938 "Lazma Law Number 29," along with the taswiyah courts that followed, settled most of the disputed claims in favor of the pump owners.[28]

Besides the land settlements, which established the legal control of private investors over land, the "Law Governing the Rights and Duties of Cultivators," passed in 1933, secured investors' control over the peasantry by redefining the relations between the cultivators, pump owners, and lazma holders. As indicated by Sir Humphry, then British High Commissioner, the origins of this law go back to 1929, when a draft was prepared by the joint efforts of a number of prominent local and political figures who were personally involved in large scale pump irrigation.[29] This was needed because, unlike the areas dominated by large estates where relations between cultivators and tribal shaykhs were already established under tribal customary law and legalized under "Tribal Criminal and Civil Disputes Regulations," there was nothing in customary or civil law to determine the nature of relations between private capital and cultivators. As clearly indicated in the parliamentary debates, this law was primarily introduced to define the labor relations between the cultivators and the merchant mullak.[30] The law was also overwhelmingly supported by the tribal large landholders because it included a clause restricting the movement of indebted tenants, in practice working to benefit both the mullak and the tribal shaykhs.

In defining labor relations, the new law granted pump owners, lazma holders, and leaseholders full rights over all decisions relating to production, including the choice of crops, choice of seeds (kinds and hybrids), water supply, harvesting, marketing, as well as the hiring of outside labor. In addition, the law held them responsible for providing proper housing for their cultivators and the payment of all taxes. As far as the cultivators were concerned, they were entitled to 50 percent of the total produce.[31]

Although the land settlements and the various laws passed in the 1930s benefited private capital and tribal landholders equally from a legal point of view, each group secured its legal privileges in a different way. This difference was to become a source of conflict, as further accumulation in agriculture (and elsewhere in the economy) was backed by the inefficient agrarian system predominant in the tribal regions. It is therefore misleading to regard the 1932 land settlement, as most sources do, as having a uniform impact on agricultural production.[32] Contrary to the agrarian system under *iqta*ʾ, agriculture under private capital began to expand, especially in the north where mechanized cultivation became more noticeable in the 1950s. As a result, in the postwar period, the bulk of agricultural production—even of staple crops—shifted north as mechanization rapidly expanded.[33]

Introduction of Machinery

Mechanized cultivation in the 1950s was undertaken by two groups: the moderate landholding peasant, under pressure to produce for the market, and the large wealthy town mullak interested in making a profit. Thus, it was in districts like Mosul and Baghdad where moderate-size proprietorship (family owner-ship) prevailed, and/or private capital was able to penetrate and control produc-tion in the capacity of lazma and tapu, that machinery became widespread. Mechanized cultivation on a large scale was therefore found in the rain-fed areas in the north, and the mid-region of Baghdad where these two types of holdings were most prominent.

In the northern region, an alliance between private capital (merchant tractorists) and peasant holders allowed for the extensive usage of machinery. Accordingly, in the postwar period, grain production in the north increased by 56 percent and contributed as much as 70 percent of the wheat produced in the country.[34] Moreover, from the 1940s, both the northern region and the mid-region surrounding Baghdad came to be the main suppliers of raw cotton for an expanding textile industry.[35]

This increase in output was primarily the result of mechanization in the 1950s as the use of tractors and combines increased from 275 in 1952, to 2,025 in 1956, to 3,181 in 1958, leading to a 50 percent increase in land cultivation between 1951 and 1958 (from 2,261,000 to 4,329,000 dunums), and to an increase in the average yield (to 126.8/dunums) within the ten years.[36]

The Iraqi economist ʿAbdul Sahib al-ʿAlwan, is of the opinion that the spread of mechanization in the north was possible due to its topography. The northern plains, flat and uniform, cost much less to mechanize than the south, where the land was both rugged and uneven due to the irrigation flow and dikes. A machine in the south, for example, would only cover 15 to 20 dunums a day in contrast to 30 to 50 in the north.[37] Yet, some areas in the irrigated zone did introduce machinery despite its relative high cost. In Baghdad province, for instance, machinery was as enthusiastically received as in the north. As reported in the 1957–1958 census there were 781 units used in Baghdad province (19.9 percent of the holdings) in 1952, and 2,219 used between 1957 and 1958. Therefore, the geographical factor cannot fully ex-plain the spread of machinery. A more satisfactory explanation might lie in the constitution of the class predominant in the areas where mechanization occurred. As Doreen Warriner verified, tractor farming in the north was car-ried out largely by a class of merchant mullak from Mosul, Arbil, and other northern towns, who came to be appropriately known as the merchant tractorists.[38]

A particularly revealing example of the important role played by merchant capital in agricultural mechanization is the case of the tribal shaykh of Shammar, Ahmad al-ʾAjil. Following "The Miri Sirf Lands Development Law of 1951," he was able to register huge tracts of land in the Sinjar region of Mosul in his name and members of his clan. Unlike the tribal shaykhs of the south, however, he and others from his clan, following the practices of the north, leased their lands over to the merchant tractorists from Mosul.[39]

The consequences of the differing class relations that emerged in the countryside became much more pronounced in the 1950s. Under the *iqtaʾ* system, deteriorating conditions led to uprisings and peasant flight. In the north and the mid-region, internal migration was considerably lower and sharecropping less prevalent. For example, in contrast to the south where 53 percent of the cultivators were sharecroppers, 17 percent of all the cultivators were sharecoppers in the north, and 30 percent in the mid-region.[40] In some northern villages, the peasants managed to keep hold of their lands and thus retained from 60 to 90 percent of their produce, in contrast to less than 50 and often as little as 30 percent in the southern estates.[41] Although the peasants, where medium-size holdings (100–1,000 dunums) accounted for only a small percentage of the rural population (13 percent), they held over five million acres or the equivalent of 31.5 percent of total agricultural land mostly concentrated in the northern villages and their plains.[42]

CONCLUSION

In certain areas of the north and the mid-region, commercialization encouraged the emergence of a more rationalized and agrarian system. The prevalence of small and free-holdings within the proximity of urban centers and commercial capital helped to arrest the development of *iqtaʾ* and at the same time it favored the expansion of a more efficient agriculture. As the south witnessed the rise of a tribal oligarchic class, these areas saw the emergence of an entrepreneurial class with interests quite different from those of the shaykhly landholders.

In the initial years of the transition (1880–1914), commoditization was restricted to the sphere of circulation, in particular to trade, usury, and leasehold. It was only in the second and third phases of commercialization (1921–1958) that mercantile capital came to exert control by directly entering into production, embarking on the rationalization and mechanization of agriculture. Whereas the prevalence of peasant holding encouraged the town mullak to lease land and machinery to cultivators for a share of the crop, the relative scarcity of landless peasants allowed the cultivators of these regions to strike better terms. At the same time, the peasants, who had access to the land, were compelled to improve the productivity in order both to hold onto the land and increase their return. By borrowing from the merchants to mechanize and by working more intensively, peasant holders were able to expand production and maintain control of their land.

The alliance between private capital and peasant holders resulted in an impressive expansion in agricultural output. By the 1950s, these regions, replacing the south, come to be the main suppliers of staple crops (and cotton) in Iraq. In spite of its success, private capital in agriculture continued to face major obstacles in the way of its expansion due to the dominance of the *iqta'* system and its powerful backer, the oligarchic class. The monarchic regime, heavily swayed by tribal landed interests, continued to pursue policies that ensured the creation of the social conditions necessary for the reproduction of *iqta'* relations, thus hindering the generalization of a more advanced, efficient agriculture.

3

Industry

Despite the emergence of nascent capitalist agriculture in parts of the north and the mid-region, agricultural development in Iraq was fundamentally restricted by the predominance of an inefficient agrarian system based on large estates. This agrarian system also proved a formidable barrier to industrial development for it was labor-intensive and characterized by low levels of productivity. As long as agricultural productivity remained low, large inputs of labor were necessary to produce enough food for the population and this, in turn, limited the proportion of the population that could be freed from agriculture to provide a labor force for industry. Constraints on the expansion of wage labor undermined the possibility of creating a home market for industrial goods, most importantly by restricting the purchasing power of the larger portion of the population.

The dominance of the *iqta*$^{\text{)}}$ system was not the only deterrent to national industrial growth. International competition was another. As a late developer, Iraqi industry could not compete with the highly capitalized and technologically advanced producers from the industrial capitalist world either on the international market or at home. Hence, an aspiring Iraqi industrial capital could only survive in a protected home market. But it was not easy to protect the home market from foreign competition given the fierce opposition to protectionism posed by an influential faction of commercial capital. Still, even with protection, local production continued to be dominated by slow-growth consumer industries. Without the development of capitalist agriculture that would have increased demand for capital goods as well as consumer goods, industrial investment was largely confined to light industries and other industries subsidiary to agriculture.

While Iraq shares these fundamental difficulties with many other developing nations, as an oil-producing country Iraq also differs from the normative model. The oil industry—a highly capitalized, highly efficient industry—appeared to offer Iraq a way out of the dilemmas of "underdevelopment." But as we will see, the growth of the industry and oil revenues accentuated, rather than alleviated, the social and economic contradictions in modern Iraq.

Involved largely in the extraction of crude oil, the highly capitalized oil industry barely engaged the domestic economy in its production process. Its machinery was purchased elsewhere. It employed very little domestic labor and generated hardly any subsidiary industries. But, while the oil industry left little impression on the domestic economy, the revenues it produced had a substantial impact. From the 1950s on, Iraq was relieved of the major predicament facing many developing nations—lack of capital. Capital alone, however, cannot initiate development. Instead of revolutionizing the economy and bringing forth widespread prosperity, oil capital helped to reinforce the social conditions and class relations which perpetuated "underdevelopment."

Due to fundamental differences in their nature, domestic industry and the oil industry will be discussed separately. The rise of domestic industry will be traced in two stages. The first stage (1920–1940) saw the formation of local capitalist enterprise following the foundation of the Iraqi nation-state. In this period, manufacturing was dominated by cottage-type industries, producing for traditional markets, and quasi-mechanized industries such as textiles, producing mainly for the government. The second stage (1940–1958) saw a spurt of industrial growth during the Second World War that was subsequently undermined by the flooding of the home market with foreign industrial goods in the postwar period.

In discussing the oil industry, I will analyze its nature and its contribution (or lack thereof) to manufacturing and other sectors, particularly agriculture. The period after 1950 is especially important due to the sharp increase in oil revenues, with dramatic impact on the national economy. The establishment of the Development Board in the 1950s and its programs will be given special attention.

DOMESTIC INDUSTRY: A HISTORICAL BACKGROUND

National industry emerged in the context of two historical developments: the formation of the Iraqi nation state in the 1920s and the contraction of the world market in the 1940s. In the inter-war period, 1920 to 1940, entrepreneurial capital found new opportunities for investment in three areas:

a.   industries which supplied the new needs and projects of a recently created nation-state;

b.   export-processing industries; and

c.   a specialized traditional market. In this proto-industrial phase, household, cottage, artisanal production, and labor-intensive enterprises prevailed.

In the second phase (1940–1958), entrepreneurial capital underwent a radical change as it began to invest in relatively long-term, capital-intensive, consumer industries. The change in its disposition was not singular to Iraq since many of the so-called "developing" nations had undergone a similar spurt of growth of national capital during the Second World War. The crisis in world capitalism and the contraction in the world market during the war were major contributors to the spurt of industrialization in Iraq and in several other developing nations. Shortages of imported goods, as much as the absence of competition, induced the various indigenous investors to move into industries once considered too risky. Despite its relative growth in the late 1940s and 1950s, national industry on the whole remained quite small and fragile. It was confined to consumer light industries, restricted to a home market, and vulnerable to competition.

By the early 1950s the circumstances that induced this growth spurt had disappeared. In the wake of reconstruction under American hegemony, the world capitalist economy had entered a new boom phase. World trade revived and foreign industrial goods began to invade local economies and impinge on their growth once again.

Nation-State, National Market, and Entrepreneurial Capital: 1926–1940

Entrepreneurial capital owed its development to:

1. government markets which were founded upon the establishment of the new Iraqi state in the 1920s;

2. agricultural subsidiaries; and

3. a highly specialized small local market.

This capital in its early stages was largely mercantalist and its investments were primarily concentrated in Baghdad, Mosul, and the port of Basra.

It is important to note that entrepreneurial capital comprised a very small part of the manufacturing sector, which remained overwhelmingly traditional. With this in mind, this section will focus mainly on the new industries which emerged in the pre-World War II period and became the base of industrial capital in the 1940s.

Government Markets and Entrepreneurial Capital

With the formation of the Iraqi nation-state, local merchant capital found opportunities for investment in industries created by the government and its newly founded markets. Three of the largest industries that emerged during this period, textiles, manufacturing, construction and building, owed their rise to government markets. It must be said, however, that even in these industries private capital would not have invested without government contracts which guaranteed them a market free of competition.

Textiles. The earliest textile factories produced cheap-quality woolen blankets, uniforms, and other cloth to satisfy the needs of a newly founded army, the military academy, the police force, and prisons. One of the first was that of ʾAzra Yaʾcub and Co. Founded in the suburbs of Baghdad, this firm started in 1926 with 10 weaving looms and 65 workers, increasing to 200 workers by 1931.[1] The second was Fattah Pasha's woolens firm, established in 1929. The firm was named after its founder, Nuri Fattah, an ex-general in the Turkish army and a member of a family actively involved in the import-export trade of grain, wool, and cloth.[2] Fattah's firm employed 300 workers, some of them women. Wages were very low and generally paid by the piece, ranging from 50 to 250 fils a day.[3] The third was founded in 1930 by a rich merchant from Mosul, Salih Ibrahim, who was the ex-partner and son-in-law of Fattah. Again, the products of these firms, like those of earlier factories were destined for government markets, which expanded in the 1930s to include the public schools.[4]

When first established, these firms were semi-mechanized—the spinning process was fully automated, but weaving was done by handloomers employed on the premises. Although both the automatic spinning machines and the handlooms were imported from Europe where mechanized looms were also available, these firms preferred handlooms for the following reasons: a) the desire to cut down on initial capital cost since handlooms were much cheaper than weaving machines; b) the market required thick and heavy fabrics and not the finer kind of fabrics that can only be produced by mechanized weaving and, most importantly; c) the availability of a great number of cheap, but skilled weavers whose artisanal skills were becoming obsolete as the handicraft industry slowly eroded under pressure of competition from cheap imported finished goods. Not surprisingly, these factories were erected in the heart of the old handicraft district of Kazimiyah in Baghdad, where an army of skilled, cheap labor was available. Kazimiyah as well offered the Iraqi firms an outlet for their manufactured yarn, especially to the small workshops and the few handloom weavers who continued to produce for a specialized home market.[5] This market centered on traditional goods that remained in high demand in both urban and rural areas, such as woolen ʿabas, turbans, tablecloths, as well as other rougher materials like sailcloth, robes, and rugs. Other small workshops needed manufactured yarn for stockings, pullovers, and various woolen garments.

In fact, the demand for traditional goods, which could not be satisfied by foreign imported cloth, attracted other Iraqis to set up similar enterprises to produce for this specialized market. An example is the rayon factory erected in Mosul, which used imported yarn, 9 power looms, and 45 handlooms to manufacture colorful and gay rayon cloth for the Kurdish tribes living in the north. As the capacity of this factory was smaller than the needs of the market, many of the traditional household weavers survived by introducing the cheaper imported rayon yarn into their weaving process.[6]

Like textiles, the construction and building industry was founded in the 1920s and 1930s in response to the new government markets and some local needs, but its market was much larger and more profitable than that of textiles. The need for public buildings, schools, administrative buildings, military structures, and the like, following the formation of the Iraqi nation, provided strong incentive to private capital to move into and expand the construction and subsidiary industries, such as brick-making, tiles, and, later on, cement. These industries were guaranteed high returns, since a good share of government revenues went to public works in the first years of the nation's formation. Augmenting public-sector expansion demand for private housing increased with the rise in the urban population.[7]

Subsidiary Industries Based on Agriculture

Industries based on agriculture were divided between those producing for export and those producing for the local market. The major export-oriented industries were date-pressing and packing, developed by the landowners and/or date traders, as well as cotton-ginning manufacturers, who were primarily British.

Export-oriented industries. Date-processing was developed in the latter part of the 19th century following Iraq's integration into the world market. At this time, Iraq was the leading date exporter, responsible for 85 percent of the world exports. The intensification of trade following British mandate rule increased demand immensely, date exports in the 1920s exceeding that of the prewar period by 100 percent.[8] Consequently, the industry of pressing and packing dates became one of the largest employers, especially once pitting was introduced.

In the 1920s and early 1930s, date-processing was dominated by petty production.[9] This industry was labor-intensive and relied primarily on seasonal, unskilled women workers, hired for much less than their male counterparts.[10] In September, hundreds of families from the Jabayish region migrated south to the Basra region for employment in the date-pressing industry.[11] Most of the hired workers were women who were contracted out by two agents to companies in Basra. They were paid in cash (50 to 300 fils a day), but, since they tended to borrow on their wages in advance, they were left mostly indebted to their agents from one year to the next. In addition to the Jabayish clans, women migrant workers and their families from all over the southern region (from Qurna, ʿAmarah, and the Muntafiq) squatted in reef huts *(saraif)* around the pressing firms for the three months of their employment.[12]

In response to international export health laws, the government in 1935 began to regulate the date industry by enforcing some health rules like requiring pressing and packaging of dates in cement buildings that had passed yearly government inspection.[13] These regulations eliminated the smaller petty-producers, led to the concentration of the industry in fewer hands, and stabilized its labor force (even though it remained seasonal). The two largest date-processing companies that emerged in the 1940s were the Middle Iraq Dates Co., with a capital of one million dinars, and the Date Industries Co., which had a capital of 100,000 dinars. The principle shareholders in Middle Iraq Dates were the prominent Shiʾi merchant landowning family, the Chalabis (Hadi and Mahmud), who also controlled large tracts of the Latifiyah agricultural lands known for cotton cultivation. The leading shareholders in the Date Industries were the Chalabi brothers again, and al-Dahwi, another Shiʾi merchant who owned date groves in Basra.[14]

In addition to dates, ginned cotton was also prepared for export. The first ginnery, the British Cotton Growers Association, was established in 1920 by a private British company. To ensure good-quality cotton, the association distributed seeds and controlled the ginning and packing of cotton.[15] Encouraged by the success of this British-owned ginnery, in 1929 Iraqi merchants and landowners involved in the cultivation of cotton decided to set up their own, the Iraqi Cotton Ginning Co.[16] Although these two ginneries, like cotton cultivation in general, were to suffer from the slump in prices caused by the worldwide economic crisis in 1929–1930, they nonetheless survived by arranging a special "bartering" agreement with Japan, in exchange for opening Iraq's market to Japanese goods.[17] By 1939, a third ginnery was established by the Agricultural and Industrial Bank.[18]

Besides these agricultural processing industries aimed for export, others both primary and secondary were producing for local consumption—cigarettes, leather-tanning, shoes, brewing, soap-making, knitting, grain-milling etc.[19] Of these, cigarette manufacturing, which had the widest market, attracted the largest capital and was the first to mechanize fully. The industry was protective, freeing producers from foreign competition and encouraging private investment. As early as 1921, the mandate government passed a de-cree forbidding the importation of raw tobacco, and imposing high duties on all imported manufactured cigarettes.[20] One can only speculate as to why this industy and no other was protected by the mandate regime. One possible reason is that the British wanted to co-opt the support of the influential Kurdish tobacco growers and merchants to the new nation-state against na-tionalist demands for a separate Kurdish state. Regardless, these measures, combined with the 1929 *Law for the Encouragement of Industry* and the *Customs Tariff of 1933,* granted local investors tax breaks on all imported capital goods and encouraged private capital to invest in the cigarette indus-try. By the mid-1930s, cigarette production had grown immensely. Most of the smaller, hand-producing firms were wiped out or taken over, under pres-sure of competition, by the larger mechanized companies. There were nine cigarette factories left in Baghdad and two in the provinces. Of the eleven factories, three were dominant.[21]

Except for the few who took advantage of these new markets linked to the establishment of the Iraqi nation-state, most private capitalists shied away from industrial investment. The risks involved, especially due to competition from cheaper imported goods, discouraged most potential investors except on the rare occasions where protection and/or guaranteed markets were offered. Most industrial production, with the exception of cigarettes, was either half mechanized (e.g., textiles) or belonged to traditional "craft" industries. Pri-vate capital flowed to safer and more profitable short-term investments like land speculation, real estate, finance, and commerce. Consequently, domestic industry remained overwhelmingly small, consisting largely of household industries and small workshops with less than five workers. Such was the case in shoe-making, knitting, leather-tanning, dairy-processing, printing, tailoring, and others.[22]

To summarize, local industry initially remained rather undeveloped. Entrepreneurial capital, small and unable to compete with industrial foreign capital, claimed only a very small slice of the national market. But change did occur. From the 1940s on, entrepreneurial capital proceeded to enter into more capital-intensive (consumer) industries. This change in the outlook of entrepreneurial capital was not unique to Iraq, for many developing nations experienced similar industrial spurts in this period. Expansion was largely triggered by the sharp decline in imported industrial goods caused by the contraction of the world capitalist market during the Second World War. The shortages in consumer goods and, more importantly, the absence of compe-tition encouraged indigenous capital to invest in local industry to fill the gap created by the war.

DOMESTIC INDUSTRIAL GROWTH: 1940–1958

In the context of an emerging small nation like Iraq, the growth of private investment in industry during this period was relatively impressive. Although investment continued to be confined to consumer and processing industries, private capital in the 1940s and 1950s became more willing to invest in long-term, capital-intensive industries.[23] Investment in industry increased from 4-million in the 1930s to 49 million in the late 1950s.[24] As industrial capitalists began to play a role in the economy, their relations with commercial capital became more conflictive as their interests diverged. The first sign of this conflict came in 1956, when industrial capitalists broke from the Chamber of Commerce to set up their own independent organization, the Federation of Industries.[25]

New economic measures taken by the government contributed immensely to the growth of indigenous industry. One of these measures was enforcing a quota system on foreign goods which, in turn, subjected all imports to state licenses. The new restrictions on imports were initiated not so much to protect industry but to reduce the widening deficit in the balance of (trade) payments. Regardless of intentions, these measures actually benefited the industrial sector.

To ease the economic pressures created by the war, the government set up an Industrial Bank providing short- and long-term loans to investors interested in industry.[26] In the 1940s, however, the bank's role in replenishing the economy was no more than a symbolic gesture due to its small overhead capital, at the time not exceeding 1 million dinars.[27] The government's lack of funds did not last long, however, thanks to a dramatic increase in oil revenues during the 1950s. The role of the Industrial Bank changed dramatically too, as its overhead capital increased to 3 million in 1952, 7-million in 1957, and 8 million in 1958.[28]

In 1950, in response to indigenous interests, the government enacted a new *Law for the Encouragement of Industry*. The law granted income and surtax exemptions for a four-year period to industries that

1.   used local raw materials;

2.   invested in capital-intensive industries;

3.   used 55 percent Iraqi capital; and

4.   employed Iraqi labor.

In addition, capital goods essential for these industries were excluded from stamp and customs duties.[29] Revisions in the law, passed in 1955, provided even better conditions for industrial capital. Exemption from income tax and surtax was extended from four to five years, and the limit on exemption was raised to a maximum of 25 percent of annual profit instead of the 10 percent allocated by the 1950 law.[30]

Despite the relatively impressive progress made by private capital, industrial expansion continued to be hampered by two significant factors: first, a slow growing consumer market and second, foreign competition, which began once again to invade local markets in the 1950s.

Domestic Textile Industry

During the wartime period, the sharp drop in imported foreign goods was most acute in textiles in general, and cotton in particular. In response to the rising demand for local fabrics, the old textile factories were driven to modernize to increase their level of productivity and improve the quality of production, and three new factories were erected, two for cotton and a third for wool.

Up to the 1940s, the indigenous woolen industry, producing for special government markets, manufactured heavy, cheap-quality blankets and fabrics. Half mechanized, these factories lacked the capacity and the technology to produce sufficient quantity or the quality desired by the private consumer.[31] The change in market demand, however, made industry-upgrading essential. The first to modernize was Salih Ibrahim, who, in 1948, set up a new plant, introduced new machinery, and mechanized the stages of both spinning and weaving. Under pressure of competition, Fattah Pasha's Spinning and Weaving Co. had to follow suit. By the early 1950s, it had installed the latest European models in weaving technology.[32] Soon after, a third textile factory was set up by the Industrial Bank as the first joint venture of its kind between private capital and the state.[33]

As a result of the new technology, productive capacity increased and, for the first time, woolen factories could meet most market demand when fully utilized.[34] Quality improved markedly as well. In contrast to the 1940s, when local woolen fabrics were renowned to be "fit for gunny bags," finer and better fabrics "commensurate with foreign products" were now at hand.[35]

The shortages in cotton textiles during the Second World War were even more severe than those of wool, since domestically produced cotton fabrics were virtually nonexistent. As imports were reduced, prices increased. So did demand.[36] In response, a joint shareholding company of private and state capital, founded the first Iraqi Cotton Spinning and Weaving Co. in 1945. Despite its large productive capacity, this mill alone was able to supply only one fourth of market needs.[37] Subsequently, a second cotton mill was erected in Mosul by the Development Board in 1956.[38]

In response to the expansion in cotton textiles, several local cotton ginneries emerged in this period. By 1957, there were eight ginneries, including the three founded before the war. Two ginneries were founded in Mosul by entrepreneurs (al-Sabunji and al-Jadir), one in Kirkuk, and two more in Baghdad.[39]

Other Domestic Industries

The expansion of local industry was not confined to textiles alone. Several already-established industries, such as manufactured shoes, soap, grain mills, date-processing, leather, and cigarettes, experienced similar growth.[40] The cigarette industry supplied 90 percent of local consumption in the 1950s and accordingly continued to reclaim the highest rates of return.[41] Although brick factories had been established in the first phase, the brick industry underwent similar growth in the 1940s.[42] Other new industries attracted private capital in the absence of foreign competition. One was the highly capitalized cement industry; the other was a subsidiary industry, vegetable oil.

Prior to the establishment of the local cement industry, all of the cement used by Iraq was imported.[43] Increased demand for cement as a result of state construction (dams, bridges, and other large projects in the 1940s and 1950s), as well as the difficulties facing imports during the war, provided the incentive for private capital to enter into cement manufacturing.

In a partnership with the Industrial Bank (20.6 percent of the shares), private investors, including the industrialist Fattah as the largest shareholder and others like al-Chalabi, al-Sabunji, al-Pachachi as principal holders, founded the Iraq Cement Co. in 1948.[44] Despite its increased capacity in the 1950s, rising demand for cement during the 1950s, especially following the state's large construction and irrigation projects, made it difficult for the company to keep up with the market needs and Iraq continued to import cement from abroad.[45]

Both the opportunity for high profits and the rise in national market demand induced private capital to establish three more cement plants. These were al-Rafidain Cement Co. in Mosul, al-Furat in Karbala with a capital of two million dinars raised primarily by al-Shabibi and al-Mirjan, and al-Mutahidah Co. in the south, which was set up by again Fattah and al-Chalabi with starting capital of two and a quarter million dinars.[46] By 1956, private capital investment in this industry exceeded seven million dinars, increasing its productive capacity to 800,000 tons of cement.[47]

By the late 1950s, the industry had attracted a total capital of twelve and a half million dinars, leading this time to a glut in the cement market. Despite a 15 percent cutback in production, these plants were by 1958 still producing between 200,000 to 300,000 tons of cement over their market needs. By 1956, Iraq was already exporting its surplus of cement to neighboring countries in the Gulf (Kuwait, Saudi Arabia, and Bahrain), and to Iran, Pakistan, and Turkey. Many of these markets, however, were to be soon lost to the more cheaper cement from Japan, sold for 6.5 dinars a ton, in contrast to Iraq's 7.25 dinars a ton.[48]

Despite the difficulties facing the industry as a whole, some were able to out-compete the others and thus reclaim high profits, as was the case with Iraq Cement Co. Despite the stiff competition, the company maintained its markets and high rate of profit. Its rate of return for 1958, for example, was 75 percent in contrast to Furat Cement Co.'s rate of 10 percent for the same year.[49]

Like the cement industry, the extraction of vegetable oil was also a result of the war and its shortages. Although smaller than cement, in both capital and scale, this processing industry was nonetheless able to achieve as much success and rates of profit as high as cement. Four major companies emerged in this period. The two largest, with a total capital of two and a half million dinars, were the Vegetable Oil Extraction Co. and subsidiaries (detergents and soap), and the Cotton Seeds Products Co.[50] The leading shareholders in the first company were the capitalist the Fattah family and a rich Mosulite family, the Hadid.[51] As with cement, most of the firm's capital was raised internally from profits.[52] Principal investors in the Cotton Seeds Products Co. were export-import merchants, mainly Simon Garibian, Iskander Markarian, and Khadduri Khadduri.[53] Smaller mechanized industries with a capital of less than a million dinars each also emerged in response to increased demand in the national market. These were the Asbestos Industry Co. (200,000 dinars), the Rafidain Milling and Trading Co. (250,000 dinars), the Iraqi Brewery Co. (450,000 dinars), al-Hajj Yunis Weaving Co. (32,000 dinars), and the National Leathermaking Co., (175,000 dinars), to name a few.[54]

Although war shortages impelled private capital to invest in industry, industrial development was far from accomplished. Domestic industry remained vulnerable to competition, confined to consumer light industries, and restricted by a slow-growing internal market. Capital accumulation continued to be hampered by an inefficient agrarian system and a highly advanced Western capitalist market. New challenges faced industrial capital in the 1950s. Protection was lifted, partly in response to pressure from commercial capital, leading to an intense competition with cheaper foreign industrial goods. Moreover, the sharp increase in oil revenues made it possible for the oligarchic monarchy to expand state-owned industries that often competed with those started by private capital.

Industrial Capital vs. Commercial Capital vs. Oligarchic Oil-Based State

In the postwar period, the sharp rise in oil revenues increased foreign exchange and eased the trade deficit crisis of the 1940s. The quota system imposed on imported goods to relieve the balance of payments deficit was no longer considered necessary. Consequently, the state, pressured by commercial interests, relaxed its regulation and began to issue import licenses quite freely.[55] While opening the market to foreign goods pleased commercial capital, it provoked opposition by industrial capitalists. Commercial capital, favoring a free market, argued that restrictions on imports contributed to economic stagnation, monopolization, and high prices, which slowed commercial interaction and weakened the consumer market.[56] Industrial capital, on the other hand, producing mainly for a domestic market, maintained that protection of infant industry was necessary for industrial growth and national development.[57] Buffetted by these competing groups, government policy lacked cohesion as it fluctuated between a policy of protection and free market.

The fluctuation in government policy is attributed, by modernization writers, to bureaucratic inefficiency and/or lack of government planning.[58] Oppositional groups as well as Marxists, on the other hand, argued the state, acted primarily on behalf of imperial capital and local commercial interests. Under the influence of international capital and the export-import branch of the commercial sector at home, the state opened markets to foreign goods and implemented free trade policies that discouraged all but minimum industrialization.[59]

The critics of modernization theory are correct to consider the context in which government decisions were made. But their framework is too unidimensional and does not explain discrepancies in state policy. While the Iraqi state had on many occasions acted on behalf of imperial power and compradore capital, it had, on others, acted independently of the will and interests of these groups. Rather than being simply an instrument of one group, the state often became an arena of struggle for contending interests and social groups. While repeatedly succumbing to the interests of commercial capital, as in the case of textiles, the state also resisted these interests, as in the case of industries such as cement, cigarettes, and vegetable oil. The oligarchic state was more differentiated than monolithic.

The government's move to relax restrictions on foreign imports posed a real threat to infant domestic industries. The high cost of production made it difficult for local products to compete with foreign goods. One striking case was that of vegetable oil. By 1953, the largest firm, the Vegetable Oil Extraction Co., was losing market share to cheaper oil from Holland.[60] In this case, the industry was able to win over the authorities and reclaim protection. Encouraged by returning profitability, the company mechanized its extraction plant to increase productive capacity in 1955, and in 1956, opened a new subsidiary plant to produce soap and other detergents.[61] By 1958, its capital increased to a million dinars and its productive capacity expanded to meet 70 percent of the market need.[62]

Although the growth of the vegetable oil industy supported the case for protection, its exploitation of the market made a stronger case against protection. Adversaries from commercial capital charged the industry with growing at the expense of the consumer, who had to pay high prices which enriched the company and its shareholders. Free competition, they claimed, was more beneficial to the consumer because it would guard against monopolization and the hiking of prices.[63]

It is true that protection allowed the Vegetable Oil Extraction Co. to monopolize the market, dictate its prices, and maximize its profits.[64] The IBRD, warning of the excessive dangers of protection, pointed out that:

> in a small country like Iraq, where the limited market affords opportunities for only one or two plants in each field and where the entrepreneurial class is small, there is an acute danger of monopoly and attendant high prices. In Iraq, this danger is aggravated by a tendency in some industries to emphasize limited production with high profits per unit rather than mass production with lower unit-profits.[65]

While the dangers posed by protection are real, one should not ignore the larger economic picture under which protectionism becomes imperative. The fundamental problem facing industrialization in Iraq was the high cost of production, which rendered these industries uncompetitive on the international market to begin with. In the case of the vegetable oil industry, for example, local production of the vegetable seeds (linseed and cotton) seemed always to fall short of the industry's needs, which compelled the company to import, at higher costs, a large percentage of its raw materials from Europe or America, thus hiking production costs and market prices.[66]

The efficiency and competitiveness of these industries was clearly contingent upon the parallel development of agriculture. Increasing the supply and lowering the cost of raw materials, however, was clearly not possible because of the dominance of *iqta'*, which discouraged the intensive cultivation of non-staple, industrial crops.[67] Instead of complementing industrialization, agriculture under the *iqta'* system posed a formidable obstacle to its progress.

Like the vegetable oil industry, local textiles were handicapped by the low level of development of the productive forces in agriculture. Of all the infant industries, textiles were hit the hardest by the open door policy in the 1950s, because production costs were far too high to render the local products competitive with imported goods. As the government succumbed to the interests of commercial capital, local textiles found themselves in fierce competition with cheaper foreign goods. Although the Iraq Cotton Spinning and Weaving Co. was capable of filling all of Iraq's requirements for the cheaper-quality cloth, the state allowed the free import of similar cloth from India. In reaction to a glutted market, the industry requested the government to impose either a complete ban on imports of all cheap fabric, or high import duties comparable to those required in other Arab countries. The government responded by raising the duties but not enough to ease the pressure of competition.[68]

The price of locally manufactured gray cotton sheeting continued to be much higher than that of Indian competitors. The industry blamed the high costs of production, since the company paid, on the average, 40 dinars for Iraqi cotton compared with the equivalent of 16 Iraqi dinars paid in India.

Despite the revival of cotton cultivation in the 1940s and its rapid growth in the 1950s, output remained comparatively low due to poor levels of productivity.[69] The company tried to cut costs by buying directly from the cultivators and by opening its own ginnery in 1953. These measures, however, could not compensate for low agricultural productivity which raised the cost of domestic cotton.[70]

Cotton was not the only textile burdened by inefficiency and the inability to compete. The woolen industry faced similar problems as protection was reduced to a minimum. The outcome was the flooding of the market with Japanese products, which claimed over 70 percent of the market by 1957. The Federation of Industries complained that local production of wool had no prospects of competing against cheaper Japanese products, selling for far less than the cost price of locally produced wool cloth.[71] Only after the industry incurred heavy losses did the government respond by raising the import tax back to 30 percent.[72] But as with cotton, this percentage was far below that required to protect the industry against competition. The Federation's attempts to seek better protection, however, went unheeded. In a final attempt to reach a workable compromise with the government, the Federation of Industries suggested that to protect the interest of local industries, a member of the Federation should be represented on the Board of Import Committee, and that restrictions be based on quantity and value rather than value alone.[73] Restrictions based on value, they objected, were often open to fraud as local importers and foreign suppliers tended to either declare fictitious prices, or cut prices to enter the market on a large scale.

The Federation of Industries argued that the high market prices of their finished products were structural rather than the outcome of deliberate hiking of prices, as was often claimed by commercial capital. Responding to their opponents' arguments that protection breed monopolization, the Federation proposed that textile industries could, under protection, meet market demand of producing good quality material at a price that would not exceed a 10 percent rate of profit.[74]

While some industries received protection and thrived, others were seriously undermined by competition and the lack of sufficient protection. But even though aspiring industrial interests won some protective measures, protection alone was not enough to unleash industrial development. The ossification of agriculture established definite limits to the growth of industrial capital. First, the high costs of production which rendered industrial products uncompetitive on the world market, and second, the small and limited home market were deeply grounded in a poorly developed agriculture. The dismal purchasing power of the impoverished mass population, poor productivity, and the vastly unequal distribution of income in agriculture, rooted in a backward agrarian system, though challenged were left unchanged. In this regard, and in contrast to state policy on protection, aspiring industrial capital could not make any headway toward policies which would have fostered the development of agriculture.

In its report of 1952, the International Bank for Reconstruction and Development (IBRD) identified the depressed economic condition of the rural population to have undoubtedly been the obstacle to industrial growth in Iraq. High levels of exploitation and low agricultural productivity drastically reduced the purchasing power of a major portion of the population. The IBRD description of the standard of living of an average fellah from the south depicts a mass population living in desperate destitution, often below the level of subsistence. The IBRD estimated the fellah's total cash income to be no more than 20 dinars for the year. An income that would usually be spent:

> on food, clothing and some low-grade domestic tobacco. Two of the most important items in food expenditure are sugar and tea. Dates, particularly in the south, and a few vegetables such as onions are purchased, but on the whole, most fruits and vegetables are beyond the reach of the fellah and are sold in the towns. . . . Clothing would consist of some cheap cotton sheeting sufficient for a few garments and occasionally a second-hand jacket, few fellahin wear shoes. Hardly any is spent on housing or furniture, the living quarters being a small mud hut . . . with few mats and cooking utensils. Soap, for example, is undoubtedly a luxury. Life is not far above subsistence level and must often be below it.[75]

These conditions in agriculture, according to the report, undermined the health and vigor of the rural population, limited the market for industrial products, and in the long run jeopardized the stability of the social order.[76]

Raising the standard of living in the countryside was, therefore, imperative for national economic growth. Accordingly, the report strongly recommended the active participation of the state in, first, the establishment of a "socially desirable class of smallholders" and the prevention of further concentration of landholdings in the hands of large absentee landlords, and second, the improvement of agricultural productivity by introducing better drainage, modern tools, fertilizers, animal husbandry, as well as machinery when possible.[77]

For the most part, then, the IBRD realized that the process of industrialization was very much contingent upon revolutionizing agricultural relations in Iraq. Yet the IBRD, along with other advisory boards and development committees (Little and Salter Reports, Majlis al-ʿImar), failed in most cases to recognize that the development of agriculture was more than a technical issue and that agricultural development required a radical transformation in the existing class and power structures.

Iqtaʾ became an even more serious barrier to development once the inflow of oil capital began. In the 1950s, following the Oil Treaty of 1952, revenues from oil increased sharply, opening possibilities for economic development throughout the social order. Instead, the proceeds were diverted to projects favoring the interests of the tribal landed classes. Rather than alleviating social inequities, oil revenues were invested in ways which reproduced the existing power/class relations.

THE OIL INDUSTRY

In contrast to domestic industry, the oil industry, which produced crude oil for export to the advanced industrial countries, was developed and controlled by international capital. Consequently, oil production was highly capitalized and highly productive. The industry also had little to no impact on the domestic economy since oil production did not draw on goods produced domestically and employed a very small percentage of the domestic labor force.[78] An "underdeveloped" nation, Iraq could hardly provide the oil industry with capital goods and other necessary materials. Therefore, the larger portion of oil company expenditures were made in western Europe and the United States. Between 1930 and 1950, in the process of building the industry, the oil company spent 90 million pounds to purchase capital goods in Western capitalist markets, in contrast to 6 million spent in Iraq.[79] It was only in the initial years of its foundation that the industry involved the local economy, mostly in the construction of infrastructure such as roads, housing, telephone lines, and the pipelines. Once production began, this highly capitalized industry engaged a negligible percentage of the local work force. Between 1929 and 1953, Iraqi oil workers represented no more than 2.7 percent of the total non-agricultural labor force.[80]

Up to the 1950s, oil production was limited, royalties very small, and its contribution to the national economy relatively slight. Oil revenues nonetheless helped to reproduce the *iqta*[3] system, supplying 15 percent of state revenues, 80 percent of which was spent on agriculturally based capital programs. Irrigation projects such as flood control, water storage and land reclamation, were assigned 58.5 percent of the budget between 1934 and 1938, and 61 percent between 1949 and 1953. The least share went to industry, which claimed 3.4 and 2 percent of state spending during those same years.[81]

In the 1950s, conditions changed dramatically. Production rates increased, royalties rose sharply, and oil became the leading sector of the national economy. All this was the result of the new Oil Agreement concluded between the IPC and the Iraqi government in 1951. The agreement, which granted the Iraqis half of the earned profits as well as higher royalties, was itself the product of a series of changes, political and otherwise, in the postwar period. One such change was the emergence of American influence in the Gulf, the other was anti-British nationalism in the region.

To compete with an already established power, American companies tried to outbid the Europeans by offering better deals to local governments. In December of 1950, for instance, the American corporation ARAMCO concluded an oil agreement with Saudi Arabia providing for a 50–50 profit share plus the expected royalties and dead-rent payments. In 1951, a similar agreement was reached with the Kuwaiti government by another American company, the Kuwait Oil Company.[82] The same year, in April of 1951, the nationalist government of Mossadaq, in an attempt to challenge British domination in the region, nationalized oil in Iran.[83]

These events triggered a strong nationalist reaction within Iraq. Taking an opportune moment to attack the regime, the nationalists charged the government of Nuri al-Sa^{c}id with appeasing British imperial interests by accepting the 1951 oil agreement.[84] In parliament, a coalition of the opposition introduced a resolution (March 25, 1951) demanding the nationalization of oil companies in Iraq.[85] The NDP paper, *al-Ahali*, while favoring nationalization, supported Iraq as a full shareholder, with rights to half of all the exported oil as a second choice.[86]

The upsurge of anti-British nationalism along with American competition forced the IPC to reopen negotiations with the Iraqi government on the basis of profit-sharing. Under the new agreement concluded in January 1952, the oil company enforced the 50–50 profit share, and also agreed to increase output. In addition, the IPC conceded to minimum royalty payments of

Table 3. Oil Revenues Compared to Total Government Revenues,
1951–1958

Year	Total Government	Oil Revenues	% Oil/Gov. Revenue
1951	44.9	13.9	39.9
1952	74.4	40.1	53.8
1953	82.9	58.3	70.3
1954	97.8	64.3	69.2
1955	125.9	73.7	58.5
1956	113.8	68.8	60.4
1957	97.6	48.8	50.0
1958	137.2	79.8	68.2

(Source: Iraq Petroleum Co., Report on Operation of Oil Companies: *9, 13)*

20 million dinars in 1953 and 1954, and 25 million from 1955 on.[87] The agreement, regarded as a triumphant success by the regime, was denounced by the nationalists as another concession to imperial interests. To the opposition, the agreement came up short on many accounts, the most important being a failure to establish Iraq's national right to the control of its resources.[88] Despite their disappointment, oil became the leading sector of the national economy following the new agreement (see Table 3).

The spectacular increase in oil revenues gave Iraq new hopes for development and economic prosperity, as "capital cease[d] to be, for all practical purposes, a constraint on the feasible expansion of the economy."[89]

Although it is true that oil revenues increased Iraq's chance to break away from the plight of many developing nations, capital was not enough to initiate development. The barriers to social and economic progress encompassed much more than the "shortage of capital," "inefficient planning," and/ or the "lack of know-how," as maintained by the modernization paradigm.[90] The fundamental problem was a structural one, grounded in the nature of class and power relations present in that period. Even when the government devised an independent board to plan development projects independent of the cabinet, the *majlis al-ᶜimar*'s policies could not be separated from the dominant power structures and the oligarchic class.

The Development Board

The Development Board was initially founded in 1950. The prime minister presided over the board while the minister of finance was one of its executive members. The other six full-time members, experts in various fields of economics and development, were appointed by the Council of Ministers for a five-year term.[91] Following the 1952 oil agreement, the board was reorganized in such a manner, according to a prominent advisory member of the board, Arthur Salter, that it fundamentally lost its independence. All decisions by the board had to be approved first by the Minister of Development.[92] Essentially, the board was entrusted with 70 percent of the oil revenues to use in programs that would raise the standard of living of the average Iraqi. The board adopted a developmental plan where the largest allocations went to agriculture, followed by roads and construction. Industry, though scoring better than before, still lagged behind the other sectors.[93]

While the board allocated the highest funding to agriculture, it ignored the most important features contributing to agricultural "underdevelopment," i.e., high concentration in landownership, low productivity, and a poor drainage system. The Development Board allocated 31 percent of its total agricultural expenditure to capital programs that emphasized flood control, water storage, and land reclamation. Productivity and·drainage hardly received any attention. In the third plan, on Arthur Salter's recommendations, investment in drainage was raised to 6 percent of the total funds allocated to agriculture.[94] In practice, however, drainage received much less funding, since the actual expenditures on agriculture reached only to 54 percent of the realized budget.

With regard to the fundamental problem of land tenure, the Development Board simply sidestepped the issue. Conscious of the fact that land reform was a problem under the present regime, Salter admitted that "successive governments felt that new legislation on land tenancy must be kept within the bounds of what will not be actively resisted by the landowners."[95] The only conceivable course left, according to him, was to go around the problem rather than attack it directly.[96] This strategy, however, also failed. The Development Board was unable to dodge the existing power structures or substantially improve the productivity of agriculture.

Although the board adopted the scheme of reclaiming state lands for distribution to landless peasants, the success of this program was marginal since a considerable part of the distributed land went to the privileged landed class, and the 20,000 poor families who were given settlements were left with inadequate drainage that rendered many of the lands unproductive.[97]

The Development Board's plans for industry were equally problematic. Its attitude toward industrialization was initially ambivalent.[98] And when it did invest in industry, the projects duplicated existing industries increasing competitive pressures on the private sector. Development Board investments in two cement plants (6 million dinars) are one striking example of public investment competing with privately owned industry. Others are the Mosul Cotton Plant and the Mosul Sugar Plant. The political opposition closely associated with industrial capital was especially critical of the Development Board's investments in light consumer industries. While supportive of government investment in large industrial projects requiring a higher concentration of capital, the Federation of Industries argued that light consumer industries should be left to the private sector.[99]

CONCLUSION

Domestic industrial capital evolved in the context of two historical events: the creation of the Iraqi nation in the 1920s and the contraction of the world market in the 1940s. Domestic industry in the 1920s and 1930s, revolving around government markets and agricultural subsidies was both labor intensive and dominated by household forms of production. The crisis in world capitalism and the shrinkage of the world market during World War II led to a spurt of industrial growth. Like many other third-world countries, the combination of shortages in finished imported goods and the absence of competition encouraged local capital to move into relatively long-term and capital-intensive consumer industries once considered too speculative. Despite its relative growth in the late 1940s and 1950s, national industry on the whole remained small and fragile and confined to light consumer industries. Its fragility was due to three interrelated factors: foreign competition, in-fighting with commercial capital, and the predominance of *iqta'* relations in agriculture. Of the three, the most formidable obstacle proved to be the *iqta'* system, which inflated the costs of production of several of the agro-based industries rendering them uncompetitive on the market, both locally and internationally. It also undermined the possibility of creating a home market for industrial goods by restricting the purchasing power of the larger portion of the population.

In sharp contrast to domestic industry, the oil industry was a highly capitalized, highly efficient industry. Developed and controlled by multinational capital, the industry initially left little impression on the economy since it generated hardly any subsidiary industries and employed very little domestic labor. In the 1950s, however, oil began to play a much more significant role in the economy as a result of a sharp rise in revenues following the Oil Treaty of 1952. Although the oil revenues increased Iraq's chance to break away from the predicament of many developing nations, capital was not enough to initiate development. As the events following 1952 clearly indicated, the obstacles to economic development encompassed much more than the shortage of capital, inefficient planning, or lack of technological know-how. The fundamental problem was a structural one, grounded in the class and power relations present in Iraq. This was evidenced in the economic strategies pursued by the Development Board—the board that was devised particularly to be independent of the cabinet and the political process. The board, unable to disengage from the dominant power/class structure, followed economic strategies that guaranteed the reproduction of *iqta$^{\circ}$* relations by expending a large amount of the oil revenues on irrigation projects that benefited mostly the traditional landed classes.

II

THE NATION-STATE:
POLITICS AND REVOLUTION

4

State Crisis and the End of the Oligarchic Monarchy

The preceding chapters traced the socioeconomic development of social classes in Iraq following the incorporation of the region into the world capitalist market. Emphasizing the importance of internal factors in the evolution of the new classes, I have argued that out of the tribal structures emerged *iqta*ʾ, a highly exploitative agrarian system based on large estates and landlord-tenant relations. The predominance of *iqta*ʾ restricted the expansion of a more efficient agricultural system that developed in areas surrounding the cities and in parts of the northern region. Characterized by low productivity and labor-intensive methods, *iqta*ʾ also proved to be a formidable barrier to industrial development, restricting the growth of a consumer market and a home market for local industry. In sum, this inefficient system was essentially incompatible with capitalist accumulation in both agriculture and industry. This chapter and the next examine the impact of this fundamental socioeconomic contradiction on political developments in Iraq in the postmandate period, more specifically from 1932 to the revolution of 1958 and the revolution's failure thereafter.

From its inception, the modern Iraqi state was largely dominated by British colonial power, which allied itself to the monarchy and the oligarchic class. A vulnerable economy, buffeted by the ups and downs of the world market, by changing conditions of, first the depression, then the Second World War, then the increasingly competitive environment of the postwar recovery, produced hardships and demands for government intervention from many societal sectors. Opposition groups began to form in the 1930s, but it was from the 1940s on that the dominant ruling elite began to face a profound political crisis. Popular eruptions increased in tempo and intensity, leading to the uprising of 1948 (*al-wathba*), which challenged the continuing alliance between the agrarian oligarchy, the monarchy, and British imperialism.

The uprising ended with the defeat of a divided opposition and the imposition of martial law until 1952, when a new period of social protest and political opposition forced the government to accede to reform demands. But, again, the brief period of reform was followed by the re-imposition of oligarchic control under the government of Nuri al-Saʿid.

This cyclical policy of co-optation and coercion did not simply respond to social pressures, but also reflected the factionalist politics within the ruling groups of the oligarchic monarchy. Class conflict within the power structure influenced many of the governmental decisions vis-à-vis the opposition, thus contributing to the course of political development in this period.

Once oil began to play a decisive role in the economy, it exacerbated the tensions within the ruling elite, which ultimately weakened the regime and eased the way for its overthrow in 1958. As the leading source of state revenue in the 1950s, oil capital helped to insulate the regime from the political opposition and other subaltern social groups outside the political structure. As the government became less dependent on the domestic economy for revenues, it became even less responsive to the opposition and subaltern classes. While the government had occasionally acceded to opposition demands, from 1954, under Nuri al-Saᶜid, it not only made no concessions but took away the few political rights that had been won previously. As the government gained increased autonomy, however, it also became more isolated from other social groups (other than those already in power), structurally weaker, and politically more vulnerable than ever before.

As the government became more rigid and repressive, the political opposition became more articulate and defiant. The increased political repression of the 1950s forced the moderates within the opposition to lose confidence in the strategy of reforming the existing regime. At the same time, the moderates shifted their political strategy, deciding now to include the Iraqi Communist Party in the National Front, thereby opening the way to a more united and stronger opposition, since the communists were one of the best-organized and strongest opposition groups. Following the defeat of the 1956 uprising, the army moved into opposition to the regime and conditions became ripe for a radical solution, which was accomplished with the help of army in 1958. The fragile unity of the opposition, however, could not be sustained in the postrevolutionary period. Driven apart by serious conflicts of interest and consequent divisions over social and economic policy, the opposition in power was itself overthrown in 1963.

This political development will be traced in the next two chapters. Chapter 4 will analyze the development of the political opposition in the 1940s and 1950s, leading to the formation of *al-Jabhah al-Wataniyah*, a United National Front which, with the help of the army, orchestrated the overthrow of the monarchy and its principal allies in July, 1958. The following chapter will analyze the breakup of the National Front and the defeat of the revolution in the period of 1958 to 1963.

THE FORMATION OF THE NATION-STATE

As part of the modernizing colonial project, the British in 1921 constructed Iraq out of the three provinces of Basra, Baghdad, and Mosul, installed a monarchy, a constitution and parliament, and created a modern administrative bureaucracy centered in Baghdad. They also contrived a mandatory power to execute their project as well as assert control over their imperial interests in the region.[1]

While constructing a unified nation-state, the British governed Iraq primarily through differentiating and classifying practices. From its inception in the 1920s, the institutions of the modern state—bureaucracy, lawmaking, administration of justice, etc.—were founded on normalizing and regulating differences between the ruler and the ruled (both European and indigenous), tribespeople and townspeople, Muslims, Christians, and Jews, and Shi³ah, and Sunni. A most striking example of exercising their power through differentiation was the institutionalization of two distinct systems of justice: the civil and criminal laws on the one hand, governing the civilian population in towns, and the Tribal Criminal and Civil Disputes Regulation governing the tribal areas, on the other.[2] Furthermore, the British invented new methods to secure their dominance, even though these techniques were often recognized as detrimental to the economic progress of the country, as in the case of boosting the political and economic power of the rising shaykhly landowning class at the expense of the development of a more efficient modern economy. This course of action also proved inconsistent with "democratic" and "liberal" values that they professed to promote.

When the British set up their mandatory power, they improvised a governmental machinery which "might be called indigenous but which would ensure, as much as possible, that the initiative and direction and definite ultimate control remain in British hands."[3] This was accomplished by giving the British High Commissioner, who headed the Council of State (the executive branch), the power of "over-ruling the decision of the majority of the Council."[4] Similarly, the mandate founded a legislative body, consisting of a senate and a Chamber of Deputies that had little authority.

In brief, under this new government, political freedoms, individual rights, and other forms of "mass representation" associated with Western liberal democracy were virtually nonexistent.[5] The first parliament introduced under British mandate rule (1924–1925) set the precedent for future elections. While the senate consisted of "twenty appointed notables," the Chamber of Deputies, hand-picked by the government, was elected through indirect balloting, instead of freely and directly by the people.[6] The seats were primarily awarded to the tribal shaykhs, aghas, and town politicians who had been sympathetic to British rule. Following this precedent, in consecutive elections most members were chosen *bi-il-tazkiya,* that is, unopposed.[7]

Instead of the Western liberal democratic model, Britain's civilizing project produced a highly contentious oligarchic monarchy that was closely allied to its imperial interests. In the first phase of its formation (1920–1932), the new nation-state successfully established the authority of the monarchy in Baghdad and the landed oligarchy (tribal shaykhdom) in the countryside.[8] It also guaranteed the dominance of Britain over Iraq, especially over its most important capital asset—the oil fields—by granting the Iraq Petroleum Company and its subsidiaries the exclusive right to explore, produce, and market the oil. The process of implanting and consolidating this modern state involved coercion and violent repression of the "rights" of many social groups that either held different aspirations or else opposed the interests of the British rulers and their allies, the landed oligarchic monarchy.[9]

In 1932, British mandate rule was terminated and Iraq was internationally recognized as independent. But the events following 1932 made it evident that Iraq was far from independent. The British, through the indigenous dominant class allied to them, continued to exert power and command tremendous authority in the affairs of Iraq. The treaty of 1932, dictated by the British and overwhelmingly backed by the oligarchic monarchy, ensured that. It granted the British the right to keep their military air bases intact. It also dictated that Iraq must consult closely with Britain in all matters of foreign policy affecting its interests, and must extend to the British in times of war or a "threat of war" all the facilities and assistance that Iraq could give on its territory.[10]

The establishment of a formally "democratic" and "independent" sovereign state that was neither democratic nor entirely independent was the context for the appearance of political opposition in Iraq. Focusing on the issue of "national independence" (both political and economic), the various opposition groups regarded the 1932 treaty as a symbol of Iraq's servitude to British imperialism as well as an expression of the deep commitment of the oligarchic monarchy to British interests. From 1940 to 1958, the question of nationhood became the fundamental political rallying point for the nationalist oppositional groups, despite their diverse and often conflicting positions.

The Oligarchic Monarchy and the Opposition

The discussion of the historical development of the political opposition will center on the three major parties—the Nationalist Democrats, the Ba'th, and the Iraqi communists—their political programs, ideologies, and the classes or social groups they most appealed to. It is important to note that organized political opposition was found mainly in the major towns and cities. One should not conclude from this that opposition did not exist in the rural areas; indeed, peasant rebellions were common, especially in the regions where large tribal estates predominated. Resistance in the rural areas was articulated not necessarily in modern political forms of expression (media and political parties), as much as in the form of oral traditions, religious, tribal, and, particularly, oral poetry—a point that should be of interest to future scholars in the field.

The political opposition was by and large nationalist in character, with the exception of the Iraqi Communist Party, which had a globalist vision of history. The two strongest representatives of the nationalist movement were al-Hizb al-Watani al-Dimuqrati (refered to from now on as the NDP, the National Democratic Party) and Hizb al-baʿth al-ʾarabi al-ishtiraki (the Pan-Arab Socialist Baʿth party).[11] Speaking on behalf of an aspiring Iraqi bourgeoisie, the National Democratic Party was aligned with the colonial state and was commited to the continuation of the Iraqi nation as a separate sovereign entity.[12] In sharp contrast to the NDP, the pan-Arab Baʿth, speaking on behalf of a much larger urban Arab audience, opposed the preservation of the Iraqi nation-state and favored instead a unified Arab nation-state.[13] The other important element of the opposition was the Iraqi Communist Party, whose political role was shaped by two interrelated factors:

a.   its failure to develop a historical analysis and a strategy that
     addressed the particularities of Iraqi society; and

b.   its uncritical acceptance of the Communist International's
     doctrine of "the two-stage revolution," with tragic consequences
     for the party as well as the nationalist revolution of 1958.

The Nationalist Parties and their Politics

Although the Iraqi nation-state was the creation of British imperial power, it was able, fairly quickly, to acquire its own internal coherence and sense of sovereignty. Rather than being simply derived from an external authority, the legitimacy of the Iraqi state was now based on the marshaling of various indigenous elements, interests, and social forces in the form of loyalty to the monarchy, or else to a territorially based national identity. The new social and political order created by the nation-state framed nationalist discourse. That is why nationalist writing, in spite of its anticolonial stand, did not dispute the basic assumptions of the colonial project. Nationalist arguments for "liberation" were hence confined within the European Enlightenment project and its modernizing agent, the nation-state. Nationalist writing, for example, never posed the need to dismantle in any radical fashion the institutional structures inherited from the mandate system, whether in the realm of administration and economy or in that of law and education. The main nationalist objection to colonialism was phrased more in terms of its failure to complete the modernizing project than in rejecting its premises. British rule, for example, was repeatedly blamed for transgressing its own professed principles and for impeding the progress of national development. Thus, the nationalists held the British responsible for creating *iqta*³, for perpetuating a backward economy, and for exploiting Iraq's natural resources to pursue their own interests.[14] The economic and political critique of British imperial power was a potent, fundamental theme in nationalist discourse. While rejecting colonialism as an "illigitimate," "alien," and "exploitative" power, nationalism at the same time affirmed the legitimacy of the colonial project itself.

As the Indian theorist of anticolonial nationalism, Partha Chatterjee, persuasively argues, nationalist thought could not just constitute itself in terms of a negation of colonialism; it also had to produce "a positive discourse" by replacing "the structure of colonial power with a new order, that of national power."[15] To demarcate its difference from colonialism, nationalist thought transformed the nation from a passive into an active sovereign entity, constructing a new political-ideological idiom, in which a reified nation displaced colonial power, subverting its authority and challenging its morality.

In the process of reappropriating the power to represent themselves as a nation rather than being represented by the British, anticolonial nationalists formulated their project as one of both "liberation" and "development." In its economic critique of colonialism, as Chatterjee argues, nationalist discourse considered the colonial project illegitimate not only because it was foreign but also because it exploited the nation's resources and created a backward economy. Development ideology thus became another essential constituent of nationalism that distinguished it from colonialism.

Nationalist political strategies and discourses reflected the contradictory realities facing not only oppositional classes in Iraq but throughout the colonized world. Chatterjee points out that in the colonial setting the emergent bourgeoisie faces the formidable task of carrying out a two-fold struggle—against the colonial power (which also represents global capitalism) and against domestic forces which block the structural transformation of a home economy. These conditions require the creation of alliances, within the framework of a nationalist movement, between the bourgeoisie and other dominant classes and social groups, as well as the support of subaltern classes, to mobilize effectively against colonial power and for national development. This strategy of gradual reform based on compromises with older ruling classes is aptly designated a "passive revolution" by Antonio Gramsci, who contrasted it with the classical "bourgeois revolution" modelled after the French Revolution with its full-fledged assault on the older feudal classes.[16] However, as Chatterjee points out, the "passive revolution" in which the national state rather than a class takes on the tasks of development, can no longer be deemed an aberration, since it represents the norm rather than the exception in the twentieth century.

Unable to establish hegemony on its own, the national bourgeoisie must seek instead to expand capitalism through an "interventionist state" which directly enters the "domain of production as a mobilizer and manager of inevestible resources." Economic development also bestows the nationalist project with the stamp of legitimacy:

> This legitimacy had to flow from the nationalist criticism of colonialism as an alien and unrepresentative power that was exploitative in character and from the historical necessity of an independent state that would promote national development. It was in the universal function of "development" of national society as a *whole* [my emphasis] that the postcolonial state would find its distinctive content. This was to be concretized by the embodiment within itself of a new mechanism of development administration, something the colonial state, because of its alien and extractive character, had never possessed. It was in the administration of development that the bureaucracy of the postcolonial state was to assert itself as the universal class, satisfying in the service of the state its private interests by working for the universal goals of the nation.[17]

Despite these common themes in nationalist discourse, there were also differences. The most striking was between "Iraqi" and "pan-Arab" nationalism. While Iraqi nationalists (the NDP) located their project of "liberation" and "development" within the confines of the Iraqi nation-state, the pan-Arabs (Baʿth) could only conceive of it within the much larger boundaries of an undivided Arab nation-state (which included all contemporary Arabic-speaking countries).

The National Democratic Party

The National Democratic Party (NDP) evolved from al-Ahali—a social club founded in the early 1930s by young, mostly urban, intellectuals.[18] Initially, al-Ahali lacked a coherent ideology and hardly any political program to speak of. In its early writings, mainly in the party newspaper, *al-Ahali*, the group raised issues relating to British imperialism and national independence, the absence of democratic rights, and called for social and economic reforms that could bring "progress" and "prosperity" as well as security to the Iraqi people within the confines of the existing regime. Al-Ahali, one could say, expressed the idealism of a new generation of Western-educated intellectuals who identified with European liberal humanism, but rejected its antihumanist and exploitative practices. Inspired by British Fabianism, they aspired to a constitutional parliamentary democracy with a highly centralized state that could foster an economic program bringing the benefits of advanced capitalism to the Iraqi people.[19]

Throughout the 1930s, the group and its newspaper, *al-Ahali*, played an important role by revealing to the literate public the social and economic injustices endured by the Iraqi people under the mandate and the oligarchic monarchy. They blamed British imperialism for deliberately failing to deliver a truly progressive democratic system in Iraq and for continuing to dominate and exploit the resources of the nation. The paper also took up the cause of the peasantry in the countryside and exposed the inequities caused by the various land settlements ratified by the national government in the 1930s. When describing the condition of the peasantry, al-Ahali, however, denied that class relations were the reason for the appalling conditions in the countryside. This position, of course, is understandable considering that the notion of class would challenge their assertion of the nation as an undivided unified subject. Instead, al-Ahali laid the blame on landlessness, rather than the exploitative landlord-tenant relations present under *iqta᾽*. Accordingly, al-Ahali supported the idea of state land distribution among the poor and the landless and suggested as well a more equitable system of taxation based on income.[20]

The group's most important role in this period was to serve as an open political forum for discussion and debate among the opposition, consisting largely of a discordant intelligentsia including progressive and moderate social democratic elements, independent Marxists, and fanatic nationalists. In the 1940s, however, this broad unity fractured and out of one of these factions emerged the NDP in 1947.[21]

In the early 1940s, the government attempted to co-opt and divide the rising popular opposition by introducing "liberal" reforms. Under these measures, the government granted all opposition the right to free press as well as the right to form political organizations, with the exception of the Iraqi Communist Party.[22] As a result, al-Ahali came to be torn between two factions: the leftist tendency that was skeptical of the government's reform program, and the social democrats who backed it. In the preparatory debates over al-Ahali's formation as an official party, the leftist faction, led by Tal᾽at al-Shaibani and Zaki Abdul Wahab, put forward two proposals: "socialism" should be included in the new party's platform, and membership should be open to all sympathizers, including independent "Marxists and others." The moderate social democrats, Kamil al-Chadirchi, Muhammad Hadid, and Hussain Jamil, who rejected class as a fundamental factor in the struggle, strongly opposed the proposal of the leftist faction primarily because the "national liberation struggle," not "socialism," was the party's immediate objective.[23]

By the time the NDP was founded in 1947, the moderate faction within al-Ahali was already in the majority. And on the occasion of the first party convention, they purged the left-wingers, renounced the notion of class struggle and socialism as divisive to the unity of the nation and reaffirmed their commitment to reformist politics by entering the election of 1947.[24]

In the initial years of its formation, the NDP, which considered itself a "progressive" party that sought change through "democratic," not "revolutionary" means, continued to attract a large number of its members from the middle strata of society—left-to-center intellectuals, students, and professionals.[25] But in the 1950s, the party came to articulate far more distinctly the interests of entrepreneurial capitalists, especially the manufacturing sector. Several of its founding and new leading members were either drawn from this class of manufacturers or had a strong foothold in it. One of its founders, Muhammad Hadid—a member of the Central Committee and the vice president of the party—came from an old mercantilist Mosulite family, and became in the 1950s the manager as well as large shareholder of the Vegetable Oil Extraction Co. Rajab al-Saffar, a member of the Central Committee and the secretary of the party, was an owner of a silk factory. Khadduri Khadduri, another prominent figure in the party, was part owner and manager of the Cotton Seeds Products Co. These three, besides other prominent manufacturing capitalists including the Fattahs, founded the Federation of Industries and were active members on its Administrative Council.[26]

In addition, the NDP tended to attract some prominent but progressive elements from the agricultural sector. Al-Chadirchi, the president of the party, came from an old Ottoman aristocratic family of landed officials.[27] The attorney Hussain Jamil, a founding and leading member of the party, came from a distinguished family of *sadah* (sayyids)—some of whom became pioneers in capitalist farming.[28] Included also was Hudayb al-Hajj Hamud, owner of 10,000 dunums of rich rice land in the province of Diwaniyah, who was appalled by the exploitation of the tenants by other tribal landlords and was renowned for his "fair" treatment of his peasantry and for returning 60 percent of the produce to them.[29]

As the NDP came to articulate the interests of the rising national bourgeoisie, its political program became markedly more coherent, especially on three issues:

1. the agrarian question;

2. the historical "developmentalist" mission of the national state as a protector and facilitator of indigenous small private capital; and

3. the Iraqi nation-state as the historical norm.

On the agrarian question, the NDP took a more cogent stand against the *iqta*[?] system and the oligarchic landed class than had *al-Ahali*. The party blamed the oligarchic class for blocking the development of both agriculture and industry and subsequently put forward a land reform that called for:

1. the confiscation of all the large landholdings alienated to the tribal oligarchy by the land settlements of the 1930s and the 1940s;

2. the distribution of confiscated lands and other state lands to the landless and poor peasants; and

3. the creation of educational cooperatives that would assist the peasants in modernizing agriculture.

Besides introducing land reform to their platform, the NDP in 1950 adopted "democratic socialism" as their new "social, political, and economic creed."[30] As explained by the NDP leader, al-Chadirchi, "democratic social-ism" stood for "state protection of both private property and national indus-try . . . support for state's control of public transportation and services that benefit the general public . . . [as well as] the state's promotion of national capital to help industrialize and develop the economy along with joint ven-tures with private capital."[31]

Essentially, "democratic socialism" represented a gradual form of capi-talist transformation under which the state was delegated the primary role of promoting development. By pooling national resources and capital necessary to industrialize and modernize the economy, the state would undertake the central role that Western history had once assigned to the bourgeoisie. The position of the NDP, one might argue, expressed not only the sentiments of an aspiring bourgeoisie but also its vulnerability as a social class. A product of the interwar period, the Iraqi "bourgeoisie" was far too fragile to transform society on its own, particularly within the context of a low level of develop-ment of the productive forces at home and a highly competitive, highly advanced global capitalist economy. The NDP adopted a political-ideological program that projected liberation and development as a national struggle rather than one representing the particular and narrow interests of the bourgeoisie.

NDP strategy, based on the largest possible national alliance, including compromises with other dominant classes as well as with subaltern classes, produced a political-ideological agenda to replace colonial power without dismantling the institutional structures inherited from colonialism and without launching a full-scale assault against the older ruling classes. Projecting a noncontradictory "national" interest in capitalist development, the NDP envisioned its nationalist revolution within the confines of the Iraqi nation-state.

For the national democrats, the struggle for liberation and reconstruction was seen as part of the process of emancipating the Iraqi nation from the grip of British imperialist power and its allies the oligarchic monarchy. Their political writings explicitly drew a line between the Iraqi nation-state and other Arab nations. While they acknowledged that the Iraqi nation was initially a construct of British imperialism, they argued that recent historical experience under European colonialism had led to the emergence of significant political and economic differentiation among the Arabs. In their discourse, they made reference only to the plurality of the Arab peoples (*al-shuᵓub al-ᶜarabiyah*) rather than to the singular Arab people (*al- shaᶜb al-ᶜarabi*) commonly used by the pan-Arabists. They rejected the notion of a single unitary Arab nation and instead called for an *ittihad ᶜarabi federali* (a regional-type federation) which would permit national autonomy by guaranteeing each of the Arab nation-states their separate territorial entities and their independent political and social institutions.[32]

The Baᶜth

The pan-Arabists, the Baᶜth, presumed an Arab not an Iraqi identity as the subject of their narrative, and envisioned the "Arab nation," and not the Iraqi nation, as the medium of national reconstruction. Deeply committed to the "revival" and "resurrection" of the historic "Arab Nation," the Baᶜth considered Iraqi nationalism a betrayal of the Arabs and their history because it was tantamount to sanctioning colonialist separatist and regionalist policy. Since European colonialism fragmented the Arab collectivity *(al-ummah al-ᶜarabiyah)* into a multitude of nations, decolonization inevitably must involve the breakdown of all the artificial boundaries and territorialities drawn by colonial administrations as well as the unification of the Arab people under "one nation—one state."

The repudiation of multi-nationalism and the recognition of the inseparability of the struggles for freedom and unity was the core of pan-Arab nationalism. To the Baᶜth, the struggle for national independence and a unitary Arab nation were one and the same. In sharp contrast to the NDP's socioeconomic rationalization for an Iraqi nation-state, the unitary Arab nation of the Baᶜth had its historical and cultural justification. It was the commonalty of language, culture, and history that provided the ideological basis for the Arab nation:

Arab nationalism is both nationalist and Arabist: nationalist in the sense that it has the basic preliminary conditions common to all nationalisms; Arabist in the sense that it has a continuous unbroken national history that extends through the various ages and civilizations. Another characteristic of its Arabness which ensured the [unbroken] continuity in its national history was the Arabic language which itself encompasses mutuality of thought, principles, and ideals.[33]

The essential character of the Arabs as a nation (an *ummah*) had therefore to be linked to a past which in the case of the Arabists goes all the way to the prophet Muhammad and the rise of Islam:

> The true birth of Arab nationalism took place with the rise of Islam. . . . Islam was revealed by an Arabian Prophet, in the Arabic language, in Arabia. We read in the Qurᵓan: 'A messenger has now come to you from among yourselves . . . ' There is a tradition that the prophet said one day: 'I am an Arab, the Qurᵓan is in Arabic and the language of the denizens of Paradise is Arabic.' . . . One of the basic aims of Islam was to replace the narrow blood and tribal ties existing among the Arabs in pagan days or the 'Days of Ignorance' by a broader and a wider 'religious patriotism' found in Islam itself. The Arabs were to be united into one great community, the Community of the Faithful—the Ummah or the Arab Nation, al-Ummah al-ᶜArabiyyah was thus a nation originally born out of Islam. Islam was the prime creator of the national life and political unity of the Muslim Arabs.[34]

The assertion of an organic connection between Islam and Arabism was also prevalent in Baᶜth writings. Michel ᶜAflaq, their Christian ideologue, influenced by earlier Arab nationalist thinkers, maintained the symbiotic relations of Islam and Arabism, "the birth of Islam was the crucial event in [our] national history," "the essence of Islam is Arabism," "Islam in its true essence emerged out of Arabism; it expressed best its genius." Reaffirming the difference between Arab nationalist discourse and that of West (which separated religion and nationalism), ᶜAflaq insisted that "there was never a contradiction between Islam and Arabism."[35]

Clearly, the question of Islam was of considerable importance to the pan-Arab nationalists. This, however, did not signify a longing to return to the "traditional" past because the linkage between Islam and nationalism was political, not religious. In the process of writing their own national narrative, the Arab nationalists secularized Islam as much as they Arabized it. ᶜAflaq, following the steps of Arab nationalists like Satiᵓ al-Husari and Abdul Rahman al-Bazzaz, spoke of religion as "a genuine expression of the humanism of man," and that "the ideals of Islam are humanism," and "the message of Islam is the creation of Arab humanism."[36]

By setting out to justify the nation as "historic," "Islamic," and "Arab," the Arab nationalists were effectively affirming that nationalism was not simply an idea imported from the West, but rather intrinsic to an Arab past that had been lost and in need of revival. The national past, therefore, as Tehmina Akhtar succinctly put it, "takes on a critical importance as the basis for the establishment of the modern nation-state through a hegemonic creation of national culture—the past is revisited, revised, and reinterpreted according to the criteria of the new nationalist elites."[37]

Like the NDP, however, the Ba⁽th party also defined itself as a "progressive" party that wanted to overthrow the old regimes through, what ⁽Aflaq called, "inqilab" and not "revolutionary" means, to establish their difference with the communists. "Inqilab," often inaccurately translated as a coup d'etat, is a slippery notion because it meant more than just the overthrow of old colonial regimes to the Ba⁽th. It also involved the process of resurrecting and modernizing the Arab nation through unification and the breakdown of all territorial boundaries.

Their progressive agenda also included "socialism" which, in their explication, was essentially "nationalistic and distinctly Arabic."[38] They rejected Marxist socialism as Western, antinationalist, and materialist. To the Ba⁽th, national unity and cohesion were the motivating force for national progress, not class conflict and internationalism. Consequently, they defined their version of Arab socialism as "spiritual," nonmaterialist, nationalist, that is, committed to the protection of private property:

> This is how we embarked on the road of a nationalistically interpreted socialism. When asked about the content of our socialism, we replied: our socialism is an Arab, nationalist one—not internationalist. And when we were asked about the difference between our socialism and communism, we answered: our socialism acknowledges mind and matter. We understand spiritualism as an idealistic value . . . which devoted itself to the whole people and not just the proletariat. We believed that class consciousness contradicts national consciousness and Arab unity; our socialism—and we stress this, accepts small-scale private property and inheritance.[39]

At the same time, the Ba⁽th did not deny the existence of deep material inequalities in the nation and the need to distribute national wealth more equally among its peoples. It also recognized the need for an Arab state that directs and plans the vital sectors of the economy on behalf of its people, without jeopardizing the right of private property.[40]

In its populist, anti-imperialist phase, the political rhetoric of Arab nationalists appealed by and large to the "petty bourgeoisie" and the middle strata of urban Arab societies.[41] In Iraq, it attracted lower-middle-class teachers, students and recently urbanized youth. It made its first appearance in Iraq in 1947–1948, Baghdad and Karbalah being the recruiting centers for the Ba⁽th in its early years.⁴² By 1952, the Iraqi Ba⁽th branch had enough followers to legitimate its official recognition by the mother party centered in Damascus. The party continued to grow in the 1950s, drawing large numbers of Istiqlal members and sympathizers into its ranks.⁴³ In general, however, the social base of the Ba⁽th party in the 1950s was largely drawn from the student population, the newly educated urban professionals, and semi-professionals in Baghdad, Nasiriyah, Ramadi, Basra, and Najaf. In contrast to the NDP, Ba⁽th leadership from 1950 to 1970 came largely from "petty bourgeois" low-income families.⁴⁴

The Iraqi Communist Party

In contrast to the nationalist formations, the Iraqi Communist Party was a Marxist-Leninist Party with an internationalist perspective and revolutionary politics. The communists took both the colonialists and the nationalists to task for denying class conflict and affirming the nation as an undivided sovereign subject that transcended class. They considered the representation of the nation-state as a unified and autonomous subject to be ideological.

While their theoretical position affirmed class struggle and internationalism, in practice, the party's revolutionary politics were constantly compromised by the doctrine of the two-stage revolution and political shifts in the position of the Communist International.

The issue of the nature of colonial revolutions was first discussed in the Second Congress of the International in 1921. In these debates, Lenin adopted the line that all colonial liberation movements were "bourgeois democratic" by character, given that the overwhelming majority of the population were peasants. He therefore upheld the position that the Comintern "must enter into temporary alliance with bourgeois democracy in the colonial and backward countries."⁴⁵ At the same time, he warned that alliance with bourgeois parties must be conditional.⁴⁶

The Fourth Congress, the last one Lenin attended, reopened the discussion, but this time with a more critical view of the national bourgeoisie especially in light of its conciliation toward imperialism in certain Asian countries. In the "Theses on the Eastern Question," the Fourth Congress stressed that:

1. temporary agreements with bourgeois democracy are acceptable and indispensable;

2. the broad peasant masses are important to the success of the revolutionary movement in "backward" countries;

3. "the objective tasks of the colonial revolution go beyond the limits of bourgeois democracy;" and

4. the young proletariat of the colonies must fight and win an independent position and be a leading force within the anti-imperialist united front.[47]

Soon after Lenin's death, open debates in the International came to a halt. Under Stalin's influence, the Comintern introduced and generalized two new doctrines that were to have fateful consequences for the revolutionary movements in both the First and Third Worlds. The first new doctrine revised the theory of the international character of the socialist revolution by introducing the doctrine of "socialism in one country." This doctrine became the ideological rationalization for the subordination of revolutionary actions in any part of the world to the interests of the Soviet state and the building of socialism in the former USSR.[48] From this point on, requirements of the Soviet government's foreign policy dictated decisions on strategy and tactics within the Comintern. The second new doctrine was a dogmatic institutionalization of Lenin's characterization of all colonial revolutions as "democratic bourgeois." Stalin's doctrine of "revolution by stages" became the standard interpretation of all revolutions in the backward colonial and semi-colonial world. Marking a clear departure from the earlier approach, Stalin's doctrine identified a separate bourgeois democratic stage of development that would have to be completed in all the non-metropolitan countries—regardless of their particular histories—before the struggle for socialism could begin. To inaugurate this stage of capitalist development, a necessary precursor to socialist revolution, the workers, peasants, and petty bourgeoisie (intelligentsia) must ally themselves with the national bourgeoisie. This "bloc of four classes" would make it possible to build capitalism and, therefore, create the autonomous industrial proletariat that was needed to carry out the second stage of the development, i.e., the socialist revolution.[49]

These two doctrines shaped the development of the communist movement in Iraq on two levels. First, on the theoretical level, the dictation of a uniform theory by the Comintern limited the possibility for the ICP to develop an historical analysis and strategy appropriate to the particularities of Iraqi society. Second, on the political level, the contradiction between the party's theoretical position and actual political developments led to a contradiction between the party's long-term strategy and short-term tactics. Ilyas Murqus, an independent Marxist-Leninist, carefully worded his critique of Arab Communism as being "characterized by the absolute separation of theory and praxis and by a large gulf between general dogma and any specific

practical activity. Loyalty to principles turns into rigid, meaningless dogmatism and political elasticity ends up as unlimited opportunism."[50]

By the time the Iraqi Communist Party was founded in 1935, the ossification of the International under Stalin was well underway. The ICP therefore did not question the leading role of the Soviet Party or Stalin's monolithic
leadership. Accepting the doctrine of the revolution by stages, the party saw
the anticolonial struggle in Iraq as part of an inevitable evolutionary process
aiming toward a national bourgeois revolution. The party saw its central role
as leading the "oppressed classes" (workers and peasants), into an alliance
(al-Jabhah wataniyah al-muwahadah) with the progressive faction of the
national "bourgeoisie" to forge the struggle for liberation, social reforms, and
the extension of democratic rights within the framework of a bourgeois state.[51]

Upholding national democracy as a separate historical stage of development, the ICP in practice subordinated "class struggle" and "revolutionary"
politics to the national struggle and the establishment of bourgeois democracy. The party's program stressed the importance of building a unified national movement to fight imperialism and end British political domination of
Iraq. Their agenda included the termination of the treaty of 1930 and the
dismantling of all foreign military bases. Besides liberation, the party's program also emphasized the need to build a national democratic government
that would unleash economic development by liquidating all feudal forms of
exploitation including large estates, create a unified national market and protect national industries from foreign competition, and control all vital natural
resources, like oil. Simply put, their program was not that much different
from that of the NDP. The differences were that the ICP emphasized the need
to organize the Iraqi working class in trade unions and enforce the eight-hour
workday, recognized the national rights of the Kurdish people, and granted
equal rights to women.[52] These reforms were seen as part of the historic task
of the anticolonial revolution which was part of creating the political and
social conditions for capitalist development.

In spite of their reformist program, the ICP's attempts to build a unified
national movement were by and large unsuccessful in this period.[53] The failure to unify the national movement was due mostly to a reluctance on the part
of the nationalists to join forces with a "divisive," "revolutionary" internationalist party which they feared would lead the movement astray, despite,
one might add, the ICP's proclamations to the contrary.[54] Dropping socialism
from the ICP agenda was often interpreted as "political opportunism" by the
nationalists.[55] Of course, the constant shifts in the ICP's political positions in
the 1940s helped to affirm rather than refute the doubts of the nationalists,
especially since these sharp "left-right" turns were dictated largely by the
International to serve the needs and interests of the Soviet Union and its

foreign policy rather than the particular needs and interests of either the Iraqi communist party or the Iraqi society.

For instance, when the Soviet Union adopted its Popular Front strategy—a mutual assistance pact with the Western democracies to combat fascism—in the 1940s, the ICP, following the Comintern's new line, not only dropped its strong anti-imperialist stand but also championed the British and the presence of their military forces in Iraq. By doing so, the ICP shunned its national struggle in defense of the interests of the Soviet Union and its allies, the British:

> In so far as the harm that befalls any part of the united world democratic front is bound to affect the Soviet Union, our party regards the British army, which is now fighting Nazism, as an army of liberation. In other words, our support of the united world democratic front means that we are on the side of the British . . . We must, therefore, help the British army in Iraq in every possible way, and in particular facilitate the transport of war materials by railways . . . "[56]

In advocating the cause of the British in Iraq, the ICP was also forced to adopt a much more conciliatory line toward the Iraqi monarchy and the landed oligarchic class. It dropped its previous strategy of the "four-class bloc" against the oligarchy for a more reformist parliamentarian road to change, as their newspaper, *al-Qaʾidah*, strongly implied:

> [We] struggle for the establishment of democracy in Iraq by pushing the present ruling authorities to respect and practice the Iraqi constitution . . . to fight against inflation and for the basic needs of the people . . . to raise the economic, social and cultural standards of the Iraqi masses, and seek the improvement of their health . . . to defend the rights and interests of the Iraqi working class . . . and to improve the general conditions of the peasantry and defend their rights."[57]

This strategy of appeasement, although adopted without reference to domestic political realities, worked favorably for the communists. It was in the 1940s that the ICP managed to organize a strong leading cadre and build a broad social base for itself. As a result of the Popular Front agreement, the Iraqi government, in league with its Western allies (Britain), began to lift its heavy-handed policy against the communists and all other radical elements. Restrictions on oppositional political activities were relaxed, exiled communists were permitted to return, and jailed members were freed.[58] It was in light of this policy that the party was able to extend its membership beyond its early cadre from the urban middle- and lower-middle-class intelligentsia to incorporate a broader social base of workers, petty traders, and many of the marginalized recently urbanized population, which crowded the slums of Baghdad and other major towns.[59]

The striking expansion of communism in this period, one might also argue, encouraged the leadership of the party to take a sharp leftward turn once the Popular Front strategy was called off by the Soviet Union.[60] With Germany's surrender, the outbreak of the Cold War, and the collapse of the Popular Front, the ICP dropped its conciliatory line and reinstated its earlier anti-imperialist, anti-oligarchic stand. This time around, however, the ICP embraced a much more confrontational line against the monarchy and the oligarchic regime. Not only that, it also adopted a much more critical view of the nationalist forces. From 1946 until the popular uprising of 1948, which will be discussed later, the ICP commanded considerable power in the urban areas, organizing a series of workers strikes, popular protests, and demonstrations challenging and provoking the authority of the Iraqi regime and its main ally, Britain.[61]

Forsaken by most of the opposition for its far-left turn, the isolated ICP soon became an easy target for the government and its repressive apparatus. In January 1947, the government arrested their main leader, Fahd, and other principal members of the Central Committee, put them on trial for national treason, and sentenced them to death by hanging. The sentence, which shocked the national democratic forces into action, was commuted under popular pressure to life imprisonment.

Although Fahd's arrest triggered a sense of gloom within the party, it soon recovered from its shock and resumed its activities with increased intensity; that is, until the second setback following the defeat of 1948 uprising when Fahd and two members of his Politbureau were put back on trial and once again condemned to death. This time, the sentence was carried out and on February 15, 1949, Fahd, Shabibi, and Zaki Basim were publicly hanged in different squares in Baghdad.

The party was once again able to gather its forces and re-enter the political scene in 1951. In the early 1950s, the politics of the ICP were, by and large, dominated by a leftist-oriented line. In 1952, for example, the ICP raised for the first time the slogan of a "People's Democratic Republic" (ʿhukm jumhuri shaʾbiʾ). This line led to a split in its ranks in 1953, and to the formation of the *Rayit-al-shaghghilah* (Banner of the Workers) by a small splintering group that refused to abandon the United Front strategy and the "national bourgeois" stage of development.[62]

During its ultra-left phase, especially between 1954 and 1955 when the leadership of the main party adopted a pro-Maoist strategy calling for armed struggle and the establishment of the peoples' revolutionary army in the countryside, the ICP became more critical of the Iraqi nationalists and less responsive to their oppositional call for a united front.[63] It was not until 1956 and the removal of the pro-Maoist ʿUthman from the leadership that the different factions of the ICP reunited their forces, reinstated the original line of "national democracy," and returned to a United Front strategy with the progressive forces within the nationalist movement.[64]

Although the ICP suffered immensely from the various shifts in its political line, the greatest blunder lay elsewhere. The dogmatic commitment to the doctrine of a separate "bourgeois democratic" stage of development proved, as I will discuss in the next chapter, detrimental to the ICP, to its cadre, and to the national revolution itself. In upholding these principles, the ICP was compelled in effect to subordinate class conflict to the national struggle and, in particular, tow the line of the Iraqi nationalists. The political implications of its alliance with the supposed "national bourgeoisie" can be seen clearly in the ICP's stance on two major issues: the national question and the agrarian question.

The ICP supported Iraqi nationalism over pan-Arab nationalism. Confined to the two-stage theory doctrine, the ICP had no other choice but to legitimate the right of the Iraqi "bourgeoisie" to a separate nation-state. In this way, the ICP's position again was not different from the NDP's.[65] By supporting a separate Iraqi nation-state, the ICP, like the National Democratic Party, opposed the pan-Arabists, especially on the importance of Arab unity in the struggle against Western domination and "underdevelopment."[66] Yet in contrast to the NDP, the communists backed the establishment of an Iraqi nation-state, not as an end in itself, but as the necessary precondition for the socialist revolution.

On the agrarian question, the ICP called for a radical land reform to free agriculture from "precapitalist iqtaʾ" and landlordism which, they argued, were fundamental fetters on the development of national economy, especially industry. In a document entitled "Semi-feudal Relations in Agriculture Retard Industrial Development," Fahd, the secretary of the party, argued that the two major factors arresting national and industrial development were:

> first, the economic penetration of world monopoly capitalism in general, and the economic and political domination of British imperialism, in particular. Second, the semi-feudal relations predominant in the countryside which impoverished the peasantry, thus undermining the possibility of creating a national market for industrial goods by reducing the purchasing power of the largest portion of the population.[67]

The agrarian revolution, from the point of view of the communists, was one of the central tasks of the national bourgeois revolution. Of course, in this regard the ICP had a point. As I have shown in the earlier chapters, the predominant shaykhly estates in the countryside not only blocked the development of a more efficient agriculture, they also arrested the growth of industrial capital in the 1950s. The problem with the ICP's position lay not so much in its recognition of the need for an agrarian revolution, but rather in assuming that there was a "national bourgeoisie" capable of carrying it out. As we shall see in more detail in the next chapter, the ICP miscalculated primarily in not recognizing the intrinsic weakness of the Iraqi "bourgeoisie" and this group's close ties to the agrarian structures.

Social Unrest and the Unification of the Opposition

In the economic crisis of the 1940s and 1950s, high inflation, and shortages in both staple and consumer goods led to increasing social unrest marked by student demonstrations, workers' strikes, and peasant flight from the countryside. Although successive governments attempted to neutralize the opposition by introducing some liberal measures, neither the oligarchic monarchy nor the British were willing to countenance fundamental political and economic reforms. Without such reforms, however, economic dislocation continued to alienate large sectors of the population. As a result, the periods of liberalization, rather than neutralizing the opposition and containing social protest, only helped to extend grassroots mobilization and embolden organized political groups. Faced with increasing opposition, the government retreated into political repression, hoping that force would succeed where co-optation failed. However, periods of repression were followed by new outbreaks of mass unrest, followed by concessions, followed by more unrest, followed by another governmental crackdown. This cycle was repeated several times between 1940 and 1958. But up through the 1956 uprising, the lack of unity among the main opposition parties allowed the regime to survive. I will now trace the process through which these divisions were overcome, leading to the national revolution of 1958.

It is important to keep in mind that a factionalized opposition faced also a factionalized ruling class. The oligarchic monarchy was by no means a unified monolithic regime. Dissension within the ruling bloc affected governmental strategies (toward the opposition) and shaped the course of political development in the 1940s and 1950s. The cyclical policy of co-optation and coercion by the governing elite was not just a response to social pressure, it also was related to dissension within the ruling bloc. For example, some of the major political insurrections in the post-mandate period were initiated by conflict within the ruling power bloc. The military coups of 1936 and 1941 expressed such dissension. Evidence strongly suggests that the 1936 coup was plotted by the palace to eliminate the king's political rivals, personified in Nuri al-Sa^{c}id and his political allies.[68] King Ghazi used General Bakr Sidqi and a pro-nationalist government, headed by Hikmat Suleiman, to stage his political coup.[69] The pro-nationalist government did not last more than a year as the coalition between Bakr, Suleiman, and the nationalist bloc fell apart leading to the resignation of the four nationalist ministers, the assassination of Bakr, and the collapse of the government.[70] The conflict between the king and Nuri was resolved with the victory of Nuri's faction.[71] The king was killed in 1939 in a "mysterious" car accident, which some believe was planned by the British and executed by Nuri.[72]

Similarly, the 1941 military coup of Rashid Ali al-Gaylani signified another conflict within the ruling elite. This time around, the discord was within Nuri al- Sa^{c}id's camp. Nuri's close associates within the army turned against him as they realized that his pro-British policies, in the aftermath of the 1940 French defeat in the war against Germany, were no longer practical as they posed a threat to Iraq's sovereignty. In turn, they backed the pan-Arabist Rashid Ali al-Gaylani who formed a new government that refused to honor the clauses in the Anglo-Iraqi treaty giving landing and transit right to British forces. The coup of 1941 resulted in the reoccupation of Iraq by British forces and the reinstatement of Nuri's faction into power.

After 1943, factionalist politics within the ruling bloc were marked by the rivalry between Nuri al-Sa^{c}id and his earlier ally, the Regent ^{c}Abdul-Ilah. Most detrimental to the regime, however, was the break between Nuri and Salih Jabr in the 1950s. As predicted by the British, this conflict had ramifications greater than the personal, as it helped to isolate and weaken the regime, paving the way for its downfall in 1958.

Prelude to the Popular Uprising of 1948

The 1948 revolt was the culmination of almost a decade of turbulent urban social protest that was nationalistic in sentiment and reformist in disposition. The workers in the railways, the Basra port, the utilities, and the oil industry, led by the communists, organized militant strikes and were able even to gain some victories. In 1944, in an attempt to appease the workers, the new "liberal" government of Hamdi al-Pachachi introduced significant labor reform, including protection of the working conditions of women workers, paid holidays, compensation for injuries, arbitration of labor disputes, and prohibition of child labor. The government also granted the right to form trade unions to all workers employed in railways, manufacturing, and the ports, with the exception of the oil industry and government workers.

These reforms, while responding to legitimate workers' protests, were also part of a political maneuver on behalf of the regent ^{c}Abdul-Ilah to discredit and undermine Nuri's position within the power structure and enhance his prestige by appealing to the opposition.[73] The liberal government took over from Nuri al-Sa ʿid, who monopolized the premiership from 1941 until June of 1944, on the orders of ʿAbdul-Ilah. This shift in the political order was encouraged by the British, even though they had little faith in ʿAbdul-Ilah, described as "a man of inferior clay," as a competent rival to Nuri.[74]

Rather than appease the workers, the labor reforms introduced by the new government encouraged more strikes. An April 1945 strike by Baghdad workers lasted over ten days, and spread to other cities and industries. The railway strike began when the workers' demand for a 30 to 40 percent wage increase was turned down by the British-managed Railway Directorate. During the strike, the Railway Directorate and the Interior Ministry threatened to cut the supply of water to the workers' living quarters and to replace the strikers with imported Indian labor. The outcome was the spreading of the strike beyond Baghdad, to Samawah (April 16), Basra (April 18), and Mosul (April 19).[75] Even after the committee that had organized the strike was arrested and the railway union suppressed, the workers continued their strike until a compromise was reached under which the company agreed on a 20 to 30 percent wage increase.[76] Despite the banning of their union, the railway workers struck again in 1946, and three times in 1948, the year of al-wathba. Similar strikes were organized by the dock-workers in Basra. Their union held several strikes in this period demanding higher wages in the face of the sharp increase in living costs.[77] In the case of the oil workers, their demands included, in addition to higher wages, the right to a union, a right denied them by the British who controlled the company. On June, 1946, when their request for higher wages was rejected by the company, 5,000 workers went on strike in Kirkuk, demanding both an increase in the wages and the right to organize. The Iraq Petroleum Company (IPC) refused to negotiate and called on the government to intervene and break the strike.[78] On the tenth day, while the strikers were holding a public meeting, the riot police charged into their meeting, killing six workers and wounding fourteen.[79] The first of its kind, this incident provoked public outrage, as it was seen as representing the government's deep commitment to the British and their willingness to sacrifice Iraqi people for the protection of British interests.[80] The incident provoked a general public strike and a mass demonstration in Kirkuk in support of the workers' strike. The national outcry this incident produced caused the existing government to fall, and forced the IPC to give in to some of the workers' demands, including higher wages, the freeing of their imprisoned fellow workers, and their right to return to work.[81]

Workers' struggles over labor issues and wages continued during this difficult period leading to the major strike and to the popular uprising of 1948, the year when inflation reached its peak.[82] The inflation and "lack of bread" triggered a spiral of strikes beginning with the railways and spreading across other industries, including manufacturing, printing workers, and oil.[83] The most militant of these strikes again was that of the oil workers. The oil workers near Hadithah and Baiji went on strike soon after the oil company rejected their request for a 25 to 40 percent wage increase. As described by the British Foreign Office then, the strike was "a disciplined subversive movement planned and directed by the Iraqi Communist Party. The leaders are known communists. The strike from the outset was organized with remarkable efficiency. They took over the plant and picketed the ferry across all roads leading into the camp."[84] The strike continued for three weeks and ended when the march down to Baghdad was stopped outside Fallujah (60 kilometers from Baghdad), and the marchers were arrested.[85]

Social discontent was not limited to workers. Students and the urban middle class living on limited income suffered as much as the workers from inflation and the economic crisis of the 1940s.[86] Unrest among the urban masses as well increased in tempo after 1945. Spearheaded by students, teachers, and the middle strata of urban society, several demonstrations protested the bankrupt policies of the government. These protests were nationalist and anti-British (anti-imperialist) in sentiment, denouncing the government, and demanding national liberation. The focus of the political struggle, moreover, transcended the borders of Iraq to embrace national liberation struggles in other Arab countries, especially in the the east (al-Mashriq). Several of these demonstrations, from the mid-1940s on, were in solidarity with the Syrians and the Lebanese in their struggle against French colonialism, and the Palestinians in their struggle against the British and the Zionists in Palestine.[87]

Successive governments tried to respond to this social pressure by periodically introducing reforms. In December of 1945, the Regent of Iraq ʿAbdul-Ilah, spoke in parliament in favor of democracy, for free election laws, and the right of the opposition to organize politically.[88] Soon after, a more liberal pro-nationalist government came to power under the leadership of Tawfiq Suwaidi.[89] Under his tenure the government lifted martial law and press censorship, granted political freedoms by legalizing political parties (with the exception of the ICP), annulled the old parliament, amended the election law, although not to the point of granting free and direct elections, and formed a committee to reopen negotiations with Britain over the 1930 treaty.[90]

There were clear limits to how far such policies could go. Fundamental reforms that might loosen the hold of the British or the oligarchic monarchy on the government or threaten their power could not be tolerated. For instance, the opposition parties were allowed to enter the 1947 parliamentary elections but the system of indirect election and government interference prevented any of their candidates from actually winning office. The victory of the landed classes in the election was considered by the British to be a victory for the government. The British consulate in Mosul testified to state interference in the election:

4. Generally speaking, the election in northern Iraq appears to have followed traditional lines. There was almost complete absence of parties and programs, the only party having a program being banned by the local authorities . . . [meaning the NDP]

5. The battle had in fact been fought before the poll and the Government were assured that people generally favorable to the regime would be elected, if only because the secondary electors, as a body, were content to follow what they were told was the Government's wishes.

6. Moreover, the government intervened in various places in the course of the election, sometimes for motives of nepotism and sometimes, more wisely, for the national good.[91]

Government interference prevented the opposition from sending more than a few members to parliament.[92] As a result, the opposition proved to be politically ineffective, unable to have any say or influence in the government or have its social and economic reform proposals taken seriously.

The opposition came up against similar limits in attempts to challenge British control. From 1947, the opposition began to focus on the national question and the 1930 Anglo-Iraqi treaty when the government of Salih Jabr reopened official negotiations with the British. For the opposition, the 1930 treaty, which ensured continual British domination over Iraq, had to be revoked. But the government remained unwilling to give up the relationship. The result was the Portsmouth Treaty of 1948 and the mass uprising known in the popular annals of Iraq as *al-wathba* (The leap).

Al-Wathba of 1948

The Portsmouth Treaty was no more than a renewal of the 1930 treaty. Instead of terminating British domination and influence, the agreement reasserted Iraq's subservience to Britain. The treaty of 1948 once more pledged to keep close economic, political, and military ties with Britain. As in 1930, the Portsmouth Treaty provided for Britain's maintaining military air bases in al-Habaniyah and al-Shuʾubiyah in the south, and at the same time pledging Britain to protect Iraq and to send its troops whenever "peace was under threat in the region."[93]

The publication of the treaty terms on January 18 triggered a strong response everywhere, in Baghdad as well as other regions of the country. The treaty sparked a three-day strike and massive demonstrations in Baghdad.

Though organized by all the opposition forces including the pan-Arabists and Iraqi nationalists, this wave of popular protest was spearheaded by the communists and their supporters.[94] The fierce popular reaction forced the Regent of Iraq to disown the treaty openly and compelled the Prime Minister, Salih Jabr, to resign and flee the country. To neutralize the opposition, the Regent called on Muhammad al-Sadr, a relatively moderate politician, to form the new government.[95] The opposition, with the exception of the communists, welcomed the change in government especially since the new cabinet's first political measure was to repudiate the Portsmouth Treaty and to promise fundamental social and economic reforms to ease inflation and social inequalities.[96] One of the first steps to be taken by the new government was to annul the old parliament and to call for a new free election that would include all parties, including the opposition (but not the Communist Party).

Despite the change in government and the new appeasement measures taken by the new government, social unrest continued to plague the country. Organized largely by the Communist Party, which was denied representation, mass protests continued through the months of February, March, and April. Their demands centered on "bread and clothes," democratic rights, freeing of political prisoners, and bringing to justice the national traitors, Salih Jabr and Nuri al-Sa‘id. Workers strikes across industries erupted during these months demanding, besides national independence, higher wages and improved social benefits. Workers were joined by the General Student Association that was formed on April 14, 1948. The British journal, *The Tribune*, alarmed by the events, described Iraq as a country on the verge of a revolution.[97]

Holding the communists entirely responsible for the escalation of social unrest, the new government set up an committee to inquire into their activities. Anticipating further disturbances, especially with the forthcoming elections, the government withdrew its earlier liberal policies and imposed martial law throughout the country. As in the previous election of 1947, interference by the government prevented many of the opposition forces from participating freely in the election.[98] The Istiqlal was able to send in four members of its party while the NDP sent in three. After the election, Sadr's government resigned and al-Pachachi took over but was soon to relinquish power again, this time to the government of Nuri al-Sa‘id.

As expected, Sa‘id's government abolished most of the liberal measures introduced by Sadr and began to take much harsher repressive measures against the opposition, in particular the communists. Blaming them for the social disturbances in 1948 and 1949, one of Sa‘id's first measures was to retry the imprisoned communist leaders, charge them with treason, and condemn them to death.[99] In addition, the government targeted the communists and their sympathizers, harassing and imprisoning their cadres and inflicting harsh penalties.[100] By the end of 1949, in fact, the government was able to drive many of them into exile or underground and to fragment the membership into smaller, sectarian groups. In its "repressive turn," the government did not focus on the communists alone, but hounded the rest of the opposition, including the nationalists and the democrats, banning their parties and censoring their press.[101]

This political pattern of opening up the system slightly to ease the pressures, closing it up again, and clamping down hard on the opposition whenever its demands became threatening continued throughout the 1940s and through the early part of the 1950s. After 1954, however, both the political and economic situation and the government underwent dramatic change.

The change can be attributed to two simultaneous yet contradictory factors: first, the intensification of factionalism within the ruling class that helped to weaken the regime and ease the road for its overthrow, and second, the dramatic increase in oil revenues that made the regime less dependent on domestic capital and more autonomous of its social classes.

In the 1950s, more dissension within the ranks of the ruling elite further diminished the power of an already weakened regime. This time around, the split occurred between Nuri al-Sa⁽id and Salih Jabr, the two most reliable and prominent political agents of the British. Salih Jabr, who assisted Nuri in 1949 to form the Constitutional Union Party, broke ranks with him and established his own party, the Popular Socialist Party, in 1951. He then joined the opposition forces to challenge the monopolization of power by Nuri.[102] Nuri's response was to push forward an amendment of the Electoral Law (Number 11, of 1946), which included an article that was regarded by the opposition, including Jabr, as "enabling Nuri to manipulate the elections with impunity" and prevent any opposition from being elected to parliament.[103] Alarmed by the split between Nuri and Jabr, the British, while trying to reconcile them, warned of the dangerous implication of their break by pointing out that "unless they could compose their differences, both they and the whole of the present ruling groups might be swept away."[104]

The 1950s marked yet another development that also had an immense impact on the course of political development in Iraq. The 1952 Oil Treaty leading to a sharp rise in oil royalties and revenues, diminished the state's immediate economic problems by eliminating the deficit and providing revenues for potential government intervention in development projects. As a result, the government became less dependent on the prosperity of the domestic economy and taxation for revenues and more willing to dispense with the co-optation of those who controlled domestic capital. As the regime became less dependent, at least financially, on the domestic economy, it became less responsive to the demands and interests of the social groups in opposition. Whereas in the earlier era the regime had to give in to some of the pressures from below, in the 1950s the state became much more authoritarian. But as the government gained increased autonomy and was less compelled to re-spond to social groups other than those already in power, it also became more isolated from the surrounding society, structurally weaker, and politically more vulnerable than ever before.

Moreover, as the regime became more repressive, the opposition became more radical. The experience of the 1940s, including futile attempts at social change through democratic means, the Portsmouth Treaty, the defeat of the 1948 *wathba*, slowly led the opposition to take a more radical line and to realize the importance of unifying forces to face their common adversary. Despite the escalation of class struggle in the 1940s, the political parties of the opposition tended to work within the confines of the existing regime and operate pretty much independently of each other. In the 1950s, the opposition came to realize that fundamental changes within the existing order were becoming less feasible, especially after 1954. As a result, they were more convinced of the need to set aside their differences and work together toward a more pragmatic political program.

The 1952 Intifadah and its Impact on the Politics of the Opposition

The 1952 uprising was the product of a new wave of unrest which swept the country in the early 1950s. A spiralling strike wave hit various industries across the country.[105] These actions culminated in a general strike across industries called by the central union in 1952. The opposition forwarded a petition to the Regent demanding the granting of all political freedoms, in-cluding free elections and democratic and civil rights to the Iraqi people.[106] Receiving no response, demonstrations were organized on November 22 and 23. Joined by workers, street vendors, and students, the opposition led a huge demonstration that was dispersed by force. Martial law was reinstated and a new military government under the army Chief of Staff, Nur al-Din Mahmud, was installed. Soon after forming his government, Nur al-Din dissolved the political parties and put their leaders in prison.[107] These policies provoked the masses even further. On November 24, demonstrations and riots swept the major urban centers, especially Baghdad and the holy city of Najaf.[108] The army was called in and opened fire on the demonstrators.[109]

Unrest in this period was not limited to the urban areas but swept the countryside as well. The 1950s, like the 1930s, marked an intensification in peasant resistance. In ʿAmarah, for example, the peasants of al-Fartous seized their lands, kicked out their landlords, and killed their guards. In response, the government sent in its troops, and forcefully pushed the peasants off the land. In May of 1950, 250 armed peasants forced their way back to their land in Kubybah after killing six guards. The government once more intervened, repressed the revolt and imprisoned its leaders. Under the Tribal Dispute, the peasants of al-Fartous were found guilty, charged with payment of customary diyyah, and forced to migrate south toward Muntafiq and the lands of al-ᶜAbd.[110] This rebellion was soon followed by another, the al-Zuraij uprising (October 1952) against the usurpation of their lands by their tribal chiefs.[111]

Even though the 1952 popular uprising was violently crushed, resistance to the existing regime continued, both in the urban areas and the countryside. Strikes erupted soon after martial law was revoked by the new government in 1953. Cigarette workers in Baghdad went back on strike. This was soon to be followed by the oil and dock workers strike in Basra (December 1953) where the British were reported to have fired on the striking workers to force them back to work. After a week, newspapers reported that the Minister of Interior on his visit to the city gave orders to arrest the strikers and to disperse their rallies by force. Eight were reported injured and one died. As a result, the city of Basra declared a one-day strike in protest of the repressive and violent measures taken against the oil workers, which in turn forced the government to reimpose martial law in Basra.[112]

The outcome of these new disturbances was the replacement of al-Jamali's government with a new one under the leadership of Irshad al-ᶜUmari, a politician known for his sympathy with Britain. In response to concerns about the danger of political unrest to the existing regime and to its own interests, the British suggested that the government introduce new political and economic reforms to ease the pressure on the regime.[113] New elections were called and the opposition entered the campaign as a one-front opposition, with thirty-seven members running for election—fourteen of whom were NDP's, eight Istiqlal, and fifteen independent, some of whom were communists.[114]

Falsification of votes and intimidation by government officials once more interfered with the election held in June 1954. Consequently, of the thirty-seven opposition candidates, only eleven were elected.The new parliament, however, was convened only once before it was dissolved again by a Royal Decree issued August 3, 1954.[115]

From this moment until the revolution of 1958, the attitudes of both the regime and the opposition toward each other changed.The coming of Nuri al-Saᶜid to power in 1954 had marked the beginning of a new era—an era of repression and unwillingness to compromise. Under his tenure, all freedoms restored in 1953 were canceled, and political parties, cultural clubs, unions, and the press were consequently banned and repressed.The new wave of repression once again targeted the communists. Saᶜid's government took harsher measures than commonly used to eliminate the communists. Besides imprisoning them, driving them underground, and expelling any government employees, workers, and students slightly sympathetic to communism, he resorted to revoking their citizenship and chasing them out of their country.[116]

At the same time, to protect the regime against external forces and mounting internal pressures, the government of Nuri al-Saʿid began to negotiate the formation of an eastern defense military pact with Turkey, Pakistan, and Iran, under the advisement of both the British and the United States, to defend the east against the "threat" of communism.[117] The Baghdad Pact provoked the national question once more, leading to another mass uprising and the birth of the Popular National Front, which prepared the way for the defeat of the oligarchic monarchy in 1958.

The Baghdad Pact and the 1956 Uprising

The Baghdad Pact was in many ways the response of Western governments and their allies in the region to the rising threat of nationalist movements and rising Soviet influence in the region. The nationalization of oil in Iran under the Mossadaq government was the first in a series of regional events that forced Britain and the United States to rethink alternatives for protecting their oil interests in the region. The second event was the Egyptian revolution of 1952 that toppled the Egyptian monarchy and the oligarchic government of the landed classes, allies of Western powers. Thirdly, the expansion of a nationalist, anti-British movement in Iraq, as well as the rising dissatisfaction with the oligarchic monarchy, compelled the British and the Iraqi government to consider seriously a military pact to protect the regime and British interests in Iraq. These concerns led to the formation of the Baghdad Pact.

Following the Baghdad Pact, which was condemned by the opposition as another sell-out to British interests, came the British-French-Israeli attack against Egypt after Nasser nationalized the Suez Canal.The Iraqis responded with another uprising in support of Egypt, and against the Baghdad Pact, the regime, and imperial Britain.

The uprising of 1956 was largely organized in the provincial towns of Mosul, Kirkuk, Basra, and most impressively in Najaf and Hayy—the stronghold of the communists and the Shiʾa ʿulamah who supported and participated in the rebellion. Baghdad, already under siege by the riot police and the army which was sent in by the government in anticipation of the uprising, remained comparatively calm.[118]

Even though the 1956 mass uprising, like the previous ones, was brutally put down by the government, its political outcome was quite significant in terms of the unfolding struggle against the regime. The opposition, particularly the nationalists, realized for the first time the limits to reform and the need for a radical change. Putting aside their ideological and political differences, the opposition in 1956 formed a United National Front (al-Jabhah al-Wataniyah). The Front included the pan-Arab parties Istiqlal and the Ba'th, the national democrats (the NDP), the Iraqi Communist Party, and various smaller coalitions and front organizations associated with the opposition. The Front's common platform consisted of complete economic and political independence, the abolition of the Baghdad Pact, destruction of iqta', the establishment of democratic rights and civil liberties, and Arab solidarity against imperialism and Zionism.[119]

As popular conflict against with the oligarchic monarchy was gaining momentum, discontent with the existing regime was also on the rise among high-ranking officers in the army.This of course was quite natural considering that the majority of the officer corps was largely drawn from the lower and poorer classes of the society, thus identifying themselves with the aspirations and frustrations of the underprivileged. The product of public education (seat of nationalist ideology) and local military academies, the new generation of officers was nationalist and had strong anti-British leanings.

Consideration of a military takeover began as early as 1952. Encouraged by the success of the military coup in Egypt, and angered by the regime's violent repression of 1952 uprising, secret cells began to form among high-ranking officers. Still, it was not until the political events following the formation of the Baghdad Pact, including the futile popular uprising of 1956 and the tripartite attack against Egypt after Nasser nationalized the Suez Canal, that the army officers began to prepare seriously for a takeover. From 1956, secret cells of Free Officers began to multiply in number, which then prompted the formation of a Supreme Committee—a committee that would take charge of the organization of the cells and plan a seizure of power.

The two officers destined to lead the coup, Brigadier Qasim and Colonel 'Arif, expressed with their divergent political views the ideological incoherence of the Free Officers and the political ambiguity of the revolution. 'Arif, the son of a draper, was an Islamically oriented pan-Arabist and a great admirer of the Egyptian leader Gamal 'Abd al-Nasser. Qasim, the son of a carpenter worker, was influenced by the national democrats and advocated liberal politics despite his rumored connections with the ICP.[120] In a similar manner, the rest of the Free Officers were politically torn between proponents of pan-Arab ideology like Rif'at al-Hajj Sirri, Nadim al-Tabaqchali, and Naji Talib, and the opponents of pan-Arabism, like the liberal Muhi al-Din 'Abd al-Hamid who leaned toward the NDP, and the radicals who espoused communism, like Wasfi Tahir and Isma'il 'Ali. In spite of the differences in their political outlook, the Free Officers, like the political opposition on the civilian front, were able to adopt a unified National Pact that included the following: first, replace the monarchy with a republican form of government; second, establish a truly representative government based on parliamentary democ-racy; third, implement a land reform; and fourth, support the Kurdish national cause within a decentralized national government.

With these principles in mind, the Free Officers, keeping in close contact with the civilian political opposition, carried out the military coup on July 14, 1958, toppling the oligarchic monarchy and establishing in its place the People's Republic of Iraq.

CONCLUSION

The Iraqi nation-state, constructed by British imperial power in 1921, was able, fairly quickly, to establish its own sense of unity and sovereignty. The legitimacy of the nation-state, rather than being derived from an external power, became in the 1930s dependent on mobilizing and organizing the various social forces either in the form of a loyalty to the oligarchic monarchy and its backer, the British, or to a territorially based national identity. The Treaty of 1932 that concluded British mandate rule and proclaimed Iraq an independent state became the focal point of political contention. The creation of a nation-state that was barely modern and hardly independent provided the context for the appear-ance of political opposition in Iraq. The question of nationhood (analogous to social and economic progress) became the key political rallying-point for all opposition groups, despite their differences and conflicting views. While the National Democratic Party (NDP) saw the struggle for independence as part of the process of emancipating the national bourgeoisie from the grip of old agrarian classes and imperialist domination, the Ba³th depicted the "Arab Nation," and not the Iraqi nation, as the medium for social and economic change. The Iraqi Communist Party, committed to the Stalinist doctrine of "two-stage theory," while taking to task both parties for denying class conflict and affirming the nation, found itself backing the national bourgeoisie and in practice towing the line of the Iraqi nationalists.

The nationalists in the 1930s and the 1940s were largely reformist in nature. After the violent repression of the popular revolts of 1948 and 1952, the opposition began to realize that reform is less likely to happen. The potential for reform ended in the 1950s, especially with the rise in the impor-tance of oil in the political economy of the nation. The sharp increase in state revenues from oil made the government less dependent on the domestic economy for its revenues and as a result less responsive to the needs and demands of the opposition situated outside the political process. This was clearly demonstrated in the 1952 and 1956 popular uprisings. However, as the government gained more autonomy, it became isolated, factionalized, and politically ineffective, thus making the path for its overthrow in 1958 a much easier one.

5

The Revolution of 1958 and Its Defeat

"The classes of the people have merged"
"Social justice and a higher standard of living to all"

Abdel Karim Qasim

The objective of the national revolution, as defined by its leaders, was two-fold: to liberate Iraq from the claws of the oligarchic monarchy and its creator, British imperialism; and to rebuild and reconstruct the nation by promoting social and economic development on behalf of its people. The revolution, in representing the "will of the nation," held "universal" goals that transcended class, ethnic, religious, and gender differences. The distinctive character of the revolutionary regime, other than being emancipatory, lay in its historical mission of reconstructing and developing the nation in the name of the whole society. Within this definition of the social good, particular interests of groups and communities had to be made to conform with and be subsumed under the general interest.

A unified, undivided, revolutionary national state with universal objectives that superceded the particular interests of social and national groups and classes proved to be self-deceiving. The national revolutionary state, despite its claim of representing the "will of the nation," became instead the arena of intense struggle whereby various groups and interests interacted, allied with, and contested each other. The outcome was the collapse of national unity and fierce social discord, leading to the impending disintegration of the national state.

In tracing political developments of the 1940s and 1950s, we have seen how the national opposition through two decades of struggle, came to realize that unification of their forces was essential, and political independence and national development was no longer possible within the confines of the existing regime. In 1956, a broad national alliance, United National Front, was formed from the various national and oppositional political groups including the communists. In the present chapter, I will describe how this broad national alliance shattered as soon as the oligarchic monarchy was overthrown. Once in power, conflicting national and class interests were sharpened, leading to the breakdown of the national coalition. Conflicting interests over the

111

strategies and plans for reconstructing the nation were articulated along two primary issues: first, unification (merger) with the United Arab Republic (Syria-Egypt), which split the coalition between those who supported the pan-Arab nationalist position and those who opposed it, and second, land reform and the split between the nationalists forces, backed by the military, and the communists. Accordingly, this chapter is divided into three sections. The first deals with the controversy over the issue of unity, the positions taken, the ideological justifications for them, the struggle for power between nationalists and pan-Arabist forces, and the defeat of the pan-Arabists. The second section addresses the land question that eventually led to the split between the nationalists and the Communist Party. The final section gives a brief analysis of why the nationalists were incapable of carrying out the "national bourgeois" revolution, which the communists assigned to them.

ARAB VS. IRAQI NATIONALISM

With the exception of the ICP, the political structure of the revolutionary national state represented all nationalist groupings involved in the United National Front and the army. Headed by Staff Brigadier ʿAbdul Karim Qasim, who also held the defense ministry, the new cabinet included two NDP, two Istiqlal, one Baʿthist, and several military and civil members who were pro-Arab nationalists.[1]

The first cabinet, however, did not survive long. The issue that promoted its fall was Arab unity. The Arab nationalists in the cabinet led by the Baʿth, the most articulate of these groups, called for an immediate merger with the United Arab Republic, headed by Nasser. This, of course, was not surprising considering their view that Arab identity and the Arab nation, not the Iraqi nation, ought to be the agent of a nationalist modernizing project. From their perspective, the national revolution of 1958 was the first stage in the struggle toward the resurrection of the historic Arab nation and the completion of Arab independence through unification. To the Arab nationalists, as discussed earlier, the Iraqi nation—a product of British imperialism—had no historical or socioeconomic foundation to justify its existence, while the Arab nation, a "historic nation," was the preferred agent for liberation and development. ʿAflaq, in "In Defense of Unity," linked, for the first time, the importance of unification to development:

> [Economic development is] a clear and simple thing when we take the Arab nation as a unit. Looking at the various economic potentialities we see that they complement each other. . . . To realize these economic potentialities and make progress, we have to take into account this link which binds the different parts

of the one homeland . . . so that we avoid building twenty ports in one region while neglecting other regions, and avoid establishing an industry in a region which does not have the raw materials . . . while we can, by unifying our economy create an industry for all of us Arabs, without having recourse to foreign capital or foreign raw material.[2]

In this respect, the "historic" Arab nation came to be fundamental not only for the struggle against imperialism, but also for the economic development of the region as a whole.

The Iraqi nationalists, spearheaded by the NDP, reiterated their earlier position by stating that a unitary Arab nation was antithetical to Iraqi national interests at this particular moment in its history. The development of a sovereign Iraq should be the principal agenda for the moment, not a merger with the UAR. It was therefore within the confines of a unified undivided Iraqi nation that the revolutionary national program of fighting against "precapitalist iqta[3]," poverty, health problems, and social injustices can be accomplished. Until Iraq resolved its internal problems and achieved economic development, "unification" (*ittihad*) as a goal could not even be considered. But once "a state of development and security" were accomplished, a federation-type *ittihad* would be possible among the liberated Arab countries—a federation, they maintained, that should guarantee the autonomy of the internal structures in each of these countries.[3]

Although national concerns composed the ideological center of the Iraqi nationalists' politics, their commitment to a separate Iraqi state, one may suggest, was also influenced by class interest. Speaking on behalf of a rising entrepreneurial class, the National Democrats' (NDP) opposition to *wihda* (merger) was quite understandable. The union with Egypt and Syria would have been more than harmful to rising capitalist interests. The product of the Second World War, national capital, as discussed in detail in chapter 3, was small, intrinsically weak, and especially vulnerable to competition even from an equally weak but historically older and relatively more developed Egyptian capital. Up to 1958, firms employing over twenty workers constituted only 1 percent of the total industry in Iraq, while over 43 percent of the total capital invested in industry belonged to the smaller firms, which employed less than ten workers.[4] Despite its fragility and the structural constraints facing it in the 1950s, the industrial wing of Iraqi capital at the same time demonstrated a promising capacity for growth. The economist Hashim Jawad, for instance, showed that industrial capital in Iraq underwent 12 percent yearly growth between 1940–1963.[5] Nevertheless, by 1958 private industrial growth, with the exception of cement, was still based predominantly in light industry and remained, by and large, vulnerable to competition. Thus, for the

Iraqi nationalists, especially those who spoke on behalf of national capital, an independent nation-state was essential for developing national industry and for the creation of a home market free of competition. This national objective, after all, had been the rationale for overthrowing the old (colonial) order. The oligarchic monarchy was overthrown precisely because it was considered a "fetter" and a "stifling" force on national growth and economic development.

Arguably, the Iraqi nationalists saw the prospect of a merger with the UAR as a new threat to a national capital that was vulnerable. A merger with Syria and Egypt would have created an open-market situation which could surely jeopardize its prospects. Iraqi industry would not have been able to compete with the relatively more advanced Egyptian industry. One need only consider the problems arising from duplication in industrial production to see how well-founded the fears of the nationalists were. In both Egypt and Iraq, the industrial complex was dominated by the production of basic consumer goods and essential intermediary materials. In both countries, textiles, cement, and food processing made up the larger proportion of industrial capital.[6] Unlike the Iraqis who had not yet reaped the benefits of their own revolution, Egyptian industries underwent a boom in the aftermath of the 1952 revolution. As a result, some of these industries, like cement, sugar, and alcohol, became fairly competitive on the world market. The share of Egyptian manufactured goods in total export increased from 9 percent in 1955–1956 to 19.5 percent by 1960.[7] By contrast, as we have seen in the chapter 3, Iraqi cement in the later 1950s was facing tremendous difficulties due to overproduction and an inability to maintain a competitive edge with cheaper Japanese cement in the neighboring markets.[8]

A similar argument can be made with regard to agriculture. By and large, Iraq and Egypt produced the same agricultural crops, mainly dates, rice, grain, and later cotton. But Iraqi agriculture operated at a much lower level of productivity, due to high salinity and the lack of interest on the part of the oligarchic landed class in improving methods of production. Iraq also lagged behind Syria in the production of cotton, despite the fact that its cultivation was expanded in response to the growth in the textile industry in the 1940s and 1950s. Yet cotton production remained confined to small numbers of town mullak and investors, and its productivity levels were relatively poor, especially when compared to the main cotton producer, Egypt.[9]

The abundance of oil capital was another important factor in the argument for a separate Iraqi nation. Oil revenues represented a major source of capital and social power, providing a great potential for development not contingent on the state's ability to accumulate through planning or foreign aid. Unlike Egypt or Syria, the Iraqi state did not have to squeeze its peasantry, raise high taxes, or make concessions to foreign interests in order to raise the capital needed for development. Iraq already had that capital, thanks to oil. The potential for utilizing oil capital to promote the economic interests of all classes made the prospect of a separate Iraqi nation-state especially attractive.

Briefly stated, a merger with the United Arab Republic was not on the agenda of the revolutionary nationalist state because it would have undermined the social power of national capital, an outcome the Iraqi nationalists were determined to prevent. By manipulating ethnic, class, and religious differences, the Iraqi nationalists, with the support of the military leader, Qasim, succeeded in subverting the pan-Arabists' merger plan with the UAR. This victory would not have been possible without the support of the most popular and perhaps best-organized political force in Iraq at the time, the ICP.

Even though theoretically the communists criticized the nationalists' notion of an historic indivisible Iraqi nation, they also opposed unity with UAR and for many of the same reasons as the national democrats. The difference was that their justification for a separate Iraqi nation-state was delivered with more sophistication. The ICP stressed the national peculiarities of the Arab countries, which they attributed to a long historical process of colonial domination and capitalist penetration. Colonialism produced an uneven development in the socioeconomic structures of these societies—an unevenness that inevitably left its mark on their class formations. For instance, the Egyptian national bourgeoisie was older and, in turn, more entrenched nationally and internationally than either the Syrian or Iraqi "bourgeoisie." Consequently, they argued, the Egyptian "bourgeoisie" was less progressive, having already made its compromises with Western capitalism. In contrast, the Syrian and Iraqi "bourgeoisie," products of the interwar period and of contemporary anti-imperialist struggle, were bound to be more progressive.[10]

The ICP predicted that the outcome of unification could only be a "Prussian" style union rather than truly "democratic," state based on equal representation. The weaker Iraqi and Syrian bourgeoisie would easily be subsumed under the stronger and more efficient Egyptian capital. A union of this sort, they argued, would no longer be an expression of the people's aspirations and desires but would be another form of imperial domination by the Egyptian "national bourgeoisie," as Aziz al-Hajj, then a leading communist, argued:

It is only natural that we oppose a "Prussian style" union and propose Ittihad. . . . We call for [a federal form of] unification that will guarantee the interests of all classes in each of the individual Arab states . . . (unification) that will take into consideration the uneven development in these countries . . . that will respect people's choice for 'democratic rule.' [W]e will not at this point support an undemocratic union that will lead to the growth and expansion (in²ash) of the Egyptian national bourgeoisie at the expense of other Arab workers, merchants and capitalists.[A]t this stage it is but natural for us to struggle on behalf of the Iraqi national bourgeoisie and its development.[11]

The key to their support of the preservation of a postcolonial Iraqi nation-state lay in the party's commitment to the theory of a two-stage revolution, socialist transformation being possible only after the full development of capitalism. The revolution of 1958, according to the party, was "national democratic" in nature and the ICP's role was to support the "Iraqi bourgeoisie" in its historic mission of developing and modernizing the economy. In a revealing editorial article, a leading figure in the Central Committee, ʿAmir ʿAbdallah, outlined the party's position on the revolution as follows:

[O]ur party supports the economic interests of the national bourgeoisie as a fundamental condition for the development of a democratic bourgeois state . . . and on this basis we raise the slogan of a "United Front." . . . The goals of this revolution are: to build democracy and get rid of the remnants of imperialism and feudalism. . . . Its supporting pillars consist of: the working class, the peasantry, the petty bourgeoisie both small and medium. The aim of the revolution is to establish social and economic reforms within the framework of capitalist relations of production. . . . We consider this revolution to be a popular revolution.[12]

By treating national democracy as a separate stage of development, the communists saw no alternative but to back capitalism and the legitimate right of the Iraqi "bourgeoisie" to a separate nation-state. In a sharp critique of Arab communism and its stand on unification, Elias Murqus, an independent Marxist-Leninist, pointed out that the communists, blinded by their dogma, essentially failed to place unity within the context of the larger historical struggle against imperialism, and consequently failed to understand that:

Arab unification was part of the national democratic-socialist revolution as it evolved and transformed into the struggle against imperialism. . . . I say, socialism is not the logical historical and strategic precondition for Arab unification; rather, it is unification that is the historical and strategic precondition for socialism and communism. The objective of unification goes beyond the limits of bourgeois national democracy since it strikes at the very foundation of imperialism. . . . The unification of 1958 was not the outcome of socialism or national democracy but was the product of a challenge to imperialism. . . . It was the outcome of an important historical moment in the struggle following the nationalization of the Suez Canal and the Tripartite attack on Egypt. . . . The termination of unity between Syria and Egypt was therefore due not to the objective historical conditions (as put by the communists) but to imperialist pressures as well as the rigidity and dogmatism of most Arab communists, Marxists, semi-Marxists and progressive intellectuals.[13]

The communists' worst miscalculation, however, followed from their illusions about the progressive and revolutionary character of the "national bourgeoisie" in Iraq. Tracing their alliance with the Iraqi nationalists who turned against them after the elimination of the pan-Arabist threat demonstrates the fallacy of their line. The following section describes the political conflicts over national unity beginning with the offensive staged by the pan-Arabists and the counter-attack by those who opposed them in support of a separate Iraqi nation. In the aftermath of their victory against the Arabists, the Iraqi nationalists, in command of the government and the military, organized against their own ally, the communists. But the Iraqi nationalists could not enjoy their victory over the communists, as we will see later in this chapter. Unable to consolidate, the NDP fractured into many splinters and, as a result, became an ineffectual political force. By the end of 1962, the social revolution was hanging by a thin thread, soon to be cut by another military coup staged by the pan-Arab forces.[14]

Political Conflict Over Unity

To force the new government to accept merger with the UAR, the pan-Arabists took to the streets. Demonstrations were organized calling for immediate union (*wihdah fawriyyah*) under the sole leadership of Nasser. ᶜAflaq, secretary and main ideologue of the Baᶜth party, flew to Baghdad to campaign on behalf of pro-union forces. The most effective campaigner for the merger, however, was ᶜAbdul Salam ᶜArif. The second military officer in command of the Iraqi forces and a dedicated Nasserite, he used his heroic role in the revolution to popularize the pro-unity cause. His fervor for union, combined with his strongly demagogic call for the elimination of class barriers based on economic inequities, was most effective among the poor population in the rural areas. His popularity also encouraged him to approach Nasser on behalf of his government without its consent.[15]

The heavy-handed campaign for merger with Egypt and Syria immediately put the Iraqi nationalists and their supporters, including the military leader, Qasim, on the defensive. Given their limited social base, the NDP had to seek the support of their ally, the Iraqi communists who took the leading role in the intimidation and physical elimination of the pan-Arab nationalists. Having the advantage of a larger popular base, especially among the landless peasantry in the south, the Kurdish population in the north, not to mention the small working class and the urban unemployed, the ICP gained the upper hand over the pan-Arabists. The Iraqi nationalists backed their efforts fully. So did the government.

On August 1, 1958, for instance, the government reinstated "People's Resistance" recruitment centers, just two months after they had been shut down because they came to pose a threat to national unity.[16] Now, the government decided that the centers for recruitment were to be directly attached to the Ministry of Defense. According to Batatu, as soon as these centers were open thousands of communist members and sympathizers enrolled.[17] Bloody confrontations—including killings and many incidents of physical intimidation—between the communists and the pan-Arab nationalists were extremely common in this period.[18]

The Iraqi nationalists and the ICP used whatever means were available to strip the Arab nationalists of their social power. Pro-union nationalists were forced out of their strong-hold, the Lawyers Guild.[19] In the Union for Construction Workers and the Basra port, workers sympathetic with the pan-Arab cause, were stripped of their union rights and privileges.[20] Another method of disarming the Arab nationalists was to discredit and demote their leadership. On August 28, 1958, ʿAbdul Salam ʿArif, second in command after Qasim and the pan-Arab official spokesperson, was removed from his post as deputy commander in chief of the armed forces. A month later, he was relieved of his cabinet position and appointed ambassador to the German Federal Republic. Rikabi, the secretary of the Baʿth Party, and the Minister of Development, was demoted to minister without portfolio. The Ministry of Development was given instead to the NDP's Muhammad Hadid, already the Minister of Finance. The Ministry of Education was transferred from a pan-Arab supporter to another leading NDP member, the Minister of Agriculture, Hudayb al-Hajj Hamud.[21]

ʿArif's defiant return to Baghdad from his exiled position as ambassador gave the government and the alliance the excuse they were looking for. On October 30, ʿArif was arrested on arrival and charged with plotting against Iraq, and the life of Qasim, its leader. On November 5, the newspaper *al-Jumhuriyah*, registered under ʿArif's name, was closed down. Its editorial members, all Baʿthists, were implicated in the plot.[22]

Isolated and without much popular support, the Arab nationalists lost their last hold on government. Only a few months after the first shift in Cabinet, a second shakeup stripped them of all their government posts.[23]

The pan-Arab nationalists were made more vulnerable by their ideological hostility to the rights of national minorities living within the "Arab nation." Their ethnic intolerance, as illustrated in the following quotation, alienated a large segment of Iraqi society, the Kurds, from their cause:

The generous Arab nation has taken all these minorities under its protection . . . to leave them the choice of either remaining within the homeland or else emigrate into their own countries, as in the case of the Armenians. . . . Arab nationalism supports the struggle of the Kurds for a Kurdish state. What are the frontiers of that state? The framework which contains Kurdish nationalism is Kurdistan as included by Turkey and Iran. . . . [The Arab Nation] will be happy to have as its friendly neighbour a liberated and democratic Kurdistan. But it is not prepared to cede off its own country to others.[24]

The Kurds, who were split between three different countries (Iraq, Iran, and Turkey), while identifying with the Arab nationalist position, especially with regard to their struggle to overcome imperialist borders, could not but oppose the pan-Arab movement on the grounds of its ethnocentric identity. The Kurdish nationalists were compelled instead to join the anti-merger camp—the camp led by an alliance between the NDP and the ICP.[25]

In a last desperate attempt at gaining the upper hand, the Arab nationalists, with the implicit help of Nasser, began to plot a takeover to save Iraq from the claws of communism.[26] Although they had hoped to spark an overall popular revolt, they only succeeded in organizing a limited revolt in Mosul on March 24, 1959.

Since the Mosul revolt has already been brilliantly documented and analyzed by Batatu, it would be redundant to describe it here. I want to emphasize, however, with the following long excerpt from Batatu, how his narrative, in sharp contrast to traditional orientalist interpretations,[27] captures the intricate interconnections and contradictions between class, ethnic, and religious identities as they played themselves out during the four infamous bloody days and nights of the revolt:

For four days and four nights Kurds and Yazidis stood against Arabs; Assyrians and Aramean Christians against Arab Moslems; the Arab tribe of Albu Mutaiwit against the Arab tribe of Shammar; the peasants of Mosul county against their landlords; the soldiers of the Fifth Brigade against their officers; the periphery of the city of Mosul . . . against the aristocrats of the Arab quarters. . . . What added to the acuteness of the conflicts was the high degree of coincidences between economic and ethnic or religious divisions. . . . Many of the soldiers of the Fifth Brigade were not only from the poorer layers of the population, but were also Kurds, whereas the officers were largely from the Arab middle or lower middle classes. Again, many of the peasants in the villages around Mosul were Christian Arameans, whereas the landlords were, for the most part, Moslem Arabs or Arabized Moslems. . . . Where the economic and ethnic or confessional divisions did not coincide, it was often not the racial or religious, but the class factor that asserted itself. The Arab soldiers clung not

to the Arab officers, but to the Kurdish soldiers. The landed chieftains of
Kurdish al-Gargariyyah sided with the landed chieftains of Arab Shammar.[28]

Class contradictions were most acute in Mosul. One could observe the
close relationship between commercial capital, town mullak, and the oligarchic tribal landed class. The social groups that backed the Mosul revolt were
the prominent merchant and town mullak families of Mosul and the "old
guard"—the tribal landed class. The interests of these social groups were
closely linked. The prominent Sunni and Christian merchant and town mullak
families like the Jalili, Kashmulah, ʿUmari, Mufti, Baytoun, Rassam, and
Sursum, for example, were firmly tied to agricultural interests. Some, like the
Kashmullah, owned large landed estates and were socially and economically
linked to tribal families, such as the Shammar.[29] The Shammar tribe headed
by Ahmad ʿAjil al-Yaʾwar and his cousins, the Farhans, came to control large
tracts of the agricultural lands in al-Jazirah following the land settlements in
the late 1940s and early 1950s. Unlike their brethren tribal owners in the
south, many of the tribal owners rented out large tracts of their lands to
merchants and town mallaks from Mosul.[30] Their support of the revolt, in
short, was economic more than ideological, as their interests were perceived
to be threatened under the new agrarian reform and by a national government
believed to be under the influence of the communists.

The revolt was a disaster. The pan-Arab nationalists were harshly and
easily crushed by the army and the communist people's militia within three
days.[31] With the victory of the anti-union forces, one thing became very clear:
the power of the ICP on the popular level was only matched by the NDPs'
entrenchment within the government. By now, the communists had control of
all the popular and professional organizations. The majority of the General
Federation of Peasant Societies constituent committee belonged to the Communist Party.[32] The same was true of the Iraqi General Federation of Trade
Unions. All fifty-one trade unions were now firmly in the hands of the communists.[33] Communists controlled the Iraqi Journalist Association, the Women's
Federation, student unions, and others.[34]

The establishment of the ICP on the popular level was matched by the
NDP's consolidation of state power. Eighty percent of the ministers replaced after the ousting of the pan-Arab nationalists were either NDP
members, ex-members, or had strong affiliations with the party.[35] This is
where the accounts of Dann, Gabbay, and others err in arguing that this
period saw "a further leap forward for the communists," rather than an
entrenchment of the Iraqi nationalists.[36] These interpretations ignore that
the NDP got the lion's share in government while the ICP, their hatchet
organization, received none.

At this point, the ICP decided the time had come to share in power along with Qasim, the NDP, and their supporters. The nationalist government, backed by the military, however, had no intention of sharing power with the ICP. With a firm hold on the government and with the backing of the army, the social democrats no longer needed to be allied with the communists. In fact, the communists were beginning to be a thorn on their side and a political force to be reckoned with, especially given the ICP's commanding popularity with the urban poor and landless peasants. Despite their frustration with the ICP, the nationalists had to avoid confrontation with the communists until the pan-Arab forces were neutralized. With the communists' public bid for power, the nationalist government decided the time had come to strike against the ICP. From April 1959 on, the nationalists began to implement a policy of systematically eliminating the ICP and its cadre. While conflict over political representation was important, the issue that brought the confrontation between the ICP and the nationalists to a head was the agrarian question.

Agrarian Reform and the Collapse of the National Front

As argued in the previous chapters, all the political forces involved in the 1958 revolution agreed on the necessity of land reform. The ICP argued that the "feudal fetters" had to be lifted in the countryside to allow for the development of capitalist agriculture. Similarly, the Iraqi nationalists saw the traditional *iqta*[3] system as hindering national development. The pan-Arab nationalists considered the relations in the countryside to be remnants of colonial rule.

As expected, three months after the revolution, on September 30, the Agrarian Land Reform Law passed. Gripped by the spirit of the moment, Qasim declared that the Land Reform intended to "abolish feudal relations . . . and emancipate its peasantry." The Land Reform, which emulated the Egyptian Agrarian Reform of 1952, however, was far less radical than Qasim proclaimed. Instead of a full-scale assault on the old landed classes, the reform essentially curbed their economic and political power. While it limited personal holdings to a maximum of 1,000 dunums in the irrigated areas and 2,000 in the rainfed areas, the law provided that landowners be paid for their seized land as well as for immovable property and trees. In addition to compensation, the law also gave the landlord the right to choose the land he would keep.[37] In many ways, compatible with the objectives of the national revolution, the land reform intended not to destroy the old landed classes as much as to neutralize them and possibly even lead them to become auxiliary allies within a reformed nation. The Land Reform, as a general project of and for the whole nation, was emphasized again by the leading figures of the revolution. For example, Qasim:

We will not persecute landlords or treat them unjustly. We will only awake their conscience towards the sons of this people, and they will march alongside the caravan of liberation and equality. . . . Our aim is to eradicate greed. . . . The small must respect the big and the big must cherish the small, so that we may form one unit serving one aim.[38]

In the spirit of the national revolution, the new law also excluded *waqf* (religiously endowed) land from confiscation.[39] By protecting the interests of the Shi'a clergy, the national government, which also feared their influence and power, was able to not only contain and manipulate class conflict but also disperse power relations in the countryside.

Affirming the law's "reformist" essence and the regime's commitment to private property, Muhammad Hadid, the NDP leader and Minister of Finance, stressed that its objective, unlike a communist program, was not to disrupt but reorganize class relations in the countryside:

By endorsing private property, providing adequate compensation to the landowners for land expropriated, allowing landlords to retain a portion of their property, and leaving control of land use to the fallahin, our progressive agrarian reform program engenders minimum economic and social disruption, gives fair treatment to all concerned, and most important of all wins the support of the intended beneficiaries. A typical communist land reform programme—characterized by collective farming, the taking of punitive measures against landlords by depriving them of compensation as well as future livelihood, and state control of land use—tends to generate social antagonism that may require employment of considerable physical force to suppress; it will disrupt the productive capacity of agriculture and lose sympathies of those who farm the land.[40]

As a consequence, the land reform, which aimed to "free" the exploited poor peasants, was constrained by its plan of accommodating the interests of the other governing groups. Accordingly, the law provided for the distribution of seized lands in small holdings of 30 to 60 dunums to poor and landless cultivators, for a price. The price for the land would be equivalent to the value of similar land, plus 3 percent annual interest and an additional 20 percent of the total value of the land to cover distribution and administration expenses.[41] The conditions for buying the confiscated land, while accommodating the middle peasant holders who already had some capital either in the form of cash or land, excluded a major segment of the rural population who were either landless or poor landholding peasants.[42] Lacking capital and access to a credit system, these peasants had little to gain from the land reform.

Although the communists acknowledged that the land reform was reformist and conciliatory to landed classes, they nonetheless initially supported it.

Commitment to the "bourgeois" stage of development was again invoked in defense of the party's uncritical adoption of the reform:

> We adopted the Agrarian Reform Law . . . not out of support for private ownership of land, but because we took into account the general condition of the revolution, the position of the Republic, the class structure of the national forces as well as the attitudes and relations of the national bourgeoisie to large estates and agricultural wealth.[43]

Despite their proclaimed commitment to a "bourgeois" land reform, however, the ICP position became the central point of confrontation with the national government when the ICP made a bid for power in 1959.

After the Mosul revolt, the ICP, aware of its popular commanding power, formally requested (in a memorandum to Qasim) its inclusion in the national government.[44] Its request ignored, the party took the demand to the people, making its rightful claim to political representation a public matter. In their campaign for power, the ICP utilized all accessible media, including its newspaper, *Ittihad al-Sha'b*, to publicize its demand. In addition, the communists organized huge demonstrations to prove their overwhelming social base among the urban poor and especially among the impoverished and landless peasants. The nationalist government, responded by accusing the ICP of provoking class struggle, becoming a divisive power, threatening "national unity," jeopardizing the security of the republic, etc.

As the ICP engaged in a war of tactics with the nationalists, it came to realize the importance of rural support in its bid for political power. Despite their initial commitment to a bourgeois land reform, the communists found themselves instead carrying the banner of the poor and landless peasants, whose interests were least accommodated under the new law. Two new strategies were adopted to strengthen the ICP's social base in the rural areas:

1. "politically" mobilizing the peasantry; and

2. pushing for a more radical land reform.[45]

In the effort to win over the subaltern peasantry to its side, the ICP began to criticize the land reform for its conciliatory line toward the older landed classes. The ICP organ, *Ittihad al-Sha'b*, ran a series of articles attacking the reform for failing to abolish all "large agricultural estates," for "compensating the landowners on their confiscated land," and especially for imposing "payments on the landless and small peasants." They blamed "reactionary elements" within the national bourgeoisie for making these concessions to the old landed classes, which had "raped state and peasant lands."[46]

To give the poor peasantry a more active voice in the national revolution, the ICP advocated the establishment of peasant societies. From December through January 1959, petitions carrying "hundreds of thousands of signatures" (*Ittihad al-Shaʿb*) were sent to the government. The campaign succeeded and peasant societies were licensed. On April 15, 1959, the "Congress for the Federation of Peasant Societies" was founded and Kazim Farhud, a communist, was elected its president.[47] To demonstrate their power, the first "Peasants' Congress" was held in Baghdad. Peasants by the thousands came to Baghdad to celebrate the occasion and render their support to the communists.[48] By May 10, 1959, *The General Federation of Peasants Societies Law* was passed; Article 87 recognized the peasants' right to organize their own societies.[49] These organizations represented a major victory for the communists and their supporters, principally the poor peasantry.

The ensuing period was marked by a political warfare waged between the ICP and the NDP over the control of the peasant societies. The NDP and their supporters were at a disadvantage since, as the ICP contended, they constituted only a minority relative to the majority of poor and landless peasants who championed the communists. By the end of May 1959, 2,267 out of the total 3,577 peasant societies were under the control of the communists.[50]

In response, the NDP, through its organ, *al-Ahali,* began a public campaign against the communists, accusing them of failing to recognize noncommunist peasant organizations and using "undemocratic" methods to control elections.[51] The conflict was not limited to words. On June 15, 1959, the NDP organized a demonstration of peasants in front of the Agrarian Reform Ministry in Baghdad to protest the meddling in their peasant organizations by the communist-controlled General Federation of Peasant Societies (G.F.P.S.).[52] The communists responded by moving in full force to prevent the protest from taking place. The outcome was a bloody confrontation between the communists and the national democratic forces.[53]

Control over peasant organizations compelled the ICP to take a harder line in favor of the poor peasantry. Through the peasant organizations, the ICP pushed and succeeded in having peasant representatives included in land expropriation and distribution committees. They also pressured the Ministry of Land Reform to improvise policies in favor of the poorer strata of peasants, such as leasing instead of selling confiscated land, and providing financial aid and credit to the poor peasants.[54]

To preempt the communists and woo the peasantry, the national government conceded many of the demands put forth by peasant societies. It also replaced the NDP minister of the land reform, the landowner Hudayb al-Hajj Hamud, with a well-known independent Marxist economist, Ibrahim Kubbeh. The latter move by the national government was made to appease the communists without giving into their demand of direct representation.[55] Under the Kubbeh tenure, new policies to speed up land distribution were introduced, including leasing instead of selling.[56]

It is important to stress that the communists' ultimate objective for mobilizing the rural population was not to drive for an agrarian revolution as much as to make a bid for political power. As noted earlier, the communists began their campaign soon after the Mosul revolt. The Central Committee first appealed directly to Qasim to include them in the government. Their request denied, the communists took their demand to the people, making their claim to political representation a public issue. A series of editorial articles appeared in *Ittihad al-Sha ͨ b*, written by leading members of the Central Committee, asserting that the policy of the party's exclusion from power was "unrepresentative of reality" and an "unjustified discrimination" against a substantial social force that had "the greatest support on the popular level."[57] Impressive mass rallies and demonstrations were organized continuously during the month of April and the first part of May. On April 16, the general meeting of the Federation of Peasant Societies was turned into a political rally for the ICP. Two days later, on April 18, a Peace Day demonstration of thousands of people was organized. A third followed with a 100,000 people marching on April 22.[58]

In view of its commanding power on the ground, the ICP adopted a more critical view of the national government. In an article entitled, "Participation of the Communist Party in Government is an Urgent and a National Necessity," *Ittihad al-Sha ͨ b* openly criticized the national government for its "unequal representation of the popular political forces" and for "blocking the official participation of the communists," despite their massive popularity. The contradiction between the existing political power structure and popular sentiments was blamed on the "reactionary elements" within the "national bourgeoisie."[59] Articles of this sort were appearing in every newspaper and journal controlled by the ICP and its followers. A final bid in this campaign was the Labor Day rally where an estimated figure of 300,000 people marched down Rashid street calling for the participation of the communists in state power.[60]

At this critical juncture, the national government could no longer sidetrack the issue, especially since the prospect of a "communist takeover" set off alarm bells worldwide.[61] The national government, which had no desire to share power with the communists, had no choice but to strike back. With the help of its repressive state apparatus, the nationalist government launched its offensive.

The Offensive Against the ICP

Arguably, the nationalist plan to undercut the communists started soon after the revolt in Mosul was crushed and the pan-Arab forces were silenced. With the danger of unification out of the way, the national government was free to strike against the ICP and its social base.

One of the first acts in the campaign against the communists was the re-enactment of the Criminal Ordinance Law. As of May, 1959, the national government instituted a revised version of the the prerevolutionary ordinance to censure political activity. Directed against the freedom to organize and associate, this law was a repudiation of one of the most fundamental principles of the national revolution. Article 107 of this law entitled the state to imprison any person engaging in spreading political and "demagogic" ideas against the republic; Article 108 directed the state to prosecute any organization that spread political (meaning communist) ideas. The penalty for violating these laws ranged from seven years to life imprisonment.[62]

The next step was the NDP's call for the suspension of their political activities.[63] On May 22, 1959, the Minister of Economy, Muhammad Hadid, a leading figure in the NDP, announced the decision to suspend his party's activities and called upon the other parties to do the same.[64] The ICP refused to follow suit. Instead, it dropped its bid for power. On May 23, the Central Committee issued the following statement: "Considering the need for unity among the national forces in the struggle to protect the Republic under the leadership of Qasim, we decided to stop this campaign."[65]

The ICP's conciliatory gestures did not deter the national government. The assault on the ICP became much more systematic following the bloody riots in Kirkuk, which the nationalists blamed on the communists.[66] As of July, 1959, the nationalists began to discredit and then methodically dismantle all popular organizations, especially trade unions and peasant societies. They were blamed for the decline in industrial and agricultural production, loss of capital, and for the general stagnation of the economy.[67]

From July 19th to August 1959, the national government arrested hundreds of rank-and-file communists and their followers. Anticommunist armed attacks were carried out against the headquarters of the party, their trade unions, and peasant societies. The beating, banishing, and killing of communists, trade union members, and peasant society members became an everyday event.[68] Police harassment, imprisonment, and forced evacuation of members of peasant societies, with the help of the landowners, were constantly challenged and petitioned against by peasant societies. Incidents of joint NDP-old guard fighting against the communists and their peasant supporters became commonplace.[69]

In the process of breaking down the ICP, the nationalist regime had to revoke all "democratic" rights and dismantle popular institutions step-by-step. On September 2, 1959, the government reinstated the Martial Law Ordinance of 1935, which abolished freedom of expression.[70] A board was established at the Ministry of Guidance to censor publications and newspapers. On September 9, a revised Peasant Societies' Law was issued. It took the right to license peasant societies away from the General Federation of Peasant Societies and entrusted it instead to provincial governors.[71] Soon after, the government proclaimed all prior peasant societies illegal because they were established without local governors' approval (September 1960). The final blow against the newly acquired freedoms was reinstatement of the Association Act in January 1960.[72] The new law required that all parties, trade unions, and societies had first to secure the approval of the Ministry of Interior before they could associate, organize, or be active. As a result, all political parties and popular institutions were now declared illegal until new official permits were issued by the Ministry of Interior. All three major parties applied for these permits. As expected, the NDP and the Kurdish Democratic Party were granted permission (February 11, 1960) but not the ICP. After a period of procrastination, the government gave the permit to an ICP underling by the name of Dauwd Sayigh and declined the request of the official Communist Party.[73]

To rally the support of the middle peasantry against the communists, the national government introduced new measures in the land reform that favored their interests. One such measure was enacted in al-Nasiriyah, Law Number 17, 1961 which recognized the rights of the sirkals (foremen) to the land they managed over the rights of the peasants who worked the land. Another measure was to redefine the landowner-peasant relationship in favor of the landowner. Special Dispute courts to adjudicate owner-peasant conflicts were canceled and land disputes were now referred to regular common courts, still under the influence of old landlords and the rich peasantry. With this law, it became virtually impossible for the poor peasants to resolve disputes over landownership in their favor.[74] This same law also recognized the rights of ownership to the lazma holder and in particular the secondary multazims such as the sirkals and clergymen. In ᶜAmarah, this law granted the primary multazims, old landlords, 200 to 400 dunums each, while the secondary multazims, the sirkals, were granted 100 to 200 dunums each. In comparison, the poor peasants of ᶜAmarah were given nothing other than the right to purchase 10 dunums of lazma lands.[75]

This law marked the beginning of the dissolution of the popular reforms won by the revolution. In its offensive against a well-mobilized peasantry, the national government could not rely on the middle peasantry, which was too small and too insignificant a force and had turned instead to the oligarchic class for support. This alliance with the "old guard" necessitated the renunciation of the earlier reforms.[76] Despite the systematic assault by the national government on the political and economic rights of the people, the ICP leadership remained faithful to its characterization of the regime as "progressive." In the face of the clear disruption of the popular revolution, and the dismantling of its institutions, the ICP leadership reaffirmed its commitment to "national rule" and its leader, Qasim. Reasserting its faith in the revival of the national coalition, the Central Committee renounced its activities of the last few months as ultra-leftist:

> In this very awkward period in the history of our country, the Central Committee decided to correct its ultra-leftist line of the last few months. . . . [The party will] emphasize instead the necessity to solidify national unity and support the ruling leaders in their efforts to protect this republic.[77]

On the agrarian question, the ICP issued a series of articles by ʿAmir ʿAbdallah reiterating its original position on the nature of the revolution and asserting the mistakes the party committed in declaring a class struggle in the countryside. Condemning its support for the landless and poor peasants as "isolationist" and "ultra-leftist," the party re-emphasized the importance at this stage of a unified peasantry to fight "feudal relations" and protect the national republic:[78]

> We never called for a radical land reform . . . because we took into consideration the class nature of the national revolution, and the close ties of the national bourgeoisie to large estates and agricultural wealth. . . . Most of the capitalist class is participating in the exploitation of the peasantry (whether) as landowners, owners of water pumps, town merchants etc., even the industrial bourgeoisie who are few to begin with have close connection with landed wealth . . . this is where the weakness lies in the national bourgeoisie.[79]

In spite of their recognition of the contradictory character of the "national bourgeoisie" including its progressive industrial wing, the ICP leadership insisted on reinstating the two-stage theory doctrine as the party's guideline.

Instead of revising its theory in accordance with the circumstances and the nature of class formation, the ICP denounced class struggle as "ultra-left" and purged three of its Central Committee members, including Salam ʿAdil and al-Haydari, for steering the party against the national revolution. The "united front" and the four-class alliance was then reinstated.[80]

The reversion to the old line helped little. The national government continued its assault against the ICP and its cadre throughout 1960 and 1961. The communists and their supporters were stripped of their leading positions in all unions and federations, Labor, Journalists, Teachers, Peasants, Students, Lawyers, Engineers, Medical, and Women's unions.[81] Communist sympathizers were removed from all official positions whether in the army or the government. Ibrahim Kubbeh was released from the Ministry of Agrarian Reform. So was Naziha al-Dulaimi, who was discharged from the Ministry of Municipalities.[82]

The offensive clearly symbolized more than an attack against the communists. It signified an interruption of the July popular revolution. The attack was not limited to the ICP alone but included all other popular and grassroots institutions won in the aftermath of the revolution. A striking case, for example, is the national government's assault on the Kurdish nationalists and their cultural and political organizations, heralding a final break in the relations between the government and the Kurds.

Brought about by a national coalition that included Kurdish forces, the July revolution was initially sympathetic to the Kurdish question. In the spirit of the revolution, one of the first acts taken by the Republic was to release all Kurdish political prisoners and to grant their exiled leaders, the Barazanis, permission to return.[83] The national government, as stated in the Provisional Constitution, promised to give the Kurds equal rights with the Arabs, promote their language and culture, and give their region a fair share of economic development and social services. Under the new freedom act, the government legalized, along with other parties, the Kurdish Democratic Party, under the leadership of Barazani, and allowed the publication of Kurdish journals and newspapers. But, as in the case of the ICP, once the KDP began to press its claims for the extension of equal national and cultural rights to the Kurds, the government responded by taking restrictive measures. One was amending the KDP program before licensing it in 1960, under the new Association Act.[84] Another was to dismiss government workers who were members of the KDP. On the second anniversary of the national revolution, Kurdish national rights were completely effaced, as were the promises made for Kurdistan's equal share in development projects. To curtail their activities, the government dismissed workers for being KDP members, suspended their newspapers, and imprisoned their leaders for publicly voicing criticisms of the government.[85]

The revolt of the Kurdish landlords (June 1961) against the implementation of the agrarian reform in the Kurdish region was seen by the national government as an opportune moment to strike against all Kurdish opposition including the nationalists.[86] Following measures like the bombardment of the

Barazani village and the suspension of the KDP by the government, the KDP joined Barazani's forces in the revolt against the republic.

By the time of the Kurdish revolt, the nationalist government, headed by Qasim, had already alienated itself from the major segments of society by declaring war against any class, social group, or party that opposed the regime. This was why the national government had to rescind its social reforms and dismantle the popular institutions already established. The leading political force in Iraq, the ICP, however, was unwilling to recognize this reality. Its insistence on the progressive nature of the "bourgeoisie" and the "national democratic" nature of the regime helped to disarm the forces of popular revolution.[87]

Yet the victory of the nationalists against the popular forces was short-lived. Structurally weak and isolated, the nationalist forces were unable to establish hegemony over society. Backed by a military junta and engaged in a futile war against the Kurdish nationalists for failure to meet their demands for internal autonomy, the national democratic forces were soon to splinter into many factions and disappear from the political scene.

The "Passive Revolution" *cum* National Revolution

As argued earlier, the constitution of the "national bourgeoisie" put constraints on its ability to consolidate control over key social, economic, and political institutions. The sources of its inability to establish hegemony were not merely subjective, i.e., tactical errors, political mistakes, etc., but primarily objective. A product of the interwar period, the Iraqi "bourgeoisie" was far too fragile to transform society radically on its own, especially within the context of a poorly developed domestic economy and an overwhelming advanced metropolitan capital.

The aspiring "bourgeoisie," as I have discussed in more detail in the first three chapters, consisted of three factions; the agricultural, the commercial, and the "industrial." All these factions, with the exception of the commercial, were structurally fragile. The agricultural faction was dominated largely by rentier capital and less so by the weaker capitalist agriculture. Commercial capital, the strongest, had little interest in long-term industrial investments. The "industrial" wing of the bourgeoisie was especially vulnerable because of its infancy, dependence on agricultural raw materials, and close social ties to agricultural-rentier wealth. Over 34 percent of Iraqi industry was agriculture-dependent.[88] The food, drink, vegetable, soap, and tobacco subsidiaries relied mostly on local agricultural raw material.[89] The second factor was the close ties, direct or indirect (through marriage), between agriculture and "industrial" wealth. The Fattahs, owners of a textile factory, major shareholders in two cement factories as well as the Vegetable Oil Extraction Co. and the

Cigarette Co., for example, were married into agricultural wealth through two families. The Damirchis, were landowners as well as main shareholders in the Date Industry Co. and the Commercial Bank of Iraq. Others were the Hadid, the Murjan, the Chalabi, etc.[90]

Another factor that added to the fragility of the "national bourgeoisie" was the conflictual relations between the relatively strong commercial and the relatively weak industrial factions. As seen in chapter 3, the rivalry between the two factions started in the prerevolutionary period, became more intense in the postrevolutionary period as the national government, assuming its developmentalist role, legislated protectionist measures to encourage private investment in industry.[91]

From the outset, the national government sought to facilitate private industry by imposing new protectionist measures and granting tax exemptions to private investors in industry. Protectionism was justified as necessary to both protect domestic infant industries against foreign competition and eliminate the deficit in the trade balance by saving on foreign exchange. In pursuit of these policies, laws which ranged from the imposition of high tariffs to restricting and sometimes banning foreign goods produced locally (wool, cotton and silk cloth, vegetable oil, soap, foreign cigarettes, etc.) were enforced.[92] Other policies supporting industry included tax breaks on the importation of raw and capital goods for production.

These policies were considered essential to promote small-scale private industries and develop a national home market. In the words of Khaduri Khaduri, the secretary of Federation for Industry, and a major shareholder in the Cotton Seeds Product Co.:

> the goal of the new national government was to develop industries so that it can satisfy the needs of the domestic market and hence free it from depending on foreign industries . . . to do so the state passed new protectionist measures in the form of high tariffs, banning or limiting imports of commodities produced locally. . . . Another is by increasing the capital of the Industrial Bank. . . . These policies are meant to protect private capital and encourage it to invest in industry; that is, in light industry. . . . Because in so far as heavy industry is concerned, it will be the responsibility of the state to develop.[93]

While helping to increase home production, these measures also allowed private industry to realize high profits on their investments. The Oil Extraction Company doubled its production capacity in two years; its profits skyrocketing as high as 70 percent.[94] The soap industry, a subsidiary of the Oil Extraction Co., increased its capital investment by 15 percent.[95] The number of factories producing ready-made clothing increased from 20 to 36 in a span of only three years.[96] Production of wool textiles, one of the most capitalized industries, doubled by 1960 and tripled by 1963; while the National Leather Co. realized as much as 40 percent of its capital in profit by 1961.[97] The rigorous protective measures pursued by the new government encouraged the flow of capital into industry. In the post-1958 period, for example, the industrial sector expanded from 37.16 percent to 43 percent while commercial capital, which had the lion's share in the previous period, declined from 43.8 percent to 26.16 percent in the post-1958 period.[98]

From the perspective of the government, which was directing a program of economic development on behalf of the whole nation, these necessary measures were intended, not just to accommodate the particular interest of private industrial capital, but also to encourage large commercial and financial capital to take an interest in industrial production.[99] Fully aware that half of the large firms in Iraq (sariffas and trade companies) still operated in the commercial sector, the government saw encouraging them to move into industrial ventures as an important potential source of capital. This, however, was not the way commercial capital perceived state policy. From its perspective, these measures were seen as undermining commercial sources of wealth.

As in the monarchic era, the import-export firms, both large and small, were the most indignant over the new protectionist measures instituted by the national government. Their wrath was voiced in a memoranda sent to the Chamber of Commerce denouncing protectionism and demanding the opening of the market to foreign goods. Similarly, their criticisms of protectionism focused primarily on the inability of local private industry to provide either the quantity needed by the poor consumer or the quality desired by the rich. In contrast to the earlier era, this time they tried to appeal to the "national-popular" ideology of the revolution by pointing out that the government's present economic plan was biased toward private industrial capital, thus violating the "universal goals" of the national revolution by simply favoring a minority over the shared interests of the nation:

> This national government, and Qasim its leader, proclaimed on many occasions that it fights all kinds of *iqta²* and puts the interests of the people over the interests of the individuals. However, we are convinced that the bans and restrictions put on the import of woolen textiles would lead to another form of *iqta²*—*iqta² sina²i* (meaning industrial monopoly) which is as dangerous as *iqta² zira²i* (referring to large agrarian estates), since [in this case] it results in the monopoly of two factories over the common interest of the people.[100]

The tension over imported goods was not limited to wool manufacturing, but included other industries like silk. Importers of Syrian silk argued that the ban on silk cloth was an unproductive policy, since local factories could neither produce the quality silk—referring to the dyes and fine intricate weaving—or the necessary quantity required by the market. In a memo the importers of silk cloth, they chastised protection because it led to the enrichment of the manufacturers at the expense of the poor Iraqi customer:

> If so why would these industries demand the limitations or prohibitions put on the importation of silk cloth? . . . First of all they cannot prove that their products are as good as the foreign . . . (second) the prices of local products are too high: these industrialists are making up to 70 percent in profit . . . not to mention the tax breaks these manufacturers are granted on the import of raw material . . . [after which] they charge the consumers exorbitant prices for low quality. . . . This, we assume, is not the goal or intention of the national government . . . because it is the small and poor consumers, in this case, who suffer from such prices.[101]

To contain further conflict between these factions, the national government improvised procedures to please commercial capital without necessarily abandoning the official "protectionist" policies. One such device, for instance, was to set up a special committee in charge of supplies (*al-tamwin al-ʾulya*), which was attached to the Ministry of Commerce, to assign a maximum for the import of woolen cloth. At the same time, the ministry promised the local woolen industry to find outside markets in case of surplus.[102]

The rivalry within the ranks of the "national bourgeoisie" also had its repercussions on the political arena. The Chadirchi-Hadid conflict within the NDP which initially was political came to express later on a much deeper conflict between the two wings. Differences within the ranks first appeared over the party's position toward the new coercive "undemocratic" measures (e.g., the Association Act) imposed by the national government. The Chadirchi faction, critical of these policies, demanded the party's withdrawal from government. Hadid, on the other hand, pushed to remain in power and favored continued support. When Chadirchi resumed the presidency of the NDP upon the request of the party leadership, he demanded the pull-out of all members from the government. Hadid refused to comply and instead resigned from the party, taking his faction along with him.[103]

But to put the split in its proper perspective, two points must be considered. The first is the role of Kamil al-Chadirchi. Chadirchi began to voice his criticism of the national government and its policies very early on, starting with the campaign against the pan-Arab movement. He opposed the forceful methods used by the national government in its campaign against the pan-Arabs and later on, the communists.[104] However—and this is crucial—

Chadirchi, due to the factionalism between the various wings within the "bourgeoisie," was unable to rally support for his position within his own party at the time. As a result, he withdrew from politics and was inactive until he was called in again by an opposition faction within the party to resume its leadership. Thus, it seems that Chadirchi became attractive only after an opposition to Hadid had developed within the NDP. The issue of the NDP's commitment to democracy then appeared to have developed along with, if not after, other issues split the party into opposing factions. From the evidence available, it seems that Chadirchi was used by the faction opposed to Hadid who was then in favor of remaining in power.[105] Due to his long-standing criticism of the undemocratic policies of the national government, Chadirchi was a natural choice for opposition leader.

The second indication that disagreement over undemocratic state policies may not have been the fundamental cause for the split was that the recent deterioration toward an authoritarian regime was the outcome of the offensive precipitated with the support of all factions. Although the offensive was launched against the communists, it led to an assault against democratic rights, and the dismantling of all popular institutions. Isolated from its grass roots, the national government was bound to become more authoritarian.

In sum, then, these two factors indicate that the split within the NDP conveyed more than just a political/personal conflict between Hadid and Chadirchi. The evidence seems to point to a much deeper schism within the ranks of the "national bourgeoisie" itself. This conflict had been subdued in the first years following the revolution in face of the more pressing need for unity against the threats of first, pan-Arabism, and second, the Communist Party. With these threats removed, the intra-NDP conflict inevitably surfaced.

Soon after the resigning from the NDP on May 6, 1960, Hadid and his supporters formed their own party, the Progressive National Party. The leadership of the new party tended, by and large, to represent the "industrial" wing of the "national bourgeoisie." In addition to Hadid, there was Khaduri Khaduri, the secretary of the Federation of Industries and a major shareholder in the Cotton Seeds Product Co., Yusif al-Hajj Elias, textile owner, and Rajab Ali al-Saffar, of the tobacco industry.[106]

The two parties, however, could not last long. Weaker once separated than they had been united, these parties became for the most part ineffective. The first party to disintegrate was the NDP. A few months after the first split, it split again.[107] The outcome was the suspension of the party and its newspaper, *al-Ahali*, as of October 1961. The National Progressive Party, which maintained close relations with the Qasim government, was luckier than the NDP. Yet, as the war against the Kurdish nationalists became unpopular, Hadid and his few followers could no longer afford to be associated with the military junta, and resigned from the government.[108] On July 1, 1962, the National Progressive Party suspended its activities in protest against the coercive measures taken by the military government, which was by then already in the process of disintegrating.[109]

Isolated from the people and involved in a futile war against the Kurds, Qasim tried to create a new popularity for his regime by proclaiming Kuwait an extension of the Iraqi nation. Kuwait, part of the Basra Province during the Ottoman period, had been conceded to the British as a protectorate in 1913 which lasted until June 19, 1962. Once the British relinquished their protectorate over Kuwait, the ruler of Kuwait, ʿAbdallah al-Sabah, declared Kuwait an independent sovereign state and immediately requested its entry into the United Nations and the Arab League. Five days after the declaration, Qasim, in a press conference, rejected Kuwait's right to sovereignty and demanded its immediate merger with Iraq.

Qasim's claim to Kuwait was not Iraq's first. Nuri al-Saʿid, just a few months before the advent of the revolution, made similar demands on Kuwait.[110] So did King Ghazi before him in 1939.[111]

Other than the historical claim to Kuwait, there was also the long-term border dispute that was as popular an issue among the Iraqis as the historical one. In fact, the border issue has troubled relations between Kuwait and Iraq since their early formation as two separate entities following the First World War. In the process of carving out and creating these two new territoralities, Britain left Iraq landlocked with no access to a deep waterway in the Gulf. Iraq resented this since it hampered its marketing ability especially "oil from the Basra because of the lack of anchorage facilities for deep draught tankers."[112] Iraq's need for a deep seaport became more urgent in the 1950s following the construction of the seaport, Umm Qasr, at the mouth of the Gulf. From this point on, Iraq had been pushing hard to reach some form of an accord with Kuwait that would allow Iraq access to the Gulf waterways. One suggestion was to have access through the islands of Warba and Bubiyan, which the Iraqis maintained belonged to Iraq but were "arbitrarily" given to Kuwait by Britain under the Treaty of ʿUqair.[113] Like earlier calls, Qasim's efforts were in vain. On July 1, British and Saudi forces moved into Kuwait to assist the Kuwaitis against a possible Iraqi attack. These forces were kept in Kuwait until Qasim was pressured into silence by Arab diplomats.

The Kuwait affair proved disastrous to Qasim's regime, both on the national and international fronts. On the Arab front, the incident helped to alienate Qasim's regime from other Arabs (like the Saudis) who at one point backed him against the Nasserite camp. It also strained Iraq's relations with the Soviet Union. On the national front, in addition to waging an unpopular war against the Kurds, Qasim's unfortunate claim to Kuwait led to ridicule and further popular disenchantment with him. This alienation was most felt in the army, which resented being forced to fight the civil war against the Kurds. The first seeds of dissent within the army started soon after the Kuwait disaster, as pan-Arab officers began to plot a military coup to remove Qasim from power. Isolated and alienated from the Iraqi people, Qasim was an easy target. On February 8, 1963, Qasim's regime was overthrown in a military coup led by his old associate, Abdul Salam ʿArif.

CONCLUSION

While the national revolution of 1958 succeeded in destroying the power base of the oligarchic monarchy, it failed to complete its historical mission of social reconstruction. I have attributed the failure of the social revolution to deep-seated ideological and class differences within the coalition that fostered the revolution. The national revolution's proclamation of universal goals that transcended class, religious, ethnic, and other differences proved illusionary. Once the oligarchic monarchy was overthrown, the national coalition collapsed, making the post-colonial state an arena of intense, often violent, struggle. The outcome was the breakdown of national unity and the disintegration of the national revolution a few years later.

Briefly stated, the conflicts over strategies and policies of reconstruction were articulated over two primary issues: first, unification (merger) with the United Arab Republic (Syria-Egypt), which split the national coalition between those who supported the pan-Arab nationalist position and those who opposed it; and second, land reform and the split between the communists and the military-backed nationalist forces.

The retreat of the national revolution had both short- and long-term repercussions. The immediate consequences were that the Iraqi nationalists, the only faction in the coalition (besides the military) left in power, were far too fragile to govern society and carry out the "bourgeois" revolution assigned to them by the communists. In-fighting within the different factions of the bourgeoisie led instead to the disintegration of their political organ, the NDP, and to its eventual disappearance from the political scene. The post-colonial government, stripped of its national and social base, was left floundering under the leadership of Qasim, while its army was entangled in an unpopular war against the Kurds in the north.

The long-term repercussions of the failure of the national revolution were even greater. The destruction of the popular movement and the dismantling of its various grassroots organizations by the national government meant more than just a temporary interruption of the national/social revolution—it signified the continuation of a policy of violence, started under the colonial state, against any and all popular/subaltern voices of difference. The strategy of silencing the opposition by sheer force was repeated more intensely and more efficiently in the ensuing years after the revolution, thus succeeding in finishing off any and all forms of participatory politics in post-colonial society. The gravest manifestation of the end of participatory politics was the emergence of one of the most relentlessly authoritarian regimes in modern Iraqi history, that of Saddam Hussein.

The defeat of the national popular revolution was one factor that eased the way for the rise of authoritarianism in Iraq. The other factor was oil. It is my contention that oil, which played a significant role in the making of the revolution, played an even greater role in the consolidation of Saddam Hussein's regime. Although the national revolution of 1958 formed a sobering threat to imperial interests, it nonetheless was incapable of seriously challenging the formidable power the IPC (Iraq Petroleum Company) and multinational capital wielded in Iraq. What the revolution did, instead, was to chip away at the IPC's authority by reclaiming from the company, under Law Number 80, the government's right to decide about future oil development. It was not until 1972, however, that the post-colonial state was able to reassert its full sovereignty over its oil fields by nationalizing the oil company. This move made Iraq instantly wealthy (oil revenues increased from £218.6 million in 1972 to £823.2 million in 1973) with enough capital to foster a distributive welfare state and initiate the capitalization of both private and public sectors of the economy. Besides making Iraq instantly rich, nationalization also boosted the prestige of the new Ba'th regime, whose authority has not yet been fully entrenched due to the persistence of dissenting voices.[114]

Oil revenues empowered the regime on several levels. The immense increase in oil revenues (reaching £29 billion in 1980) from both nationalization and the sharp rise in oil prices after the formation of OPEC, gave the Ba'th regime more economic autonomy and much greater political power. This wealth transformed the Iraqi state into the principal determining force in the political economy of Iraq. As the agent instead of the facilitator of capital accumulation, the regime began to utilize its new wealth, not only investing in the infrastructure and other social welfare projects, but also restructuring the economy by building both the private (through subcontracting to private capital) and public sectors. In the process of reconstruction, the regime created its own social base—a new satellite urban class whose wealth was totally dependent on its privileged access to the ruling Ba'th, a small, highly centralized group of people within the Regional Command Committee.

Besides being the engine driving capital accumulation, the Ba'th regime spent enormous amount of its wealth on importing the latest technologies of coercion and in building a highly sophisticated surveillance system, consisting of massive armed forces, a private militia, and a secret police service, to bolster and maintain its leadership. With this mighty system of coercion and in the absence of participatory politics, force became the convenient method of solving conflicts, both local and international. On the domestic scene, coercion—ranging from forced migration, mass deportation, and execution to the use of poison gas, imprisonment, and torture—was commonly and invariably used against organized resistance groups like the communists, the Kurds, and the Shi'a Muslims (al-Da'wa), as well as against ordinary people voicing their opposition.

On the international level, force as the solution to conflict is evident in the recent wars started against Iran and Kuwait in 1980 and 1990. The disastrous war against the Islamic revolution of Khomeini, launched on behalf of the Arab Gulf states as well, was expected to end quickly and spectacularly for the Iraqis. Instead, the war turned into a nightmarish, endless war of attrition, lasting eight years and costing both sides staggering human and economic losses. In addition to the loss of over 100,000 soldiers and the destruction of the city of Basra and its surrounding oil fields, Iraq was left mired in debt (estimated at between $60 to $80 billion), most of which was to Saudi Arabia and Kuwait.

The Ba'th regime, politically shaken and economically drained, became more dependent on its surveillance system and less on its satellite of domestic support to maintain power during the war. Once the war ended, the regime immediately set out to reconstruct the economy and rebuild its support base by investing heavily in capital-intensive projects. To raise the capital needed for reconstruction, the Iraqi government started to put pressure on OPEC members to reduce production and increase oil prices. The Iraqi campaign, while backed by Algeria, was rejected by many Gulf states, including Kuwait, which refused even to lower production to meet its own quota, and Saudi Arabia, which flatly rejected any price increase. Faced with resistance, Iraq once again resorted to force and in August, 1990, sent its armed forces to invade and annex Kuwait. Underestimating the significance of oil to imperial interests, Iraq once again entered a conflict far beyond its physical and human means because of its mistaken assumption that the conflict with Kuwait was an "internal matter" and, therefore, a regional problem. Not surprisingly, the Gulf War of 1991, under the auspices of the UN, quickly became an international conflict, spearheaded by the United States and fully backed by the old imperial guards headed by France and Britain. Of course, Iraq's diminutive forces had little chance against the mighty power of this alliance, which—in less than a week—was able, with air power alone, to crush the Iraqi army and convert its equipment to ashes, having lost little to nothing on its side. It is quite ironic that this colossal defeat of the armed forces of the authoritarian Iraqi state, at the hands of an even mightier coercive force headed by the United States, which virtually destroyed Iraq as a modern nation-state and brought its people to the brink of starvation, spared the regime of Saddam.

III

EPILOGUE

Epilogue

The most powerful as well as the most creative results of the nationalist imagination in Asia and Africa are posited not on an identity but rather on a difference with the "modular" forms of the national society propagated by the modern West.

Partha Chatterjee

When a project is translated from one site to another, from one agent to another, versions of power are produced. As with translations of a text, one does not simply get a reproduction of identity. The acquisition of new forms of language from the modern West, whether by forcible imposition, insidious insertion, or voluntary borrowing, is part of what makes for new possibilities of action in non-Western societies.

Talal Asad

REFORMULATING THE NATIONAL QUESTION[1]

This epilogue addresses some of the more recent writings on the nature of colonial and post-colonial nationalisms. It expands the historical analysis of the book and explores some of the current debates about the issue of nationalism and the nature of colonial state. The thrust of the argument is that colonial power as a modern power is distinctive because of its transformative nature; in the sense that it inserts itself and reconstitutes the domain.

Mainstream Western nationalist thought assumes that nationalism and the nation-state are an integral part of the story of liberty, industrialism, democracy, and progress. Based on the classical European liberal experience, this model served as the norm for analyzing subsequent versions of nationalism, including those that emerged in the non-European, colonized world. The success of non-Western nationalisms is judged according to whether they display the same characteristics as the European model. Since the non-Western variations of nationalism have not reproduced an identical version of the classical model, they came to be seen as "lacking," non-rational (reads revivalist), unprogressive (antimodern), and oppressive (antidemocratic).

In his recent work, *Nations and Nationalism since 1780*, Eric Hobsbawm adopts a historical and therefore a more critical approach to the study of nationalism. He raises two significant points:

143

1. there is "no *a priori* definition of what constitues a nation," and

2. there is no such thing as a "*historic* nation." Nationalism is a construct of modernity or rather, as he puts it, a modern product of capitalism, industrialization, and mass communication.

Although Hobsbawm problematizes the idea that nations are based on a "historic" language, "primordial" culture, he still embraces the liberal criterion that only nations with viable economies and large territories are deserving of independence. This is where I consider his analysis flawed. Hobsbawm continues to subscribe to the nineteenth-century liberal version of nationalism as the standard by which to judge the legitimacy of other nationalisms. This position becomes even more visible when he addresses the nation-state and the question of nationalism in the context of twentieth-century non-Western states. Disregarding the historical and colonial context, he employs what he terms the "normative" model (despite having shown it to be inapplicable even to much of Europe) in order to judge the anticolonial movements and postcolonial nationalisms, thus reaffirming the Eurocentric view of history that regards the West the only true subject of history.

A different and perhaps a more judicious study of nationalism is the work of the Indian scholar, Partha Chatterjee. His two books on Indian nationalism, *Nationalist Thought and the Colonial World* and his more recent *The Nation and its Fragments*, are theoretically more relevant than Hobsbawm's because they are critical of the liberal accounts of nationalisms and because of their focus on non-Western forms of nationalism. Informed by the French post-structuralist critiques of modernist meta-narratives, Chatterjee locates the problem of liberal nationalism not so much in "bourgeois" knowledge (since Marxists, like Hobsbawm, also adopt the same approach) as in its presumption of the universal sovereignty of post-Enlightenment rationality.

While critical of the post-Enlightenment project, Chatterjee, however, does not abandon Marxism in its entirety, as did the French post-structuralists.[2] Instead, he uses the Gramscian notion of the "passive revolution of capital" to make another critical yet vital point—that the non-Western model of the modern nation-state is, empirically speaking, the "norm" and not the aberration. By making this point, he shifts the debate from the West to the East by positing non-Western nationalisms as central to theorizing about the modern nation-state.

Chatterjee starts with the central question of how Indian nationalist thought, which rejected European domination, on the one hand, accepted "the very intellectual premises of 'modernity' on which colonial domination was based." Through a critical reading of Bengali nationalist writings, Chatterjee concludes that anticolonial nationalism, while embracing some modes of post-Enlightenment rationality in the material domain of state, economy, science, and technology, rejected it in the inner domain which has the marks of an authentic culture upon which the idea of the nation could be imagined. While nationalism sought to reconstruct the outer domain in the image of the West (through the importation and establishment of Western political-economic apparatuses), it circumscribed the inner domain as the site of distinction and essential identity. It was in the latter domain—of religion, family, language, and community—that antinationalist thought, according to Chatterjee, launched "its most powerful, creative and historically significant project: to fashion a 'modern' culture that is nevertheless not Western."[3]

In the process of reappropriating national power, he argues, anticolonial nationalism also designated the project as one of both "liberation" and "development." In its economic critique of colonialism, nationalist discourse regarded the colonial project illegitimate not only because it was "alien" but also because it expropriated the nation's resources and did not sufficiently modernize the economy. Development rhetoric thus became another essential constituent of nationalist discourse.

Chatterjee points out that in the colonial setting the emergent bourgeoisie faced the formidable task of carrying out a two-fold struggle—against the colonial power and against domestic forces which blocked the structural transformation of a home economy. These conditions required the formation of alliances, within the framework of a nationalist movement, between the bourgeoisie and other dominant classes, as well as the mobilization of subaltern classes, to struggle effectively against colonial power and for national development. This strategy of gradual reform based on compromises with older ruling classes is appropriately designated a "passive revolution" by Antonio Gramsci, who contrasted it with the liberal "bourgeois revolution" modeled after the French Revolution with its full-fledged assault on the older feudal classes. Chatterjee, however, in contrast to what Gramsci had assumed, notes that the "passive revolution," in which the national state, rather than a class, takes on the tasks of development has been the "norm" rather than the exception in the twentieth century.

Likewise, the postcolonial state earns its legitimacy through the broad mobilization for development. To maintain the coalition and its legitimacy, the national state needs to create, what Chatterjee calls, a " 'synthetic hegemony' between civil society and precapitalist community." This means adopting a development plan founded on reform and molecular change (i.e., the "passive revolution") instead of a revolutionary transformation and the eradication of precapitalist classes. This is where he locates the contradiction in the postcolonial nationalist project since what was often defined by the state

as "important for the economic development of the nation" did not necessarily correspond with the sentiments and needs of the "popular," thus producing
contradictions in state policy and legitimacy.[4]

Although Chatterjee's account of non-Western nationalist thought is both
provocative and incisive, his discursive discussion of the autonomous, sovereign inner domain is problematic because it fails to emphasize sufficiently
the participation of modern colonial power in the constuction of such a domain. As the formation of modern Iraq demonstrates, the inner/outer domains
as the ground of an indigenous emancipatory struggle were unimaginable
without the categories and concepts applied by the colonialists in the process
of extending their rule.

Like the nation of India, Iraq was also constructed by the two modern
powers of global capitalism and the nation-state. Whereas capitalism began
to have its transformative power on the three Ottoman provinces of Basra,
Baghdad, and Mosul in the latter part of the nineteenth century, Iraq—as a
unified territorial entity with recognized borders—was only borne in the aftermath of British occupation in the First World War. Britain, using both
military force and modern technologies of power, carved Iraq out of the three
provinces, gave it a modern rationalized bureuacracy, a new system of law,
of education, an army, a police force, etc., and on top installed a monarchy
and a parliament, emulating England. With the pretext of awarding Iraq
England's "gifts of efficient administration, of impartial justice, honest finance,
and [of] security . . . ," the British launched their modernizing (imperial)
project.

While the British colonial project clearly drew on Western models of
political institutions and social practices, its rule, as the many recent histories
on colonialism have also shown, was extended through practices of classification and differentiation.[5] In Iraq, British rule was highly dependent on the
application of distinctions founded on religion, ethnicity, and other categories
to establish its dominance. This can be seen in the way the British created
measures to regulate the tribes as opposed to towns and civil society. The
application of legislative and administrative regulations founded on isolating
and defining discrete social groups succeeded not just in normalizing the
tribes as "tribes," but also in naturalizing ethnic identities (Arabs, Kurds,
Assyrians, Turkomans), producing religious differentiations (Christian, Jewish, and Muslim, both Sunni and Shiʾa) as well as creating class distinctions
(capitalist, precapitalist). This is not to say that such distinctions did not exist
in precolonial times, but to simply emphasize that they did not constitute
discrete entities within a regulatory system and that therefore the boundaries
under which they functioned were far more flexible and porous than what
later became the case. Governing through difference, the British constructed,

in other words, what Chatterjee described as the inner and outer domains with conflictually differentiated precapitalist and capitalist communities, elites, and classes.

Therefore, when the European project was translated to Iraq via the mandate, it did not (and could not) produce an identical version of the original because of the improvisational character of modern power when applied to a different field of social elements, possibilities, and circumstances. As demonstrated in chapters 1 and 2, British rule was pragmatic (e.g., the land policy in the south) and highly flexible in that it relied on a constant adaptation to local conditions as well as the exploration of new opportunities within which to insert power. To extend its dominance, the mandate had to both invent new technologies as well as draw on those practiced elsewhere in the colonies. This meant that existing ideologies, social divisions, and conflicts were exploited and elaborated by the British, not as obstacles to rule, but as its instruments.

The British, for instance, drew heavily on their Indian experience to normalize conditions after their occupation of Mesopotamia. Within a week of their occupation, they set up a police force "modelled along Indian lines" and a civil administration fashioned after the "administrative methods and practices" developed in India. Then they divided the country into political districts similar to "British India, with a British officer at each key position, responsible to the central administation, to which voluminous reports and statistics were dispatched in accordance with Indian practice for every aspect of life within the division," even "the very titles borne in India, Civil Commissioner, Political Officer, Assistant Political Officer, Revenue Officer, Judicial Officer, and others were reproduced in the Iraq administration."[6]

When borrowing was not enough, they improvised. This is best illustrated in the legislation of the civil justice system. A special code, known as "Iraq Occupied Territories," was first devised to replace the "inefficient" Turkish system with the Anglo-Indian judicial system. The code was soon revised to give the power of amending the "Indian Law to meet local conditions," and the "power to make rules of procedure for the better execution . . . " of the law.[7] The final product was a civil and criminal law of justice that was an amalgamation of both the Anglo-Indian and Ottoman (Turkish) systems of law.[8]

A more striking example is the different strategies invented and inserted to achieve British dominance in a rebellious (tribal) countryside. The creation of the Tribal Criminal and Civil Disputes Regulations Act in 1916 (amended in 1924) to govern the tribes that could not be assimilated into the body politic of civil society represents one such strategy. This distinct system of justice informed by a rich body of knowledge, which ascribed to tribes intrinsic social, cultural, and economic characteristics that set them apart from and in opposition to towns and centralized authority and was fashioned after the Indian Frontier Crimes Regulation, was adopted to govern the tribal areas through the "natural leaders of the tribes: the shaykhs." British political officers were subsequently granted the power to "invoke a tribal majlis or other arbitrating body to deal in accordance with tribal custom, with all cases in which any of the parties concerned was a tribesman."[9] The Regulation Act drawn by the revenue commissioner of the time, Henry Dobbs (who was renowned for his wide experience in India, Persia, and Afghanistan), was "an adoption of the system so successfully developed and applied in Baluchistan [in 1875] by Sir Robert Sanderman."[10] Its purpose was to aid in the settlement and pacification of the tribes "by giving effect to tribal opinion obtained by arbitration," and by giving the shaykhs "a recognized place in the political and legal system."[11] Such legislations as the Regulation Act and the land tenure system discussed in chapter 1, were the key to disciplining and governing tribes.

This is not to say that these practices were offered as an alternative to repression; violent force indeed was an integral part of administrative requirement. When (tribal) resistance persisted in spite of the insertion of "traditional" and other regulatory practices, the British resorted to force. And similar to other technologies, repression was also open to new inventions to accomodate local conditions. In the early years of occupation the British depended heavily on their ground forces to maintain order. The high cost of keeping a regular army, combined with the loss of many British lives and ground battles in the irrigated zone of southern Iraq, made the British rethink the wisdom of using conventional methods when the air force had proven more effectual against the tribes. After the 1920 revolt, the British abandoned their ground forces for a cheaper and more efficient air force, using principally their bases in Habaniyah and Sha'baniyah and the method of bombing to discipline rebellious tribes and others.[12] This knowledge, as recent events in the Gulf War clearly demonstrated, was not wasted on the "allied" troops who applied similar (but more advanced) tactics in their effort to discipline Saddam Hussein.

It should be noted that modern power was not just improvisational, it also was transformative. Iraq, a recent creation of the Europeans, was able fairly quickly to attain its internal coherence and sense of sovereignty. Its legitimacy, as discussed in chapter 4, rather than being simply derived from an external power, became based on the mobilization of the various indigenous elites, classes, and communities in the form of loyalty to the oligarchic monarchy (and British imperial power), or else to a territorially based national identity (Iraqi or Arab).

It was within this new social and political order created by the modernizing nation-state, capitalism not excluded, that anticolonial nationalism emerged. That is why nationalist discourse did not dispute the basic assumptions of the colonial project. National "liberation," as illustrated in chapter 4, was thus argued within the confines of the European Enlightenment project and its modernizing agent, the nation-state. Even when they differed (e.g., pan-Arabists vs. Iraqi nationalists), the nationalists never posed the need to dismantle in any radical fashion the institutional structures and legislations inherited from the mandate system. As in India, the main nationalist objection to colonialism was that the colonialists did not modernize enough. The nationalists denounced the British for abandoning the modernization project, for supporting the precapitalist *iqta$^{\circ}$* system at the expense of the modern sector, and for expropriating the country's oil. While nationalism rejected colonialism as a foreign and exploitative power, it affirmed at the same time the legitimacy of the modern project itself.

In the process of appropriating the power to represent themselves, the nationalists, however, adopted a new political-ideological idiom which stressed that the Iraqis/Arabs did not need an external agent to usher them into modernity because they were capable of transforming the nation on their own. The national revolution of 1958 was thus envisioned as an act of empowerment (empowerment of the nation/the people), an emancipatory struggle with the aim of implementing the modern project, not abandoning it. The national revolution accordingly never sought to dismantle the colonial state and its institutions, whether in the domains of administration and law or in those of economy and politics. This meant that the forms of social and political organization set up by the mandate power continued to dominate postcolonial Iraq, despite the termination of "direct" British control and the relative novelty of the system installed. This is precisely what renders "independence" and postcolonial nationalism problematic.

The national revolution assumed that the nation-state was an undivided subject with a singular will and an essence that transcended class, ethnicity, religious, and other differences, and this is where the problem was. A unitary nation with "developmentalist" universal goals that superseded the particular interests of social groups, national and ethnic interests, and communities, proved self-deceiving. The national revolution, as explained in chapter 5, was turned instead into an arena of intense struggle where the various political groups and communities interacted and contested each other. Its failure to maintain a proper balance between what was considered socially "good" for the nation and its conflicting differentiated elements resulted in the collapse of national unity, in violent social strife, and then in the disintegration of the national revolution.

It should not be understood from this that the national postcolonial regime was just an extention of colonial power. Inasmuch as nationalist rule relied on forms of modern power, it adopted, produced, and shaped the conflicts that took place in the aftermath of the revolution. The nationalist regime, in other words, participated in the creation of new forms of politics, organizations, and powers which allowed the various local elements, diverse interests, and communities to act, or not to act. The proliferation of political divisions as well as national, ethnic, and religious identities (e.g., the Mosul revolt, the Kirkuk massacre, the Kurdish revolt), for example, opened up new public spaces and opportunities both for supra-nationalist and sub-national separatist projects, as well as for the national postcolonial regime to maneuver and insert its power.

It is also inaccurate simply to assume that the emergence of these ethnic and religious divisions and social conflicts were a product of and inherent to an archaic Arab/Islamic culture. The post colonial state, using modern technologies of power, tried to insert its *control* by producing ethnic differentiations (Turkomans/Kurds/Arabs) and regulating political and national distinctions, hence creating conflicts that eventually subverted its nationalist homogenizing project.

Epilogue 149

NOTES

INTRODUCTION

1. Majid Khadduri, *Republican Iraq: A Study in Iraqi Politics since the Revolution of 1958* (Oxford, 1969), 10.

2. Phebe Marr, *The Modern History of Iraq* (Westview Press, 1988), 151.

3. Uriel Dann, *Iraq Under Qassem: A Political History:1958–1963* (London: Pall Mall, 1969), 2/3.

4. Samir al-Khalil, *Republic of Fear* (Berkeley, 1989), 214.

5. Talal Asad had already rebutted the theoretical viability of a separate nomadic mode in "Equality in Nomadic Social System?" *Critique of Anthropology* 3 (Spring 1978), 57–65.

6. Robert Fernea and William Roger Louis, eds., *The Iraqi Revolution of 1958: The Old Social Classes Revisted* (London, 1991),

CHAPTER I

1. Charles Issawi, *The Fertile Crescent, 1800–1914*. (New York, 1988), 6. Modernization analysis is also prevalent among Arab writers. *See* Abdul-Wahab Matar al-Dahiri, *Introduction of Technology into Traditional Society* (Baghdad, 1969), 92.

2. Charles Issawi, ed., *The Economic History of the Middle East: 1800–1914* (Chicago, 1966), 163–64.

3. Muhammad Salman Hasan, *al-Tatatuwwur al-iqtisadi fi-l-ʾIraq 1864–1958* (Beirut, 1965), 207.

4. *See* Imad Ahmad al-Jawahiri, *Tarikh mushkilat al-aradi fi-l-ʾIraq 1914–1935* (Baghdad, 1978). He was greatly influenced by Salman Hasan's writings.

5. Samir Amin, *Imperialism and Unequal Development* (New York, 1977); *The Arab Nation* (London, 1978).

6. Robert Brenner, "The Origins of Capitalist Development: a Critique of Neo-Smithian Marxism," *New Left Review*, 104 (July–August, 1977), 25–100. Critical of the neo-Malthusian model which places great emphasis on the economic factor of population in bringing about the collapse of feudal Europe, Brenner in "The Agrarian Roots of

European Capitalism" shows once again how class relations and class conflict (i.e., the politics of classes) were central in bringing forth the historical changes in pre-industrial modern Euorpe. T. H. Aston and C. H. E. Philpin, *The Brenner Debate: Agrarian Class Structure and Economic Development in Pre-Industrial Europe* (New York, 1985).

7. One can trace its modern usage to the British, who were the first to employ the term (incorrectly) to describe the tribal landholdings in modern Iraq. Since then the term *iqta³* came to serve, especially for opposition political groupings and Marxist intellectuals, as a generic term to denote and describe the pre-capitalist, feudal character of these estates. Modern *iqta³* required new methods of control including the direct control and management of the agricultural process by the shaykh landholder/owner.

8. Even though the Ottomans ruled over the provinces of Baghdad, Basra, and Mosul (which constitute modern Iraq today) since the nineteenth century, their control varied considerably over the centuries. It was not until 1831 when the Ottoman army defeated the Mamluks that the provinces were reclaimed by the Porte and reintegrated into the Empire. These provinces, like many others in the Empire, had relative administrative and economic autonomy until the Ottoman centralization policies in the mid-nineteenth century.

9. The best-informed geneological study on Iraqi tribes, including the Kurdish, is the four-volume work of ⁽Abbas al-³Azzawi, ⁽Asha³ir al-³iraq (Baghdad, 1956). Another is Abdul al-Jalil al-Tahir, *al-³asha³ir al-³iraqiya*h (Beirut, 1972). The most useful studies on the Kurdish tribes are Martin van Bruinessen, *Agha, Shaikh and State: The Social and Political Structures of Kurdistan* (London, 1992); and C. J. Edmonds, *Kurds, Turks and Arabs: Politics, Travel and Research in North-Eastern Iraq 1919–1925* (London, 1957).

10. According to Edmund Burke, these stereotyped images were the product of the colonial period and served to legitimize and establish French colonial rule over Algeria and Morocco. Edmund Burke, "The Image of the Moroccan State in French Ethnological Literature: A New Look at the Origin of Lyautey's Berber Policy," in Gellner and Micaud, eds., *Arabs and Berbers: From the Tribe to Nation in North Africa* (London, 1973), 175–99.

11. French writers point to and reinterpret Ibn Khaldun, a fourteenth-century indigenous social theorist, who in the *Introduction* (*al-muqadimah*) to his voluminous study of Islamic history, delineated a cyclical theory of the rise and fall of Islamic civilization based on the dialectical opposition of two modes of life: *al-⁽umran al-hadari* (civilized mode) vs. *al-⁽umran al-badawi* (bedouin mode).

12. Gellner, E., *Saints of the Atlas* (London, 1969). This interpretation does not exclude Marxists, like Yves LaCoste whose *Ibn Khaldun: the Birth of History and the Past of the Third World* (1978), is no more and no less than a dialectical rehash of the tribal/ town dichotomy.

13. It is important to emphasize that the production of this body of knowledge was interwoven with colonial strategies and practices because the production of these texts not only conditioned practices but was conditioned by these practices, hence the proliferation of writings on the tribes before and during the period of colonization.

14. Quoted from P. H. Ireland, *Iraq: a Political Development* (London, 1937), 137–38.

15. Blunt, *Bedouin Tribes*, vol. 2, 205.

16. Ibid., 229.

17. Ibid., 204, 207–8. These writings are best represented by travelers such as Ann Blunt, who travelled with her husband S. Wilfred in 1877, and published *Bedouin Tribes of the Euphrates*, in 1879 based on their their travels; and W. F. Ainsworth, *A Personal Narrative of the Euphrates Expedition*, which is a historical geographical exploration of the region, published in London, 1888. Other than the traveler, British agents and officers serving in India traveled and collected information about the tribes and the region that proved crucial for the takeover of Mesopotamia by the British during the First World War. Representatives of this class of explorers are: Commander Felix Jones of the Royal Indian Navy, who was given the assignment by Turco-Persian Boundary Commission, and in the *Narrative of a Journey to the Frontier of Turkey and Persia through a Part of Kurdistan* (published in Bombay in 1857), he gives a thorough description of the routes and the geography of the region as well a detailed discussion of the tribes; Captain Mark Sykes', *Dar-ul-Islam* (London, 1904) description of the tribes in Kurdistan was used as an important source of information for the British when they entered the war with Turkey in 1915; E. B. Soane, *Through Mesopotomia and Kurdistan in Disguise* (London, 1909) disguised as Shi²a moslem from Persia, Soane was able to collect massive historical material regarding the country and its people. In 1919, he appears in Mesopotamia as a British major who was assigned the position of the political officer responsible for the administration of northern Iraq. Captain T. C. W. Fowle, *Travels in the Middle East* (London, 1916); G. E. Hubbard, *From the Gulf to Ararat* (Edinburgh, 1916); C. J. Edmonds, *Kurds, Turks, and Arabs: Politics, Travel, and Research in North-Eastern Iraq 1919–1925*; T. Lyell, *Ins and Outs of Mesopotamia* (London, 1923); A. Musil, *The Middle Euphrates*; Gertrude Bell, *Review of the Civil Administration, 1914–1920*; Great Britain, Admiralty, Intelligence Division, *Handbook of Mesopotamia* (London, 1916–1917) 4 vols.; A. T. Wilson, *Clash of Loyalties* (London, 1930), 2 vols.

18. Ghassan al-ᶜAtiyyah, *Iraq 1908–1921: A Socio-Political Study* (Beirut, 1973), 22–23.

19. Ibid., 26.

20. Hanna Batatu, *The Old Social Classes and the Revolutionary Movement in Iraq* (Princeton, 1978), 13–14.

21. Ibid., 27–28.

22. The transhistorical notion of the tribes is not just typical of the works on the modern tribes, it is a strong feature of the writings on early Islam. Note, for example, F. M. Donner's, *The Early Islamic Conquests* (Princeton, 1981) which unabashedly uses the tribes of Iraq in the nineteenth century to draw conclusions on the economy of the Arab tribes in pre-Islamic Arabia. *See* chapter I, notes 18 and 19.

23. There are a few scholars like J. Berque, T. Asad, and Martin van Bruinessen who have already argued that there is no such thing as a "typical" tribe, yet their observations have been generally overlooked by the historians in the field. *See* J. Berque, *Structures sociales du Haut-Atlas* (Paris, 1955) and T. Asad, "Ideology, Class, and the Origin of the Islamic State," *Economy and Society* 9 (November, 1980), 450–73; *The Idea of an Anthropology of Islam*, (Center for Contemporary Arab Studies, Georgetown University, Washington D.C., March, 1986); M. V. Bruinessen, *Agha, Shaikh, and State: The Social and Political Structures of Kurdistan.*

24. While the estimated price for an average Arabian horse ranged from 50 to 300 pounds; a celebrated Arabian pure-bred horse, like the Kochlani, can sometimes be purchased "at the price of 800 or 1,000 crowns each." Ann Blunt, *The Bedouin Tribes*, vol. I, 313; vol. 2, 269.

25. Batatu, for example, points out that: "The People of the Camel regarded all the other groups with the same undiscriminating contempt. . . . From their point of view, any manner of living other than that of bearing arms was unworthy and shameful. Being more mobile and possessed of superior fighting qualities, they were often able to assert their dominance in the tribal world." Batatu, *Social Classes*, 68. In agreement, al-ᶜAtiyyah says: "the Beduins (as warriors) disdained manual work and regarded cultivators and craftsmen as inferior to themselves . . . ." al-ᶜAtiyyah, *Iraq*, 22.

26. In her travel account, Ann Blunt, for example, describes the extensive movement of ᶜAnaizah as follows: "Camel owning bedouins are perpetually on the move. The ᶜAnaizah wander as far south in the winter as to within a few days march of Jabal Shammar. . . . They may travel in exceptional years two thousand miles between November and May. No sheep accompany the southern journeys. Those who belong to the ᶜAnaizah are left behind in the upper plain with weldi Aghadait and other tributary tribes." Blunt, *Bedouin Tribes*, 166–67; *see* also Talal Asad, *The Kababish Arabs* (London, 1970), 15–30, especially the section that deals with the ecology and technology of livestock herding.

27. ᶜAshair al-Ajwad had their permanent dira on the two banks of the Euphrates between Shatra and Nasiriyah. al-Tahir, *al-ᵓAshaᵓir al-ᶜiraqiyah*, 63.

28. Ibid., 170; 178. "Some members of the clans would take off with the flocks during the season leaving behind other members to look after and prepare the land for winter cultivation . . ."

29. "Tribal lazma was essentially a form of corporate property . . . and included all the lands on which a tribe or tribal group reserved exclusive rights of possession, whether for pasture or cultivation." Individual lazma is the cultivated areas which "were customarily distributed in parcels among the members of the tribe and its affiliates who were entitled to a sahm (share) . . . families and individuals who acquired a lazma claim became sahib lazma whose land was heritable, could be sold, rented or mortgaged." Albertine Jwaideh, "Aspects of Land Tenure and Social Change in Lower Iraq during the Late Ottoman Times," in Tarif Khalidi, ed., *Land Tenure and Social Transformation in the Middle East* (Beirut, 1984), 336–37.

30. Shakir Salim, *Marsh Dwellers of the Euphrates Delta* (1962), 96, 98. It should be pointed out in this context that these tribes were already undergoing proletarianization as a result of the disintegration of the old economy based on transit trade.

31. Bani Malik, the largest contingency within the Muntafiq confederation consisted of three great leagues: Bani Khiqan, al-Majara, and Albu Salih. The land they occupied included Suq al-Shuyukh, the district of Albu Salih, which includes shat al-Gharraf and Shat al-Bid³ah all the way to Qurnah, and other areas in Diwaniyah, Hillah, and Huwayzah. *See* al-Azzawi, *ʿAshaʾir al-ʾiraq*, vol. 4, 30.

32. The authority of the Shamiyahh shaykhs was often described as "autocratic"— the rice-growing tribespeople were especially known for their respect and obedience to tribal authority. *See* al-Jawahiri, *Tarikh al-aradi fil-Iraq*, 102; also Great Britain, *Administration Report of the Shamiyah District for 1918*, 67.

33. As part of the Tanzimat, the Ottoman state in 1838 declared a new tax reform under which the old tax system including *iltizam* was abolished. The most important feature of this reform was that the tax would be collected directly by salaried state agents (muhassil). This new system was too difficult to enforce in the countryside, which compelled the treasury to reinstate the tax-farm system in some areas, giving two-year rights to collect taxes on the auctioned estates to the highest bidder. This decree was followed by another in 1847 authorizing the extension of leases to five years at a time. This form of landholding continued to be practiced in certain regions of the empire until the declaration of the Land Code of 1858. Stanford Shaw, "Nineteenth-Century Ottoman Tax Reforms," *International Journal of Middle East Studies*, 1975, vol. 6: 421–59.

34. S. Haider, "Land Tenure in 19th Century Iraq," in *The Economic History of the Middle East: 1800–1914*, ed. C. Issawi (Chicago, 1966), 171. The size of estates varied from region to region depending on the crop and the organization of the tribes. Estates ran from thousands of dunums to tens of thousands and sometimes even exceeded a hundred thousand, especially in the winter-crop areas. In contrast, in the rice areas, few estates exceeded the size of a few thousand dunums and most were less than a thousand acres. Date plantations were even smaller.

35. S. Haider, "Land Problems of Iraq" (unpublished Ph.D. thesis, London University, 1942), 201, 311.

36. Although many references are made to *talʾiyah* during the Ottoman period, no references are made to the term after Britain occupied Iraq. One can perhaps assume that *taliʾyah* was absorbed within the privatization project carried out in the post-Ottoman period.

37. "The individual estate *(muqataʾah)* was divided into tracts *(qitaʾ)* subleased to the shaykhs of the clans or sub-clans, which were in turn divided into plots *(sahm, khait, talʾiyah, nagshah,* etc.) of ten to fifty dunums of winter crop areas and ten dunums or less in rice areas." S. Haider, "Land Tenure in Nineteenth Century," 171.

38. Most Western analysts have failed to recognize the importance of customary rights as distinct from legal rights, with a few exceptions, such as Albertine Jwaideh, who

was among the first to show that customary, in contrast to legal, rights "conveyed a much more profound sense of property." A. Jwaideh, "Aspects of Land Tenure and Social Change in Lower Iraq During the Late Ottoman Times," in *Land and Social Transformation in the Middle East*, ed. Tarif Khalidi (Beirut, 1984), 335–50; Abdallah al-Fayyad, *Mushkilat al-aradi fi-liwa'-al-Muntafiq* (Baghdad: al-Tijara wa-l-tiba'a Press, 1957): 35,148; F. al-Mizhir al-Fir'awn, *al-Qada' al-Asha'iri* (Baghdad, 1949).

39. Individual *lazma* represented the individual shares (*sahm*) of land allocated to different units (*fakhd* and *bayt*) or individual tribespeople. Ksarah was another form of naqshah practiced among the Hindiyah and Shamiyah producing tribes, while *mugharasah* represented another form of ta'abah practiced in date groves of the mid-region.

40. Haider, "Land Tenure," 642–43; al-Fir'awn, *al-Qanun al-'asha'iri*, 170.

41. Both naqshah and ta'abah were identified with labor-intensive crops, like rice and dates. Tal'iyah (choice land) "was granted in perpetuity as a kind of super naqsha since it was exempted from the payment of tax" as in mulk. Besides the strongest holdings under super *naqshah, tali'yah*, and *ta'abah*, there were others like imperfect *naqsha, kasr al-hijara, matluqah* and *shikarah*—most entrenched forms of tenancy in the mid-Euphrates. Albertine Jwaideh, "Land and Social Transformation," 338–39; Fai'q al-Fayyad, *Mushkilat al-aradi*, 134; 148–49.

42. M. S. Hasan, "Population Movements, 1867–1947," in Issawi ed., *The Economic History*, 157.

43. "Lower Iraq and the Gulf had been the major distribution points for the export of live animals—particularly horses and camels, to the Arab provinces and India throughout the eighteenth and nineteenth centuries." Hala Fattah, *The Development of the Regional Market of Iraq and the Gulf 1800–1900* (University of California, Los Angeles Ph.D., 1986), 126.

44. Ibid., 35. "Tribal merchants formed commercial arrangements with tujjar from the city, indicative of profitable alliances between town and countryside. Trading 'corporations' emerged to take advantage of important monopolies of land and sea transport. . . . Finally, occupational specialization existed throughout this regional network, tying livestock supplier to transport agent and both of them to the resident trader of Bombay."

45. In describing the wealth of Ruwala, the ruling tribe of 'Anaizah, Blunt says: "We looked down over the plain of Saighal and saw it covered as far as the eye could reach, with a countless multitude of tents and mares. . . . We have estimated the whole number of tents to be 20,000 and of camels at a 150,000, and at the sight, I felt an emotion of almost awe, as when someone first sees the sea." Blunt, *The Bedouin Tribes*, vol. 2, 136. Describing their horses, she says: "The Ruwala were possessed of immense numbers of mares, and had the reputation of having the monopoly of some of the best strains of blood. It was to their shaykh Sha'lan, the prince of the desert that 'Abbas Pasha (Ottoman wali) sent his son to be educated, and from whom he bought most of his mares." Blunt, *The Bedouin Tribes*, vol. 2, 136; vol. 1, 37.

46. ʿShaykh Thuwayni, the great grandfather of al Sᵓadun and the founder of Suq al-shuyukh was known for his travels through Kuwait, Gharraf, and Basra with "tents of goods and merchants," and was famed for his loans "of hundreds of coins in silver and gold to merchants and traders." Sulyman al-Dakhil, "Suq al-shuyukh," *Lughat al-Arab* (December, 1912), 246.

47. The banker (sarraf) and the head clerk of Nasir Saᵓdun were townspeople from the city of Baghdad. Manahim Danial was his sarraf and Naᵓuwm Sarkis was his clerk. Yaᵓqub Sarkis, *Mabahith Iraqiyyah*, vol. 3, 318.

48. By the mid-1800s, al-Zuhyr spread their control over Basra and the Arab tribes surrounding the port, which came to threaten British interests as much as it undermined Ottoman authority in the area. As a result, the Ottomans and the British joined forces along with the Muntafiq leading tribes to forcefully push this household out of Basra, and later on out of their own town, Zubyr, thus, ending the rule of this powerful house. *See* Nuwwar, *Tarikh al-Iraq al-Hadith*, 466.

49. Al-Dakhil, "Suq al-shuyukh," 247.

50. In fact, the Muntafiq tribes, famed for their Arabian horses, were more entrepreneurial in their approach to horse trade than other horse-breeding tribes, like Shammar and ʿAnaizah. Blunt points out that to accommodate the new demands of the Indian market after its colonization, the "Muntafiq, once celebrated for their horses, have allowed the purity of their breed to be tampered with, for the sake of increased size, so necessary for the Indian market which they supplied. It was found out that the cross-bred animal of mixed Persian and Arabian blood, would pass muster among the English in India and would command a better price for their extra height. The produce is known in India as Gulf Arab." *See* Blunt, *The Bedouin Tribes*, vol. 2, 225–26.

51. Al-Haydari, Ibrahim ibn al-Sayyid, *Kitab ʿunwan al-majd fi bayan ahwal baghdad wal-basra wal-najd* (Baghdad, 1869), 94–98, 168–71; al-Tahir, *al-ᵓAshaᵓir*, 319.

52. Blunt says: "Weldi Haddadin are entrusted every winter by the citizens of Aleppo and Mosul with thousands of sheep, which they account for in the spring to their owners." Blunt, *The Bedouin Tribes*, vol. 1, 225.

53. The value of seaborne trade in 1845 and 1846 was estimated at 280,000 British pounds. After 1875, exports increased in value to an annual average of nearly 800,000 pounds. Cf. Roger owen, *The Middle East in The World Economy: 1800–1900* (London, 1981), 180; 274–75.

54. Salman Hasan estimates that the share of nomadic tribes in the rural population declined dramatically in this period: from 35 percent in 1870 to 17 percent in 1905 (and 5 percent in 1947), while the size of the rural population increased by one third between 1867 and 1905. Sedentarization was most spectacular in the central region whose nomadic population decreased from 23 percent in 1876 to 1 percent in 1947, leading to an increase in the peasant population from 41 percent of total population in 1887 to 83 percent in 1930. cf. Hasan, "The Growth and Structure of Iraq's Population," 158–59.

55. The Hindiyah dam was officially inaugurated in 1890. The expenses for building the dam (estimated at LT. 30,480) were raised by the treasury of the wilayah, the saniyah (sultan's estates in the wilayah), and local landowners. The dam was reconstructed in 1913. The governor of Baghdad agreed with Nasir Saʾdun, the paramount shaykh of Muntafiq, on the building of the Jazaiʾr dam and that Nasir would finance it and supply thousands of workers from his tribes. Issawi, *The Fertile Crescent, 1800–1914* (Oxford, 1988), 350–51; al-Bustani, *ʿIbrah wa-Dhikrah*, 147.

56. The output of dates was 60,000 tons in 1887, 91,000 tons annually between 1909–1913. Exports of dates increased from 44,000 tons in 1887 to 65,655 tons annually between 1909–1913. Exports of grain also increased but not as impressively: 24,600 tons of wheat and 33,900 tons of barley were exported between 1888–1895; 11,800 tons of wheat and 36,200 tons of barley between 1896–1903; 15,400 tons of wheat and 46,800 of barley between 1904–1911; and 19,000 tons of wheat and 77,200 tons of barley between 1912–1913. Hasan, *al-Tatatuwwur al-iqtisadi*, 25; 103; 170–75.

57. The main tribal trading towns came under direct Ottoman control were the towns of Zubyr, Deyr al-Zur, the depot of ʿAnaizah and Shammar tribes, and the building of al-Nasiriyah as a new center in the heart of Muntafiq land to compete with Suq al-shuyukh.

58. The Tanzimat, which started in the early nineteenth century, encompassed more than just reforming the taxation system. It aimed at the restructuring and "modernizing" of all Ottoman institutions, including the army, the bureaucracy, and law as well as religious and civil institutions. The principal aim of the Tanzimat was to reassert the power of central government and extend its rights over the provinces.

59. The French absolutist state based on taxation and office also developed in conflict with landed property. The monarchist state increased its control through its ability to get between the landlords and the peasants, to ensure peasant freedom, hereditary, and fixed rent. Cf. R. Brenner, "The Agrarian Roots of European Capitalism" in *The Brenner Debate* 288–91. In the case of the Ottomans, the state, in alliance with the peasantry, was able to extend its rights over some parts of the rural provinces (i.e., Anatolia) but was unable to do so in others.

60. Yaʾqub Sarkis, a leading authority on the Saʾdun, points out that in 1860 the *mashyakha* and the land were put up for auction with two bidders competing, Mansur Saʾdun and his uncle Bandar. Bandar won the iltizam for three years for almost 15,000 purses. Nasir al-Saʾdun in 1866 raised 8,677 purses of tax a year in contrast to 4,900 purses raised by his father in 1860. Sarkis, *Wathaʾiq*, 67,72; 255–57.

61. G. Bell, *Civil Administration*, 22.

62. Shaykh Muhsin al-Hadhdhal of ʿAnaizah abandoned his tribal shaykhdom in favor of becoming the qaʾimaqam of the Mussayyib district along the Euphrates. Farhan, the shaykh of Shammar was granted the title of pasha by the Ottoman governor Midhat Pasha. The Saʾduns of al-Muntafiq were offered the governorship of Basra. Along with their new official positions, these leaders were granted tapu rights. *See* Haider, "Land Tenure," 167.

63. Nasir Saʾdun was known to have forced members of his ruling house to register lands in their names. He was also famed for acquiring deeds of large tracts of rich cultivable lands around Basra, Shatra, and Gharraf for himself, his family and his associates when he became a governor of Basra in the 1870s al-Tahir, *al-ʾAshaʾir*, 51–52; 308.

64. "The installation of Ottoman regiments in Khamisiyah, Shatrah, Hai, and other parts of the Muntafiq gradually emboldened the Saʾdun family in their dealing with their component tribes. They did not find it necessary to consider the wishes of their tribes, because they did not need their military support any longer. They used government forces in their midst to affirm their claims as landlords . . . they claimed mulkiyah (rent of 20 percent) as well as the miri or government revenues (20 percent)." Haider, "Land Problems," 579.

65. Haider, "Land Tenure," 164–66.

66. Wadi al-ʿAtiyah, 1954, *Tarikh al-Diwaniyah: qadiman wa-hadithan* (Najaf, 1954), 51–53.

67. Ghassan al-ʿAtiyyah, *Iraq*, 27.

68. Although saniyah lands were to be found in Hillah-Diwaniyah and Basra districts, the largest holdings were those rich lands occupied by the tribes of albu-Muhammad and albu-Durraj in the ʿAmarah district. Although the saniyah estates in ʿAmarah were auctioned every five years to the shaykhs, the duration was subject to arbitrary termination. In contrast, the tribes of the saniyah lands continued to consider their holdings as lazma in the Hillah-Diwaniyah district and as taʾabah in the date groves of Basrah. All saniyah domains reverted to state land administered by a special department, *Amlak Mudawarah*, after the Young Turks revolution and the dethronement of Sultan Abdul Hamid II in 1908. Jwaideh, "The Saniya Lands of Sultan Abdul Hamid II," in Maqdisi, ed., *Arabic and Islamic Studies*, 327–35.

69. Ireland: *Iraq*, 47.

70. Ibid., 60; 61.

71. G. al-ʾAtiyyah, *Iraq*, 244. Similarly, the British Acting Civil Commissioner in Baghdad in 1920, critical of the landed shaykhs' claims, admitted to the unfairness of British policy in supporting them: "In the light of our experience of past three months . . . we must plead guilty in various administration matters affecting tribes . . . we have as a matter of policy backed the shaykhs and supported their authority."

72. Great Britain, *Administrative Report of the Nasiriyah District for the Year 1919*, 1919.

73. al-Tahir, *al-ʿAshaʾir*, 28–32, 52–54.

74. F. Sluglett and P. Sluglett, *Iraq Since 1958: From Revolution to Dictatorship* (London, 1987), 12.

75. Khaiyun al-ʿUbeid, described by British officer, A. Haldane, as "the most influential man in Shatra district, whose good services in preventing the spread of

insurrection in the Hai" and for joining, along with his followers "the British forces put down the insurrection." Lieutenant-General Sir Aylmer L. Haldane, *The Insurrection of Mesopotamia: 1920* (London, 1922), 220, 290.

76. al-Tahir, *al-ʿAshair*, 20–1; 164–68, 236–37; al-Firʾawn, *al-ʾQadaʾ*, 341; Haldane, *The Insurrection*, 22, 27, 105–6.

77. Great Britain, *Report on Iraq: 1932*: 13–15; *see* also Wilson, *A Clash of Loyalties*, 76–96.

78. Batatu, *Social Classes*, 95, 103.

79. Great Britain, *Report on the Administration of Iraq 1920–1922*, 20; Wilson: *A Clash of Loyalties*, v. 1, 78

80. In the settlement, the British conceded:

1. 7.25 percent mulkiyah share to be collected and paid to those landlords who were in actual possession of the Ottoman title deeds (tapu);

2. in cases where such deeds were not in the possession of the landlords, their share was to be held in government treasury until such a time when a final resolution was reached among contested claimants;

3. in the meantime, the so-called mallak could not interfere in the production process which would thus remain under the sole charge of the sirkal or lessee.

Although this settlement did not refute the property rights of landlords, it did represent a partial victory for the cultivating ʿashaʾir and their sirkals.

81. Great Britain, *Report by his Majesty's Government to the Council of the League of Nations on the Administration of Iraq for the Year of 1928*, 150. In rice areas of lower Hindiyah (in the districts of Shamiyah and Abu Sukhair), the government official, Ahmad Fahmy, found in 1925 that of the total cultivated area in these two districts which amounted to 74,300 dunums, 32,800 were held directly by individuals (afrad) and smaller sirkals, and the remaining 41,500 dunums were held by the shaykhs with over 100 dunums each. Similarly in Suq al-Shuyukh, the peasant proprietors, who were called the naqashah, held by far the greater part of the land in the district and particularly in the date plantations. Peasant holdings also existed on a considerable scale in the areas of Dhaghara where rice and shitwi (winter) crops are grown and in the shitwi and date plantations of Jarbawiyah below Hilla. Haider, *Land Problems*, 631–62. On the Dhaghara district, *see* Fernea *Shaykh and Effendi*, 39–49.

82. The British, for example, reported the following land disputes over boundaries and rights in the ʿAmarah in 1925 between:

1. Shaykh Hasan Saʾid of Huwwar and Shaykh Ziara of umm al-ʾayn;

2. Shaykh Muhammad al-Hajj Hasan of Dahamiah and Shaykh Abdul
    Hasan al-Rouki of al-Jamila;

3. Shaykh Muhammand Hasan of al-Dahamiah and Shaykh Majid
    al-Khalifah of al-Majr al-Kabir. Great Britain, *Report on the
    Administration of Iraq 1924–1925*, 18.

83. Great Britain, *Special Report by His Majesty's Government to the League of
Nations on the Progress of Iraq during 1920–1931*,183–85.

84. Grain exports increased after the evacuation of the British occupying forces
once the mandate system was set up. During 1922–1923 over 150,000 tons were exported,
and between 1923–1924 over 200,000 tons. During 1924–1925, the harvest was poor and
exports dropped to 50,000, went up again between 1926–1927 to 181,000 tons; was close
to 150,000 tons in 1930, and 200,000 tons again in 1931. Ibid., 217.

85. Based on Dowson's 1932 study of land tenure in Iraq, the law classified three
types of land tenure: mulk, waqf (religious endowments) and miri-lazma. Under miri, the
state recognized the rights of all tapu holders to be the same as mulk with the exception
of a certain payment to be made to the state in the form of rent. The customary right of
miri-lazma was deemed binding by law. In practice, lazma rights addressed the interests
of the pump-owners, mostly urban capitalists, who were eligible to reclaim land in the
case of defaults in payments by direct producers, as discussed in chapter 2.

86. *The Land Settlement Number 29*, 1938.

87. Hasan Muhammad ʿAli, *Land Reclamation and Settlement in Iraq*, 63–65.

88. Ibid., 63–65; Batau, *The Old Social Classes*, 108–9; Gabbay, *Communism and
Agrarian Reform*, 33–35. Besides the 1932 law, the other laws were *The Sale of Miri Sirf
Lands of 1940*, later amended in 1945 as *The Dujailah Project*, and the *Land Settlement
of 1952* which was an amendment of the 1938 law.

89. In Kut, the lands were expropriated by shaykhs such as Muhammad al-Habib
Amir, the paramount shaykh of Rabiʾah who under the settlement of 1938 was awarded
211,315 dunums in lazma by the settlement committee in charge of the district. These
lands did not include the over 160,000 dunums already in his possession in tapu and mulk.
Under the same claims, his brother Habib was also granted the equivalent of 200,000
dunums. Over half a million dunums of state land was alienated to two leading members
of the paramount households of al-Yasin and al-Amir. al-Suwari, *al-Iqtaʾ fi-l-Kut* (1955):
34–35, 80–81.

90. Batatu, *Social Classes*, 111, 130–31.

91. Ibid., 122. Khairallah was said to have possessed over a million dunums. In the
Hai region of Muntafiq, half the cultivated land was claimed by two brothers Balsam and
Abdulla al-Yasin, the shaykhs of the Mayah tribe.

92. Despite the fragmentation in land holdings in this region, the repercussions were
not acute, as might have been the case elsewhere (e.g., Egypt) because the ratio of labor
to land is very low. al-ʾAlwan, *Dirasat fi-l-islah al-ziraʾi* (Baghdad, 1961).

93. Jwaideh, "Saniya Land," 350. This does not mean that the cultivators them-selves had control over land as Jwaideh (1984) and others point out. In the process of the long struggle between landowners and tribespeople, many of the lands came to be the de facto possession of the sirkals or the smaller shaykhs. Zaki Khairi, *al-Hizb al-shuyu[*]i wa-l-mas[*]alah al-zira[*]iyah* (Baghdad, 1974), 56.

94. al-ʿAlwan, *Dirasat fi-l-islah*, 18.

95. Government of Iraq, *The Agricultural and Livestock Census of* 1952 and 1958.

96. The following quotation is typical of many modernization writers: "The fallahin were too ignorant to compute the size of their debt or the value of their crop. . . . Because of the lack of incentive for the fallahin to work, members of the landlord's family were often employed on the large estates as supervisors." Gabbay, 29.

97. Abbas al-Nasrawi, *Financing Economic Development in Iraq* (New York, 1967), 68.

98. At its peak, agriculture contributed 42 percent of the government revenue in 1911, falling to 11.7 percent in 1930, and to 7.7 percent in 1940. In contrast, indirect taxation represented 46.5 percent in 1926, 50.6 percent in 1930, and 32.25 percent in 1940. Batatu, *Social Classes*, 106–8; Peter Sluglett, *Britain in Iraq: 1914–1932* (London, 1976), 232.

99. Oil revenues represented no more than 0.4 million Iraqi dinars in 1931, but increased to to 40.1 million Iraqi dinars in 1952, 58.3 million in 1953, and 73.7 million in 1955. F. Jalal, *The Role of Government in the Industrialization of Iraq 1950–1965* (London, 1972), 10.

100. Between 1951 and 1958, capital programs in agriculture were given priority—34.4 percent of the total developmental budget was assigned to this sector. A. Salter, *The Development of Iraq: A Plan of Action* (Baghdad, 1955), 101.

101. The 1950s was marked by peasant revolts: the al-Uzayrij revolt in ʿAmarah in 1952 and 1953; the Shamiyya peasant revolt in 1954; Rumaytha (Diwaniyah) peasant revolt in 1955; the Dhaghara and Rumaytha revolts in Diwaniyah in April 1958 (a few months before the revolution).

102. According to government reports, 44 percent of the total land in Iraq was under cultivation in 1957. *The Census of 1958*, 6; Salter, *Development of Iraq*, 190.

103. Besides having the state apparatus to enforce their control over the land, the landlords under tribal customary law maintained their own armed guards—the hushiyah or shabibah—to enforce their control and extract the necessary surplus from the peas-antry. Batatu, *Social Classes*, 150.

104. "The farmer finds the soil becoming salty and uses more water to wash it away, then the excessive use of water raises the water table and increases salination of the soil by evaporation." Salter, *Development of Iraq*, 17; 193.

105. "Consideration might be therefore given to the imposition of a levy to pay the cost of subsidiary canals. Construction of such canals should be optional with the landowner because failure to build them across one man's property might deny the benefits of drainage to adjoining properties." IBRD, *The Economic Development of Iraq* (Baltimore, 1952), 18; al-Nasrawi, *Financing Economic Development*, 66.

106. Salter, *Development of Iraq*, 55.

107. According to the IBRD, tractor ploughing could increase yields, by 20 to 50 percent through more effective destruction of weeds and partly through better preparation of the soil. IBRD, *Economic Development*, 19.

108. As early as the 1940s, less than one third of the 3.2 million dunums of agricultural lands in ʿAmarah was put under cultivation, the rest being either abandoned due to salination or left fallow. The Government of Iraq, *Census of 1952*, 7.

109. Batatu, *Social Classes*, 142–43. An example of the intensification in the exploitation is the 1933 law, the *Law Governing the Rights and Duties of Cultivators*, which legally defined the relationship of the cultivator with his landowner and sirkal. Included was a clause that restricted the movement of peasants when in debt. For detailed information on this law, *see* al-Jawaheri, *Tarikh mushkilat al-aradi*, 340–56.

110. Abdul Razaq Zubair, "al-Islàh al-ziraʾi wa-l-mushkelat al-hijra min al-rif ila-l-madina," *al-Thaqafah al-Jadidah* 5 (August, 1969): 16.

111. When the cultivating tribes of al-Uzairij revolted against their landlords in 1951 and 1952 in ʿAmarah, they were brutally put down by the shaykhs' armed militia who then burned the rebels' houses and threw their families off the land. *See* Zaki Khairi, *al-Hizb al-shuyuʾi*, 46. The brutal retaliation of the shaykhs against the peasants who revolted left the cultivators with little option but to flee the area. According to Warriner, "rural exodus . . . proceeded at the rate of ten lorry loads a day for Baghdad." Warriner, *Land Reform and Development* (Oxford, 1962), 152–54.

112. The *Law for Granting Lazma Rights in ʿAmarah*, according to Warriner, would have "allowed the shaykh and his family to secure most of the land, because it provided that a secondary multazim (shaykh's agent/sirkal) who was a close relative of the shaykh might be regarded as a primary multazim, so that the shaykh could nominate members of his family as his lessees or agents, entitled to a half share in any part of the holding which the shaykh decided. After the shaykh's own share of half the total holding had been deducted and the members of his family had taken half shares in the remainder, there was little left for the cultivators. Further, since the area of holding contained both cultivated and uncultivated land, the shaykh and his family might claim the whole cultivated areas as their property, leaving only the uncultivated and the uncultivable to the fellahin." Warriner, *Land Reform*, 153.

113. Ibid., 154. Besides pressure for reform coming from the peasantry, new industrial interests arising in the towns were beginning to put pressure on the state to

reform agriculture as they were negatively affected by its retardation. Also, pressure from outside, especially the Egyptian revolution of 1952 and the land reform that followed, compelled the oligarchic state to introduce new reforms in order to ease the rising social discontent. One such law was *The Law Determining the Share of the Cultivator in the Produce* (1952), which prohibited special levies, at the same time that it put a limit of 50 percent on the landlord's share.

114. The 1957 census recorded the number of people migrating to Baghdad that year as 378,996 (representing 29 percent of its total population); 30 percent of the migrants came from ʿAmarah and 10 percent from Kut, and 48 percent of the 88,819 migrants to Basra moved from ʿAmarah.

115. Warriner, *Land Reform*, 156.

CHAPTER 2

1. Haider, "Land Problems," 558, 568, 626–27.

2. Ibid., 561, 540–43.

3. Bell, *Civil Administration,* 54.

4. Jwaideh, "Land and Tribal Administration," 463.

5. Dowson, *An Inquiry into Land Tenure*, 19; and Bell, *Civil Administration*, 54.

6. Batatu, *Social Classes*, 293.

7. Hasan, *al-Tatawwur al-iqtisadi*, 144–45.

8. Batatu, *Social Classes*, 289–90.

9. Ibid., 292–95, 314–15.

10. Great Britain, Colonial Office, *Special Report by his Majesty's Government in the League of Nations on the Progress of Iraq during 1920–1931* (London, 1931), 183–85.

11. Great Britain, *Administrative Report 1929*, 153.

12. Great Britain, *Administrative Report 1927,* 58. W. H. Himburg pointed that Iraq had the potential to become a new source for raw cotton. To follow up the intention of the mandate, a private company, the British Cotton Growing Association, erected a modern ginnery with a capacity of 10,000 bales per year, and to encourage the growers to continue cotton cultivation, often paid higher than prevailing market prices.

13. Great Britain, *Administrative Report 1924*, 65, 95. Concessions given to Asfar et al: "Eastern Irrigation Ltd. which included the study and the development of the Habaniyah reservoir and the Falujah Barrage which will allow in time the annual irrigation of 312,000 acres in cotton, 312,000 in wheat, and 312,000 acres in barsim.

While the Diyalah scheme, on the other, will result in providing 500,000 acres of cotton, 500,000 acres of wheat and another 500,000 of barsim."

14. Great Britain, *Administrative Report of the District of Mosul Division 1921*, 18.

15. Great Britain, *Administrative Report 1923–1924*, 70; *Administrative Report 1926–1927*, 53. Others followed suit. King Faisal, for example, introduced cotton on his royal estates at Khaniqin. The Association of Local Landowners and Agriculturists, consisting of entrepreneurs and town mullaks, rented religious-endowed lands from the awqaf authorities for the purpose of raising cash crops, especially cotton.

16. Great Britain, *Administrative Report 1927*, 165; *Administrative Report 1929*, 150; *Administrative Report 1930*, 137

17. As explained by a British official: "The great majority of the cultivators employed on cotton farms are engaged on the terms of the ordinary share system in vogue locally. By this system the cultivator is regarded as the part owner of the crop and receives at harvest time a share varying from 30 to 50 percent of the gross crop. The onus of providing irrigation, either by flow or by lift, falls on the proprietor or employer. This system is age old in the country and although it is not well suited to the needs of industrial agriculture on large estates, it is maintained partly by the conservatism of the people and partly by the fact that proprietors have not sufficient capital to employ labor on wages. Where wages are paid, and this occurs only on a few estates, a good cultivator is paid Rs.25 to Rs.30 a month." Great Britain, *Administrative Report of 1927*, 29.

18. Great Britain, *Administrative Report 1926*, 58. The British claimed that "the most hopeful aspect of cotton cultivation in Iraq was the cost of production which was probably lower here that in America."

19. Great Britain, *Administrative Report of 1931*, 209. *The Administrative Report of 1929*, 29, also states that "on many estates on which cotton crops are being grown, the laborers have hereditary tribal rights of cultivation, and it is not wholly correct to regard them as hired laborers since they cannot be dismissed."

20. Great Britain, *Administrative Report 1929*, 29

21. Great Britain, *Administrative Report 1930*, 37. The report also indicates that only 3,300 bales were exported in 1930, and by 1931 it declined to 1,000 bales.

22. Sabah al-Durrah, *al-Tatawwur al-sina'i fi-l-'iraq, al-qita' al-khas* (Baghdad, 1958), 94; 96. According to Durrah, cotton cultivation expanded immensely in the 1940s to 15,000 tons a year. In the early 1950s, production increased to 20,000 tons and to 44,000 tons by 1957. Ittihad as-Sina'at reported that in 1951, 401,109 dunums were put under cotton cultivation. At the same time, the report indicated the concern of industrialists over the low levels of productivity in cotton production.

23. Great Britain, *Special Report 1920–1930*, 209.

24. Most of the British reports, including Dowson's, indicate that urban private capital was the main investor in pumps. In accounting for pump installation according to region, the British report of 1930 indicates that Baghdad district, where town-mullak form of ownership prevailed, had the highest installation of pumps: 1,025 of which 909 on the Tigris, 77 on Diyalah, and 39 on the Euphrates. Kut comes second having 327 pumps installed; however, 318 of the total were installed on the Tigris river—i.e., on the Dujailah project which was a state project. In ʿAmarah where non-capitalist agriculture also prevailed, there were only 139 pumps installed and according to the British report of 1929, they were by and large installed by the smaller sadah town mullaks. Dowson, *An Inquiry*, 27–29. Batatu likewise points to town people, like Jamil Zadah, who invested capital in pumps and, as a result, were able to acquire titles to newly reclaimed miri lands. Batatu, *Social Classes*, 165. Another account reports that private investment in agriculture has brought more than half of total area of land cultivation under irrigation by 1944. Out of the total acreage in 1944 (4,241,718), 2.2 million acres were irrigated by pumps. al-Daheri, *Introduction of Technology*, 118.

25. Great Britain, *Administrative Report 1920–1930*, 209.

26. Great Britain, *Administration Report on Iraq 1930*, 134. According to British reports, the fallah's indebtedness in the aftermath of the world crisis was most severe in the pump areas where townspeople pump owners, in competition with each other, had offered extravagant advances to the fallah, and the fallahin had in consequence become indebted for as much as Rs.600.

27. Grain exports increased after the evacuation of the British occupying forces once the mandate system was set up. During 1922–1923 over 150,000 tons were exported, and between 1923–1924 over 200,000 tons. During 1924–1925, the harvest was poor and exports dropped to 50,000, went up again between 1926–1927 to 181,000 tons; was close to 150,000 tons in 1930, and 200,000 tons again in 1931 Great Britain, *Administrative Report of 1931*, 217.

28. al-Jawahiri, *Mushkilat al-aradi*, 332–40.

29. FO 371/17858, "Law Governing the Rights and Duties of Cultivators," London, 1934.

30. For detailed information on the debates in the Iraqi parliament and public reaction to the law, see al-Jawahiri, *Mushkilat al-aradi*, 340–56.

31. Ibid., 348–49.

32. The traditional historiography, including Salman Hasan, Batatu, and al-Jawahiri etc., do not differentiate between the class of mullak and the large landowners and tend to address the land settlements as uniform, having the same effect on both of these social groups, thus not recognizing their contradictory interests.

33. Warriner, *Land Reform and Development*, 129–30.

34. Ibid., 118; also Government of Iraq, *Census of 1958*, 14.

35. Durrah, *al-Tatawwur al-sina'i*, 94; 96; Ittihad al-Sina'at, *Yearbook 1957–1958* (Baghdad, 1958), 16–17.

36. Government of Iraq, *Census 1952, 1958*, 12; Sana al-'Umari, *Intaj wa-istihlak al-hintah fi-l-'iraq* (Baghdad, 1980), 15; 74; 132; 134; 164. One must take into consideration the difference in fertility of the soil and the productivity of the land when comparing the rain-fed north with the irrigated south. The average yield in dry farming areas is naturally much less (162.2 per dunum) than the irrigated areas where the average yield is expected to be as high as 337.7 per dunum. The discrepancy between the average and the actual yield was enormous in the south, according to at least one study of the agricultural productivity of wheat, since the actual yield covered by the study (1950–1966) was no more than 171.9 per dunum.

37. Al-'Alwan, "al-Taqadum al-fanni wa-l-takniki fi-zira'at al-'iraq," *al-Iqtisadi* 1 (July, 1961), 47–49.

38. Warriner, *Land Reform and Development*, 138–39.

39. Ibid., 160; Khasbak, *al-Iraq al-shamali* (Baghdad: Matba'it Shafiq, 1973), 207.

40. Khayyat, *al-Tatawwur al-tarikhi li-hiyazit al-aradi*, 278.

41. Warriner, *Land Reform and Development*, 138.

42. Khayyat, *al-Tatawwur al-tarikhi li-hiyazit al-aradi*, 278; The Government of Iraq, *The Census, 1952*, 22. In the Mosul province, smaller size holdings were more common as 76 percent of the agricultural lands were held by family proprietors who use farm labor. According to the government Agricultural and Livestock Census of 1952, the average landholding was 128 dunum, of which 95 percent were under 400 dunums, 72 percent less than 100 dunums, and 40 percent under 60 dunums.

CHAPTER 3

1. Durrah, *al-Tatatwwur al-sina'i*, 145–46.

2. Batatu, *Social Classes*, 316–17; Hasan, *al-Tatawwur al-iqtisadi*, 147.

3. Durrah, *al-Tatawwur al-sina'i*, 146.

4. Kathleen M. Langley, *The Industrialization of Iraq* (Cambridge, 1967), 62.

5. Ibid., 39. Like Fattal & Co., which was the largest shop of this type. It had over 20 hand-operated machines, employed 40 workers, and produced 360 pairs of stockings per day.

6. Ibid., 63.

7. For more information on this sector, *see* Langley, *Industrialization*.

8. According to Mudhafar Hussain Jamil, the high profits reaped from imports of dates encouraged its cultivators to expand production of date trees on their land, thus

sacrificing the quality of the fruit. Mudhafar Hussain Jamil, *Siyasit al-ʿiraq al-kharijiyah* (Cairo, 1949), 540.

9. In the 1920s, pressing dates was carried out either by the date merchants or the date growers on the farms of the latter. Each season, they set up simple huts made of hay or reeds called "jarathi." Durrah, *al-Tatawwur al-sinaʾi*, 236; and Mudhafar Jamil, *Siyasit al-ʿIraq*, 541.

10. According to Langley, as many as 50,000 workers were employed in pressing and packing following the introduction of the pitting process. Mudhafar Jamil concurs but Salman Hasan questions the authenticity of such a high figure contending that the date-pressing industry in the 1950s (according to the Industrial Census of 1954), did not exceed eight thousand. Langley, *Industrialization*, 45; Hasan, *al-Tatawwur al-iqtisadi*, 289.

11. Shakir Salim, *al-Jabayish*, 366.

12. Durrah, *al-Tatawwur al-sinai*, 240; Salim, *al-Jabayish*, 369.

13. Durrahh, *al-Tatawwur al-sinaʾi*, 234-35. According to Durrahh, there were twenty such establishments founded in 1935.

14. Batatu, *The Old Social Classes*, Table 9–13, 276–81.

15. With these improvements, the British company claimed to have obtained better prices in the Liverpool market for Iraqi cotton than that obtained for the "Middling American" cotton. Langley, *Industrialization*, 37.

16. Ittihad al-Sinaʾat, *Yearbook 1957–1958*, 18.

17. Langley, *Industrialization*, 64.

18. By the late 1930s, cotton cultivation began to pick up again as the following figures indicate: 1935, 4,405 bales were prepared for export; 1936, 9,477 bales and 1937, 20,000 bales. Government of Iraq, *The Agricultural and Industrial Bank Yearly Report 1937–1938*, 1–3.

19. For more details on primary and secondary industries for local consumption, consult Durrah, *al-Tatawwur al-sinai*, 127–43; 165–202.

20. Langley, *Industrialization*, 64.

21. These were the Rafidain Co., owned by Sayyid Abdullah Lutfi, one of Iraq's leading tobacco merchants; al-Ahliyah Tobacco Co., a shareholding company with the largest shares belonging to the textile financier Fattah and his family; and the ʿAbbud Tobacco Co., the first mechanized factory established by a Lebanese merchant. The total capacity for cigarette production increased to an estimated 10 million cigarettes a day by the mid-1950s. Saʾid Kittanah, "al-Tibgh fi-l-Iraq," *Majallet al-ziraʾa al-iraqiyah* 8 (July–August, 1953): 685–88; Durrah, *al-Tatawur al-sinaʾi*, 200.

22. Hasan, *al-Tatawur al-iqtisadi*, 298.

23. For example, from 1950–1956, the percentage of imported capital goods rose from 17 percent to 50 percent of the total. *See* Jalal, *Role of the Government*, 107.

24. Durrah, *al-Tatawwur al-sina⁾i*, 63.

25. The Federation of Industries was founded in 1956. Sulayman Fattah headed the Board of Directors while Rajab al-Saffar, Muhammad Hadid, Adib al-Jadir among other industrialists were members. The Federation represented 40 million Iraqi dinars in industrial capital. Ittihad al-Sina⁾at, *Yearbook 1956–1957*, 22.

26. Abdul Ghani al-Dalli, "al-Mashari⁾ al-sina⁾iyah fil-⁾iraq wa-musahamat al-masraf al-sina⁾i," *Majalat ghurfit tijarit baghdad* 12 (January–February, 1949): 37–45; Industrial Bank, *Yearly Report 1947–1948*, 1–5.

27. Dalli, "Mashakil al-Sina⁾a al-wataniya fi-taqrir al-masraf al-sina⁾i al-Iraqi," *Majalit ghurfit tijarit Baghdad* 11 (September–November, 1948), 547–50.

28. Industrial Bank, *Yearly Report 1958*, 1–3.

29. Langley, *Industrialization*, 256.

30. Ittihad al-Sina⁾at, *Yearbook 1956–1957*, 10.

31. As the largest textile factory in 1945, Nuri Fattah's had 5,200 spindles and 50 looms while Salih Ibrahim's factory had 1,600 spindles and 25 looms. *See* Langley, *Industrialization*, 141. The production of the three factories available in the 1930s was no more than half a million square yards of woolen or a mixture of wool and cotton fabrics. Also *see* Hasan, *al-Tatawwur al-iqtisadi*, 294.

32. Langley, *Industrialization*, 97.

33. As a joint shareholding company, this factory had the advantage of raising 250,000 dinars as the initial capital which then was increased to 1.5 million (1956). Industrial Bank, *Yearly Report 1957*, 2.

34. Hasan, *al-Tatawwur al-iqtisadi*, 293.

35. *See* Langley, *Industrialization*, 97. As reported by the Industrial Census of 1954, employment in these industries increased as well, to 9,058 workers. Their sales averaged to 4 million dinars and their capital investment to 2.5 million.

36. The wholesale price of white cotton shirting rose from 0.6 British pounds per 40 yards in August of 1939, to 9.35 pounds in August of 1943, to 16 pounds by 1944. Durrah, *al-Tatawwur al-sina⁾i*, 105; Langley, *Industrialization*, 141.

37. It was designed with 27,000 spindles, 615 automatic looms, and a productive capacity of 10 million tons of cotton yarn a year (1.5 million tons went to small household producers), 15 million square yards of cotton and silks yearly, and over 30 million yards medium-quality cotton fabric (gray sheeting).The initial capital was 150,000 ID, raised to 900,000 ID in 1949, and 1,200,000 ID in 1951. Ittihad al-Sina⁾at, *Yearbook 1958–1959*, see Tal⁾at al-Shaibani, "Dirasah fi-iqtisadiyat al-qutn al-ʿiraqi," 5.

38. With 3.5 million dinars, the Board set up the mill with 25,000 spindles and 630 automatic looms, and a production capacity of 16 million meters of very fine cotton fabric.

Ibid., 39; Adib al-Jadir, "Sina ʾit al-ghazl wa-l-nasij," *Majalit al-zira ʾah al-ʿiraqiyah* 10 (May–July, 1955), 299–310.

39. Ibid., 18. The total capital involved in ginning, according to the Federation was 684,000 dinars. *See* also Isma ʾil Abdul Ra ʾuf, "Tatawwur sina ʾat al-halj wa-atharuha fi-l-tijarah al-qutniyah," *Majalit al-zira ʾa al-ʿiraqiya* 10 (May–July, 1955), 314–18.

40. The Trading and Milling of Iraqi Grain established in 1949 with a capital of 150,000 dinars, 20 percent of which was contributed by the Industrial Bank.The Middle Iraq Dates Co. with a capital of 1 million dinars with the Chalabis as the main shareholders. Durrah, *al-Tatawwur al-sina ʾi*, 250.

41. For instance, the Rafidain Cigarette Co. claimed an 81 percent rate of profit and al-Ahliyah a 60 percent for the year 1957. Hasan, *al-Tatawwur al-iqtisadi*, 296–98.

42. By 1949, there were 11 brick factories, employing over 33,000 workers, and a total capital of over 100,000 dinars in contrast to 5,000 dinars and 13 factories in the 1930s. Hasan, *al-Tatawwur al-iqtisadi*, 305.

43. Ittihad al-sinaat, *Yearbook 1957–1958*, 172. In 1935, 45,000 tons of cement were imported and over 80,000 tons by the mid-1940s.

44. The initial capital was 200,000 dinars, increased to 1 million in 1950. In 1954, the company paid 40 percent in dividends and in 1955, it was able to raise its capital investment to 750,000 dinars and to pay 20 percent of its returns in dividends. By 1955, its capital investment was once more increased to 1,750,000 dinars, which was raised from its capital gains. *The Industrial Bank Reports of 1954 and 1955.*

45. In its first five-year development plan, the Development Board (90 percent of whose budget was raised from the oil royalties), allocated 100 million dinars to irrigation projects, the construction of roads, bridges, and other buildings. Durrah, *al-Tatawwur al-sina ʾi*, 260; Hasan, *al-Tatwwur al-iqtisadi*, 312–14.

46. Batatu, *Social Classes*, 278

47. Ittihad al-Sina ʾat, *Yearbook 1957–1958*, 176. Besides private investment, the state through the Development Board erected two more plants to fill the gap. With a capital of 5 million dinars, the board established the Sirinjar and the Hammam al-Alil Cement plants in the northern region, where several irrigation dams were under construction.

48. Ittihad al-Sina ʾat, *Yearly Report 1957*, 176; Hasan, *al-Tatawwur al-iqtisadi*, 312–14. Japanese cement was sold for 6.5 dinars/ton in contrast to Iraq's 7.25/ton. In the case of Iran, Turkey, and Pakistan, local production of cement decreased the need for imports.

49. Hasan, *al-Tatawwur al-iqtisadi*, 314–15.

50. Vegetable Oil Extraction Co. started with a capital of no more than 30,000 in 1940, but by 1946, expanded to 150,000 dinars, and by 1957, to 1 million dinars. Hamdi Muhammad Sartawi, "al-Tawasu ʾ fi-intaj al-zayt fi-l-ʿiraq," *al-Tijarah* 16 (January, 1953), 54.

51. Ittihad al-Sina'at, *Yearbook 1957–1958*, 22.

52. Ibid. The company's rate of profit, according to the Ittihad, exceeded 60 percent in 1948.

53. Batatu, *Social Classes*, 310.

54. Ibid., 276–81. Table 9–13 which lists the Iraqi capitalists worth over 1 million Iraqi dinars.

55. Jalal, *Role of Government*, 111.

56. *Majalit al-Tijarah*, 5–6 (Baghdad: Chamber of Commerce, 1952), 355. The article in this journal called for the reduction or cancellation of tariffs on imported goods as one way of improving the purchasing power of the consumer. At the same time, the article points out that "the tariff system enforced today had caused great difficulties for the local traders . . . ."

57. Ibid., 586. "The absence of foreign competition during the war made the local capitalists, who realized high amounts of profits during the war period, become aware of the dangers of competition and need for protection. . . . With the end of the war and the lifting of the protection, however, the enthusiasm of private capital for industrial investment showed a definite decline." The article then went on to defend the quota and the tariff law of 1948 which restricted the imports of goods produced locally and encouraged the import of raw material and capital goods.

58. In reference to Sir Arthur Salter, Arthur D. Little, Edith Penrose, Iverson among others.

59. See al-Durrah, Sabah, "Hawl al-burjuwaziyah al-sina'iyeh fil-'iraq" *al-Thaqafah al-Jadidah* 2 (May, 1969), 193–99.

60. Industrial Bank, *Yearly Report 1954*, 31.

61. Langley, *Industrialization*, 156.

62. Ittihad al-Sina'at, *Yearbook 1957–1958,* 138.

63. Ja'far Humaydi, "al-Zuyuwt al-nabatiyah bayn himayit al-Muntij wa-himayit al-mustahlik," *Majalit al-Tijara* 18 (July, 1955), 17–19.

64. As noted by Ittihad al-sina'at, the company in 1958 realized 60 percent profit, the highest rate of return recorded since its inception. Ittihad al-sina'at, *Yearbook 1961*, 23.

65. IBRD, *Economic Development*, 40.

66. "Raw material supply also affected the vegetable oil extraction plant. Since it could not obtain an adequate and steady flow of vegetable oil seeds (i.e., cotton, sesame, or other oil-bearing seeds) from Iraqi sources, the company was forced to supplement its needs from higher-cost imports and from time to time was forced to curtail production because of lack of material." Langley, *Industrialization*, 158.

67. Ittihad al-Sina³at, *Yearbook 1957–1958*, 98.

68. Even though the duties were raised from 66 to 154 fils, they were still considerably lower than those imposed in other Arab countries like Syria (336 fils) and Lebanon (365 fils) that were facing similar difficulties. Langley, *Industrialization*, 152.

69. Cotton production in Iraq increased after 1945, especially after the rise in demand for non-dollar cotton and in world prices after 1945, and especially following the outbreak of the Korean conflict in 1951. The area of cotton cultivation expanded immensely after 1949, increasing from 34,289 dunum in 1947 to 232,726 dunum in 1957. The yield, however, was poor and tended to fluctuate from one year to the next. The average yield was 132 in 1936, 192 in 1950, and 170 in 1957. Ittihad al-Sina³at, *Yearbook 1957–1958*, 68; 18.

70. Ibid., 153; 157. During 1951–1952 "an American observer estimated that it took three women all day to plant a quarter of an acre, and that even with their low wages of 100 fils (25 cents) per day, the cost per acre was $3. Mechanical equipment would have been less expensive even though the tractor driver received about five times as much as unskilled labor."

71. Protection was reduced from 33 to 12. See Ittihad al-Sina³at, *Yearbook 1958–1959*, 18; 43.

72. Ibid., 24.

73. Hasan, *al-Tatawwur al-iqtisadi*, 370–71.

74. Langley, *Industrialization*, 152–53.

75. IBRD, *Economic Development*, 133.

76. Ibid., 6.

77. Ibid., 15; 18–23.

78. The Oil Company employed no more than 2.5 percent of the labor force. Al-Eyd, *Oil Revenues*, 15.

79. Abu-el-Haj, "Oil Industry," 7.

80. Ibid., 4–5.

81. Jalal Farhang, *Role of Government*, 6, 10, 37–38.

82. Langley, *Industrialization*, 165.

83. For more information on the nationalization of Iranian oil, *see* E. Abrahamian, *Iran Between Two Revolutions* (Princeton, 1982).

84. While the agreement increased the royalties from four to six gold shillings per ton of crude oil, the value of the gold was based on the official rate set by the Central Bank in England rather than on a free-floating market rate.

Notes

173

85. Ja³afar Abbas Hmaydi, *al-Tatawurat al-siyasiyah fi-l-ʿiraq 1941-1953* (Najaf, 1976), 646-54. The coalition consisted of NDP members and other independent nation- alists. They formed al-Jabha al-sha³biya, headed by Taha al-Hashimi, al-Shabibi, and al-Chadirchi.

86. Iraq as a full share-holder was prefered over the 50–50 profit-share proposed by others in the opposition. *al-Ahali* 10, 11, 13, 14, 15, July 1951.

87. Langley, *Industrialization*, 166; and Al-Eyd, Oil Revenues, 16.

88. For more information regarding the position of the opposition on the oil issue, *see* the NDP pamphlet, *Qadiyat al-naft al-ʿiraqi* (Baghdad: al-Ahali Press, 1952), 63–74.

89. Jalal, *Role of Government*, 10.

90. Economists like Farhang Jalal, Al-Eyd among others, attribute the failure of or the slow growth in development programs in Iraq to poor plan implementation caused by administrative inefficiency, over-ambitious plans, and technical factors. Jalal Farhang, *Role of Government*, 69–77, Al-Eyd, *Oil Revenues*, 69.

91. Jalal Farhang, *Role of Government*, 15.

92. Salter, *Development of Iraq*, 56.

93. It is important to point out in this context that the actual development expendi- ture fell short of the programmed revenues. Between 1951 and 1958, the average planned expenditure in agriculture was estimated at I.D. 178.2 million, while the actual expendi- ture did not exceed 81.2 million, or 51.2 percent of what was initially planned. Covering the same period, industry's planned funds were 71.2 million dinars, while the actual expenditure was 34.8 million dinars. The rest of the revenues, as Al-Nasrawi argued, were left idle—i.e., invested in short-term securities in the London market. *See* Al-Eyd, *Oil Revenues,* 24; Nasrawi, *Financing Economic Development*, 58.

94. Most of the expenditure of the DB went to the construction of Wadi al-Tharthar, Habaniyah flood control, Dokan and the Derbedi-Khan depressions. Nasrawi, *Financing Economic Development*, 60.

95. Salter, *Development of Iraq*, 54

96. Ibid., 55.

97. Nasrawi, *Financing Economic Development*, 70; also Chapter 1.

98. According to one source, "forced industrialization with the aid of tariff protec- tion or government subsidy might lead to inefficiency and waste of economic re- sources . . . " See Arthur D. Little, *A Plan for the Industrial Development in Iraq* (Cambridge, 1961), 3.; Salter, *Development of Iraq*, 73; and Carl Iverson, *Monetary Policy in Iraq* (Baghdad, 1954), 147; 227.

99. Ittihad al-Sina³at, *Yearbook 1960–1961*, 58. As Khadduri Khadduri, the Secre- tary of the Federation pointed out, "private sector is deeply committed to the necessity of

a planned state economy in a country like ours that has not completed its economic development. Such a policy will prevent extemporaneous [irtijal] behavior in the industrial domain." Also, see the NDP economic program in chapter 4.

CHAPTER 4

1. The European civilizing/modernizing project (grounded in the universalization of the Enlightenment principles of liberty, progress, secularism, equality, human rights etc.) is premised on the Orientalist representation of non-Western cultures as static, unchanging essences locked into past eras of universal history, incapable of transforming themselves and attaining progress without the interference of the west. This conception provided the context for the colonization of non-Western societies. Accordingly, the High Civil Commissioner, Arnold Wilson, for example, viewed his mission as bestowing England's "gifts of efficient administration, of impartial justice, honest finance, and of security on backward peoples, who, in return for these services were to assume places in the economic and defensive system of the Empire." Ireland, *Iraq: A Study in Political Development* (London, 1937), 141.

Aware of the project's ambiguity, Wilson quotes his imperial archetype hero, Cromer of Egypt, arguing that the project is "striving to attain two ideals, which are apt to be mutually destructive—the ideal of good government, which connotes the continuance of his [English] supremacy, and the ideal of self-government, which connotes the whole or partial abdication of his supreme position. Moreover, although after a dim, slipshod, but characteristically Anglo-Saxon fashion, he is aware that empire must rest on one of these two bases—an extensive military occupation or the principle of nationality—he cannot in all cases quite make up his mind which of the two bases he prefers." Cromer quoted in Wilson, *Clash of Loyalties*, 72.

2. P. W. Ireland, *Iraq: A Study*, 85. Regarding the administration of tribal areas, Ireland points out that both Percy Cox and Henry Dobbs, who served as High Commissioners, were of "the view that the governing of tribal areas can be best attained by making use of the natural leaders of the tribes: the shaikhs. . . . Their efforts were directed towards building up forms of administration of justice which, while conforming as far as possible to Western standards, were based on tribal organizaton of the shaikhs as instruments of government," 89–90. The tribal Criminal and Civil Disputes Regulation was, in fact, drawn up by Dobbs who served as the Revenue Commissioner and supervised the administration of the occupied territories between 1916–1917, and as the High Commissioner between 1923–1929. The regulation , as observed by Ireland (85), was drawn on the lines of Indian Frontier Crimes Regulation.

3. Ibid., 203–4.

4. Wilson, *Loyalties*, 245.

5. According to Wilson, the Acting High Commissioner, "the extension of the plebiscite to the rank and file of the inhabitants was both impractical and unnecessary." According to Wilson, the "masses were too illiterate, too ignorant and dependent on their leaders to merit consideration." Ireland, *Iraq: A Study*, 166.

Notes

175

6. Regarding the re-election of the Chamber of Deputies, Ireland pointed out that "without exception," it was "rigidly controlled by the Government, often under pressure from the [British] Residency as in 1928, 1930 [principally because the Treaties of 1928 and 1930 were to be ratified by the newly elected chambers]. In all districts except Baghdad where the electoral body is not so amenable to control as elsewhere, the confidential orders of the Government to the provincial officials proved sufficient to secure the election of its candidates whether they were residents of the district or even known there. Thus in 1925, all but four of the government candidates were returned . . . in 1928, the deputies returned from Basra ʾAmara, Diyalah, Duleim, Hilla, and Arbil were government candidates." Ireland, *Iraq: A Study,* 431–32; *see* also Batatu, *The Old Social Classes,* Table 6–1, 103 on the first Assembly.

7. These methods scarcely improved in later years despite the ending of the formality of indirect elections by Decree No. 6 of 1952. Except occasionally, for some of the seats of the larger towns, royal parliaments continued to be picked rather than elected.

8. "Examination of the statute books of Iraq . . . seems to suggest that the deputies have not failed to make free of their position. Many of the financial measures granting remission of arrears in revenue (law number 38 of 1927; number 55 of 1929; numbers 38, 43, and 69 of 1931; numbers 1, 5, 10, 34, and 35 of 1932; numbers 8, 10, 13, and 14 of 1933), and of other financial legislation (the Pump Law of 1926; number 72 of 1926; number 38 of 1929; number 37 of 1930; number 66 of 1931), while passed by the Chamber for the benefit of Iraq as a whole . . . have especially favored the land-owning class which has been predominant in Parliament." Ireland, *Iraq: A Study,* 432–33 (including notes 1 and 2).

9. The histories of the manifold revolts—e.g., the popular revolt of 1920, the 1919 and 1930 Kurdish rebellions, as well as the many peasant uprisings against their shaykhs—and their violent repression testify to the manner in which the British established the modern regime.

10. The conditions attached to this treaty were similar to the British-Egyptian Treaty of 1922 which declared Egypt an "independent sovereign state" following the National Revolution of 1919.

11. Al-Istiqlal party (Independent Party) was also a nationalist party that played not a small role in the politics of the 1940s and 1950s. Formed in 1941 out of the Muthana Club, it reached its height of activism between 1947–1952, attracting over 5,000 members, mainly "retired army officers and government officials." The party was designated by many as "right-wing" with "fascist" tendencies. Its politics as determined by its program, however, were not very different from the other nationalists. It was "populist," "reformist," and "modernist" in outlook. Since it was pan-Arabist in sentiment, many of its members joined the ranks of al-Baʿth once the party began to lose its political momentum in the mid-1950s. *See* Batatu, *Social Classes,* 298–300.

12. The Kurdish Democratic Party held similar views but from a Kurdish perspective. On this subject, *see* Saʾd Jawad, *Iraq and the Kurdish Question 1958–1970* (London, Ithaca Press, 1981); Majid ʿAbdu-l-Rida, *al-Qadiyah al-kurdiyah fi-l-ʾiraq* (Baghdad, 1974).

13. Although the Istiqlal played a more important political role in the 1940s than the Ba᾽th, the Ba᾽th and its ideology was much more significant in the 1950s, during and after the revolution. That is why I have chosen al-Ba᾽th over Istiqlal for analysis. Moreover, the political program of al-Istiqlal did not seem to differ much from that of the NDP. They called for a similar land reform, a more equitable system of land distribution, protection of local commercial and industrial enterprises, etc. The fundamental difference that can be drawn between Istiqlal and the NDP was that Istiqlal was less committed to democracy, while in practice, it was more opportunistic and tended to cooperate more with the oligarchic state and the ruling groups. Another difference was their extreme hostility to communism especially in regards to the national question. For a history of the party, *see* Muhamad Mahdi Kubbah, *Mudhakarati fi samim al-ahdath 1918–1958* (Beirut,1962).

14. Opposition to iqta᾽ was articulated more clearly in the 1940s than in the earlier nationalist discourses of the 1930s.

15. Ibid., 42.

16. Gramsci treated the "passive revolution" as a case of "blocked transition," agruing that compromise with the feudal classes inevitably arrested social transformation.

17. Chatterjee, *The Nation and its Fragments: Colonial and Post Colonial Histories* (Princeton, 1993), 203; 205.

18. The al-Ahali group consisted by and large of recent graduates of Arab and Western universities. They included ᶜAbdil Fattah Ibrahim, Mohammed Hadid, Darwish al-Haidari and others who were originally graduates of the American University of Beirut. Mohammed Hadid did his graduate work at London School of Economics while Fattah Ibrahim did one year of graduate work at Columbia University in New York. Other leading figures included Hussain Jamil, a graduate of Law school in Damascus, and Abdul Qadir Isma᾽il, Jamil Abdul Wahab who formed their own cultural club in Baghdad, prior to the formation of al-Ahali. Fu᾽ad Hussain al-Wakil, *Jama᾽it al-Ahali f-il ᶜIraq* (Baghdad, 1976), 161–64.

19. Personal interviews with Muhamad Hadid, one of the founding members of al-Ahali, and Dr. Fadhil Hussein, author of *Tarikh al-hizb al-watani al-dimoqrati* (Baghdad, 1963), on March 15, April 20, 1983.

20. *(Sawt) al-Ahali*, September, 23 and 24, 1942; January 5, 28, and 29, 1943.

21. The right-wing nationalists within al-Ahali were represented by Khalil Kinnah and Jamil ᶜAbdul Wahhab who were sympathetic to national socialism. They resigned their positions in the late 1930s. The left wing were ᶜAbdul Fattah Ibrahim, Zaki Abdul Wahhab, and Tal᾽at al-Shaibani. The social democrats were Muhamad Hadid, Hussain Jamil, and Kamil Chadirchi. The Marxists were Yusif Mitti, Yusif Isma᾽il, Salman Fahd among others. The first split in al-Ahali took place in April of 1946 when Abdul Fattah Ibrahim and Aziz Sharif, two left-wing members, left the Group. Ibrahim established his own group, Hizb al-ittihad al-watani, which included several communists. Aziz Sharif formed al-Sha᾽b Party (People's Party) that was backed by the Syrian Communist Party, while Zaki Khairi formed the National Revolutionary Committee with Sharif al-Shaikh.

Hussein, *Tarikh al-hizb*, 103,108–9; Gabbay, *Communism and Agrarian Reform*, 57; Batatu, *The Old Social Classes*, 587–89, 420.

22. Batatu, *The Old Social Classes*, 476.

23. For a transcript of the debate between the left and right wing tendencies before the formation of the party, cf. F. Hussain, *Tarikh al-Hizb*, 132–204; and Kamil al-Chadirchi, *Mudhakarat Kamil al-Chadirchi wa-tarikh al-hizb al-watani al-dimoqrati* (Beirut, 1970), 185–86.

24. Hussain, *Tarikh al-hizb*, 205. Left members Abdul Wahab Zaki and al-Shabibi resigned after they lost to the moderates.

25. According to Batatu, the "party attracted a large following particularly in Baghdad, Basra, and the middle Euphrates and by April 1947 counted 6,961 members, 50 to 60 percent of whom came, according to the party's secretary, from the middle walks of life, and comprised merchants, shopkeepers, small property owners, craftsmen, students, teachers, lawyers, and other professionals." Batatu, *Social Classes*, 306; also *see* Hussein, *Tarikh al-hizb*, 113–16, on the debates regarding the party's program.

26. Federation of Industries was founded in 1956. Its first president was Sulayman Fattah, its vice president Rajab al-Saffar (NDP), members included Muhamad Hadid (NDP), Khadduri (NDP) among others. Ittihad al-Sinaʾat, *Yearbook 1956–1957*, 3–4.

27. Batatu, *The Old Social Classes*, 302.

28. As discussed in chapter 2; also *see* Batatu, *The Old Social Classes*, 301.

29. Ibid., 814.

30. Hussain, *Tarikh al-hizb al-Dimoqrati*, 275.

31. al-Chadirchi, *Mudhkarat*, 516, 523, 185–90.

32. Interview with al-Chadirchi recorded by Hussein, 337.

33. Michel Aflaq, *Fi-sabil al-Baʾth*, 103.

34. Zeine Zeine, *The Emergence of Arab Nationalism* (New York: Caravan Books, 1958), 130; see also Satiʾ al-Husri, *Muhadharat fi-nushuʾ al-fikra al-qawmiyyah* (Beirut, 1948); A. A. Duri, *The Historical Formation of the Arab Nation* (London, 1987).

35. Michel ʿAflaq, *Fi-sabil al-baʾth* (Beirut: Manshurat dar al-taliʾa, 1959), 123; 55.

36. Ibid., 43; 55.

37. Tehmina Akhtar, "Thinking the Nation: Historiography, Education and the Minority Question in Egypt," 10 (unpublished paper).

38. "When I am asked to give a definition of socialism, I can say that it is not to be found in the works of Marx and Lenin. I say: socialism is the religion of life, and its victory over death. By giving work to everyone and helping them to develop their talents it keeps the patrimony of life for life." Bassam Tibi, *Arab Nationalism*, 171.

39. B. Tibi, "Islam and Modern European Ideology," *International Journal of Middle Eastern Studies* 18 (1986), 23.

40. See the party's constitution of 1947, especially Articles 26, 27, 29, and 39.

41. I would like to suggest a connection between the pan-Arabist commitment to unification and the breakdown of territorial borders and mercantilist interests engaged in regional trade.This group's economic interests and political status had been severely undermined by the creation of the wire-fenced, legal frontiers between Syria and Iraq. This thesis, however, has to be empirically established.

42. The first group was founded by Syrian students n Baghdad. The second, in Karbalah, was founded by an Iraqi student, Sa'dun Hamadi who was recruited to the Ba'th while studying in Beirut. From these two groups, other cells were founded among the urban university and high school students. Hmaydi, *Tatawwurat siyasiyah*, 656–58.

43. Ibid., 661–62.

44. According to Batatu, "25.5 percent of the members of the Iraqi commands originated from the classes of low income, 38.3 percent from the classes of lower middle income, and 29.8 percent from the classes of middling income . . . it will be further noticed that the majority of (53.8 percent) of the members of the Iraqi commands of 1952–63 came from the underprivileged Arab Shi'a sect." Batatu, *The Old Social Classes*, 748.

45. Fernando Claudin, *The Communist Movement from Comintern to Cominform* (Middlesex, 1975), 261.

46. Lenin points out that alliance with bourgeois parties should take place "only when they are genuinely revolutionary, and when their exponents do not hinder our work of educating and organizing in a revolutionary spirit the peasantry and the masses of the exploited. If these conditions do not exist in these countries, the communists must combat the reformist bourgeoisie." Cited in Claudin, 265.

47. Ibid., 267.

48. Ibid., 77. "The theory of "socialism in one country," having become the theoretical foundation for Comintern strategy, signified, in the last analysis, that the world revolution, in all of its phases and episodes, was to be subordinated to the requirements of building socialism in the USSR."

49. For a critical analysis of this theory and its implication on the communist movements in Europe and in China, see Claudin, *Communist Movement*.

50. Tibi, "Islam and Ideology," 24.

51. *Min watha'iq al-hizb al-shuyu'i, kitabat al-rafiq al-Shabibi* (Baghdad, 1974).The book consists of a series of documents written by al-Shabibi who was a member of the Central Committee of the Iraqi Communist party in the 1940s.

52. Ibid., 94–124; especially the document entitled, "Liberation and National Independence."

53. Except for the short period in 1936 following Bakr Sidqi's military coup when the communists joined forces with al-Ahali to form the "Popular Reform Society" to defend and mobilize support for the coup. The Front collapsed in less than a year when the new government of Bakr Sidqi turned against the communists in an attempt to appease the tribal landed class in the south. Batatu, *The Old Social Classes*, 444.

54. For an analysis of the difficulties facing the formation of a united front, refer to the ICP document entitled, "al-Inᵓikasat al-salbiyah fi tafsir al-jabhah al-muwahadah fi-l-harakah al-wataniyah" ("The Negative Impressions of the United Front on the Nationalist Movement") in Shabibi's, *Kitabat*, 33–56.

55. In distinguishing the NDP's political discourse from that of communism, al-Chadirchi had the following to say: "We believe deeply in democracy . . . (yet) we do not want to achieve change through socialist revolutionary methods, we aim to achieve it through democratic methods, bit by bit. . . . Our political philosophy tends to lean towards the politics of the Labor Party in Britain—the party which represents all classes rather than one particular class." Chadirchi, *Mudhakarat*, 183, 337. In due time, however, the nationalists were forced to change their position as they began to realize in the 1950s that without a united front, the national struggle was more or less futile.

56. Batatu, *The Old Social Classes*, 525.

57. *al-Qaᵓidah*: June 5, 1943.

58. Gabbay, *Communism and Agrarian Reform*, 53.

59. Batatu, *The Old Social Classes*, 512; 516.

60. As Claudin points out, the spectacular expansion of the communist movement particularly in Europe and Asia filled the communists with a "euphoric optimism about the prospects for revolution throughout the world." Claudin, *Communist Movement*, 307; 311.

61. In 1946, the League Against Zionism, and the National Liberation Party (front organization for the CP) organized a demonstration in Baghdad in which over 3,000 students and workers took part. Unable to disperse the demonstrators, the police fired live ammunition at the crowd killing one and wounding several. Most of the leadership was arrested as a result. Batatu, *The Old Social Classes*, 532; Humaydi, *Tatawwurat siyasiyah*, 153; 156.

62. On the struggle between the right and left tendencies within the leadership in this period, *see* Najm Mahmoud, *al-Siraᵓ fil-hizb al-shuyuiᵓi al-ᵓIraqi qadhaya al-khilaf fi-lharakah al-shuyuiᵓiya al-ᵓalamiyyah* (Beirut, 1968), 17–19.

63. In the first half of the 1950s, the NDP, according to Chadirchi, tried unsuccessfully to reach out for the ICP to join a united front. Chadirchi, *Mudhakarat*, 540. The exception was 1953 when the ICP under the leadership of Hussain Ahmad al-Radi, reinstated the slogan "national democratic government" in congruence with the softening of the left line of the Cominform and the communist movements in the neighboring

countries (mainly Syria). During this year, the CP entered into a short-term alliance with the progressive nationalist forces in preparation for the elections of 1953, which took place in the early part of 1954. This alliance did not last long because in 1954, Hamid ʿUthman, a pro-Maoist, took over the leadership of the party and geared it towards an outright struggle with the state. He raised the slogans of "general political strike," "armed struggle," and called for the building of people's resistance army in the countryside. Batatu, *The Old Social Classes*, 675–78.

64. The change in the leadership in 1956 was considered by some as "right deviationist" policy that was dictated by Moscow. *See* Mahmood, *al-Siraʾ fi-l-hizb*, 15–19. With the ousting of Uthman, *al-Qaidah, Rayat al-shaghghilah* and *al-Nidhal* ceased publication. As of July, 1956, the united communist party issued a new journal, *Ittihad al-Shaʾb*. Batatu, *The Old Social Classes*, 711.

65. In this period, the NDP's and the ICP's programs were similar, not just on the issue of the nation-state. As of 1947, the National Charter of the Communist party dropped its "socialist" and "revolutionary" program and adopted instead a reformist line that called for "true independence," a "genuinely democratic regime," the "revival of the Constitution," and for the "development of the economy."

66. The first document touching on the issue of Arab unity was written by Fahd and appeared in *al-Qaʾidah*, September 8, 1943. Although the historical circumstances (union between Jordan, Syria, and Iraq as then proposed by the British) which produced this document were radically different from the 1950s period when the pan-Arabists became popular, this document nonetheless continued to be used as the reference and the rationale for the Iraqi communists' opposition to unity. The document states: "to raise the slogan of unity (merger) is not too pragmatic at this point due to the great diversities in the social and economic levels of development among the Arab countries. Therefore, we propose an Arab Federation (*ittihad ʿarabi*) as the more viable alternative for the moment, a kind of union which will allow only independent Arab countries to join, if they choose to. Within this federation, the autonomy of the political structures of each of these countries must be respected."

67. Min wathaʾiq al-hizb, *Kitabat al-rafiq Fahd* (Baghdad, 1967), 207.

68. The reports dispatched by the British Ambassador, Archibald Clark Kerr to Anthony Eden, disclosed the complicity of King Ghazi in the military coup, based on Bekr Sidqi's admission that the "movement, of which he was the head, was being carried out with the knowledge and the approval of King Ghazi." Kerr also confessed that based on "first hand observation of the King's behavior" that "I am bound to say that I, too, gained the impression that it [the coup] came as no surprise to his Majesty." Great Britain: FO 371/20014/62780; E7147; E7180; E7145/1419/93, November 16, 1936.

69. The new government included leading members of al-Ahali, Jaʾfar abul-Timman, al-Chadirchi, and Yusif ʿIzz-al-Din Ibrahim. Critical of the "despotic acts of the former government and its arbitrary measures," the new government under the leadership of the "National Reform Force" presented a reform program similar to al-Ahali's. *Al-Ahali*, November 6, 1936.

70. From the start al-Ahali group did not trust Sidqi Bakr, who established his reputation by brutally crushing the revolts of the Assyrians in 1933, as well as tribes in the south in 1935, and Kurdish revolt led by Barazani in the north. The nationalists resigned from the government after Bakr's barabarous repression of the Diwaniyah tribes in 1936.

71. Nuri al-Sa³id derived his power from the shaikhly landed class and old mercantile interest. Great Britain: FO E7266/489/93, letter from Cornwallis to Eden dated November 6, 1943.

72. British involvement is suggested in the following dispatch after the 1936 coup: "HMO may therefore be faced in the future not only with the problem of the political future of Iraq, but also with the problem of the dynasty. In that connexion it will be recalled that we have already given preliminary consideration to the possibility of alternatives to King Ghazi (*see* E3984/308/93)." Great Britain, FO 371/ 20014/62280, November 16, 1936. On Nuri's alleged participation in the plot, *see* Batatu, *Social Classes*, 338–42.

73. Abdul-Ilah's political power improved after the 1943 amendment of the king's power, which the regent exercised, was passed by the parliament. The amendment gave him the power to dismiss the prime minister.

74. The British fully backed Nuri al-Saᶜid until 1943 when they began to raise doubts about his governorship, calling for a more "honest" and liberal government, as the following letter from the residing British Ambassador to Eden in 1943 openly stated: "I attacked his Excellency for the endless failure of his governments to tackle the economic problem honestly and boldly, for the manner in which they have tolerated dishonesty and inefficiency in the public services, for the resultant weakness and corruption of the police, the unreliability of the army, the mishandling of the Kurds, the shameless land grabbing carried on by prominent personalities, the general lack of courageous leadership, and the wide gulf between the government and the people." (Great Britain, FO E 7266/489/93, November 6, 1943.)

75. Batatu, *The Social Classes*, 617. Over 60 percent of the 11,000 Iraqi railway workers, according to Batatu, were either communist members or sympathizers.

76. Humaydi, *Tatawwurat siyasiyah*, 154–55; 426–27.

77. Organized also by the communists, the dock workers, who were mostly employed by British agencies, went on strike in 1947, 1948, and 1952. Talib Abdul Jabir, *Rub³ qarn fi tarikh al-harakah al-³umalliyah* (Baghdad, 1960), 45.

78. The oil industry employed 12,000 workers between 1947–1953. The level of wages received by labor in the oil industry was much higher than that received in other industries. According to 1948 index, the oil worker was paid an average of 357 fils/day in contrast to 258 fils in other industries. Their wages here do not include the fringe benefits offered in the oil industry, including hospitalization, housing, and clinics. The annual income of unskilled oil workers was estimated by the economist Ribhi Abul-Haj at 128 dinars a year. Abul-Haj, "Oil Industry," 5.

79. Humaydi, *Tatawwurat siyasiyah*, 438.

80. Ibid., 322–23; 560. According to Humaydi, the newspapers of the opposition groups, like *al-Ahali, al-Watan,* and *al-Usbah* among others were suspended and their leaders were put in prison.

81. Ibid., 426–29; 440. The agreement reached included:
1. the setting up of a special committee to investigate the killing of the workers; and
2. the banning of the arbitrary firing of workers. The workers, however, were denied once more the right to unionize.

82. According to Batatu, even though workers' daily wages in 1948 increased by 400 percent over the 1939 level, the official price of food index, based on the requirements of an unskilled labor, reached 805 points higher than the 1939 standards. Batatu, *The Old Social Classes,* 472–73.

83. Workers' strikes included those in al-Habaniyah and al-Shuʾubiyah British military bases in June of 1952, followed by the one in Basra port in August. In November of the same year, strikes unfolded in the textiles, cigarette, and printing industries etc. For more information, *see* Razzaq Ibrahim Hasan, *Tarikh al-harakah al-ʿamilah fi-l-Iraq* (Beirut, 1976), 106.

84. British Foreign Office, FO 137/68479; 68467; 68481, 1948.

85. Batatu, *The Old Social Classes,* 626–27.

86. Ibid., 472–73.

87. Humaydi, *Tatawwurat siyasiyah*, 145; 158. In 1945 protests in support of the Syrian and Lebanese struggle against French colonialism were organized in Baghdad. In the same year, another demonstration was organized to protest the Balfour Declaration and the Zionization of Palestine. Law students went on a strike in January of 1947 protesting British domination and its policies against the Iraqi and Palestinian people. The government riot police moved in and violently repressed the strike.

88. The move to liberalize was not just a response to social pressure from below, but also expressed the rivalry between the ʿAbdul-Illah and Nuri al-Saʾid's ranks. ʿAbdul-Illah, who was described by the British as "a man of inferior clay," did not have the backing of the British as did his opponent, Nuri, who was considered a shrewd and reliable agent despite his "dubious acts." The liberalization policies enacted by ʿAbdul-Ilah, one might say, were meant to co-opt the nationalists to boost his weakened position within the power structure.

89. Swaidi, a pro-nationalist, was naturally unpopular with the British as the following statment illustrates:" He has the reputation of being somewhat crooked . . . and he is not a man of outstanding ability . . ." British Foreign Office, FO 371/20795, 1937.

90. Humaydi, *Tatawwurat siyasiyah*, 174–76.

Notes

183

91. Great Britain, FO 371/61589; 61685; 61664, Beaumont to Hugh Stonehewer Bird, 1947.

92. Ibid.The three NDP members who won in the election were Mohammad Hadid, Hussain Jamil, and Khadduri Khadduri. *See* Fahdil Hussain, *al-Watani al-dimoqrati*, 230.

93. Humaydi, *Tatwwurat siyasiyah*, 510–18.

94. For more details on al-Wathba and the role of the communists, *see* Batatu, *The Old Social Classes*, 546–66.

95. Saleh Jabr and Nuri al-Sa'id, who pushed the agreement through, continued to support it against rising opposition and after its renunciation by the new government, headed by al-Sadr: "The recent receipt of report from Baghdad that Saleh Jabr and Nuri Pasha Said have been organizing opposition to the present Iraqi government and doing propaganda in favor of the recently signed Treaty of Portsmouth, on the ground that Iraq's friendship with Britain must be maintained. . . . Saleh Jabr and Nuri Pasha have turned in the first place to the tribal leaders for support. This is, of course, quite natural since, with few exceptions, the tribal leaders of Iraq are firm adherents of the British connexion." But even the British came to realize that their strategy to depend on the old guard was no longer enough to sustain the existing regime: "it would be a grave mistake on their part to ignore the younger educated classes of towns, particularly the capital." Great Britain, FO 371/68447/62947, M. T. Walker, February 26, 1948.

96. The NDP and al-Istiqlal were asked to join al-Sadr's government, the NDP refused while the Istiqlal relented. *See* Hussain, *al-Watani al-dimoqrati*, 229–30.

97. *The Tribune*, April 14, 1948. In April, the textile workers went on strike demanding higher wages and better social benefits. The second-largest strike was on April 17, organized by the railway workers demanding flour and higher wages and their union back. The strike spread across the city to include printing press, bakery, city sanitation workers. Soon after, the oil workers joined the strike. "Musahamah fi-kitabit tarikh al-harakah al-naqqabiyah," *al-Thaqafah al-jadidah* 41 (December, 1972), 57–67.

98. On government interference in the elections see, British Foreign Office, FO 371/58447; 68449; 68451; 68452, 1948; also Humaydi, *Tatawwurat siyasiyah*, 450–53.

99. Great Britain, FO 371/ 75130, 85127, 1949.

100. Prison sentences of suspected communists and communists ranged from 5 to 15 years in hard labor.

101. *Al-Ahali*, for example, was shut down and the NDP leader, al-Chadirchi was put on trial for criticizing government policies in the opening article. For the trial of Chadirchi, see Hussain, *al-Watani al-dimoqrati*, 248–51.

102. As explained by the residing British Ambassador, Troutbeck, "Stated in its simplest terms the rivalry between Nuri and Saleh is of course the struggle between those in power who want to stay there and those out of power who want to replace them. Hence the identity of the feeling between the supporters of both sides which is increased by the

religious partisanship, the rivalry between Sunni and Shi³a, with which the struggle for power has become identified." Saleh Jabr was the first Shi³ah to become prime minister.

103. The opposition objected to two articles:

1. "The article providing for penalties of imprisonment up to two years and/or a fine up to ID 500 for anyone making defamatory statements on the conduct of the elections once these have been completed . . ."; and

2. "the substitution of the municipal Council for the mukhtar and notables as the body which chooses the committee of inspection whose task is to supervise the elections in each district."

Great Britain FO 371/8734/63127, Report by Troutbeck, July 3, 1952. The opposition, including Jabr, were strongly in favor of free and direct election. *See* memo of the Istiqlal, NDP, and Jabr's in al-Hasani, *Tarikh al-wizarat al-ᶜiraqiyah*, v. 8, 321–37.

104. Despite their bitter struggle, "there was no essential difference of attitude or policy between "Jabr and Sa³id. Both their parties "derived their strength from the tribes," Gt. Britain FO 371/98734/63127, Sir Troutbeck, July 3, 1952.

105. 1. The Iraq Spinning and Weaving Co. (a British managed company with Abhdul Ilah as its largest stockholder) went on strike against "overtime without pay" and "arbitrary firing";

2. the cigarette workers of Abbud Cigarette Co. over wages;

3. the butchers of Najaf and Kufah over the legalization of their union;

4. the Iraqi workers in the military base of al-Habaniyah over wages; and

5. the Basra port workers over wages and working conditions.

See FO 371/ 98734; 98759; 98784, 1952; and Chadirchi, *Mudhakarat*, 625.

106. The NDP, Partisans for Peace (ICP front organization), al-Jabha al-Sha³biyah (organized by dissident politicians) and pan-Arab Istiqlal party.

107. Hussain, *Tarikh al-hizb al-watani*, 318.

108. With the exception of Mosul, most of the other major towns joined in the uprising. As summarized by Chadirchi, the uprising was characterized by:

1. a unified opposition;

2. a popular uprising not confined to students and workers;

3. for the first time, people voiced their hostility against the monarchy and called for its fall;

4. the regime called in the army to protect it. Chadirchi, *Mudhakarat*, 571–72.

109. In Baghdad alone, 18 were killed and 80 wounded. For more details on the uprising, *see* Batatu, *The Old Social classes*, 669.

110. Khairi, *al-Mas³alah al-fallahiyah*, 166–67.

111. Ibid.

112. Chadirchi, *Mudhakarat*, 652.

113. "Her Majesty's government should express publicly their concern to see reform and development advancing more quickly in Iraq. I therefore also emphasized the close connection between the stability in Iraq and our defense arrangement . . ."; British Foreign Office, FO 371/104665/ 63127, reported by T. M. Troutbeck to Anthony Eden, March 21, 1953.

114. al-Chadirchi, *Mudhakarat*, 636.

115. Batatu, *The Old Social Classes*, 686–87.

116. Humaydi, *Tatawwurat siyassiyah*, 185.

117. al-Hasani, *Tarikh al-wizarat*, vol.10, 56–61.

118. Batatu, *The Old Social Classes*, 751–56; al-Hasani, *Tarikh al-wizarat*, vol.10, 127–40.

119. Gabbay, *Communism and Agrarian Reform*, 59.

120. Khadduri reports Qasim's liberal views and his close contact with the NDP, while Batatu seems to accept Qasim's communist connections. Khadduri, *Republican Iraq*, 30–31; Batatu, *The Old Social Classes*, 793.

CHAPTER 5

1. Members of the Sovereignty Council and first Cabinet included two NDP members, Muhamad Hadid as the Minister of Finance and Hudayb al-Hajj Hmud as Minister of Agriculture. Two from al-Istiqlal, Siddiq Shanshal, its secretary, as Minister of Guidance, and Muhamad Kubbeh, its president, as a member of the Sovereignty Council. Fu³ad al-Rikabi, the secretary of al-Ba³th, was given the Ministry of Development. Staff Colonel ᶜAbdel Salam ᶜArif, a well-known Nasserite became the Deputy Prime Minister and Minister of Interior, while Staff Brigadier Naji Talib, also a Nasserite, was given the Ministry of Social Affairs. It is important to note that al-Istiqlal party was pan-Arabist in sentiment. Batatu, *The Old Social Classes*, 812–13.

2. Michel ᶜAflaq, *Choice of Texts from the Ba³th Party Founder's Thought* (Italy, 1977), 13.

3. On the occasion of the first year celebration of the unity between Egypt and Syria, al-Chadirchi gave a speech that appeared in *Ittihad al-Sha³b*, February 17, 1959. He

pointed out that, "every revolution needs a period of regroupment of its forces to secure national stability and build the necessary democratic institutions. . . . [even though] we still hold the belief that the Arabs constitute 'umma wahidah,' they live in 'several separate provinces' and these provinces will inevitably unite in a federation (Ittihad) based on democratic provisions. . . ."

4. Of the total capital of 53.4 million Iraqi dinars, 23.4 million belonged to small firms which employed less than 10 workers. *See* chapter 3.

5. Hashim Jawad et al, *Taqyyim al-nimow al-iqtisadi fi-l-ʾiraq* (Baghdad, 1962), vol. I, 202. Hashim Jawad also served as the Ambassador of the national revolutionary state to the UN in 1958 and as the Minister of Foreign Affairs in 1959.

6. In Iraq, textiles and cement accounted for 25 percent of gross output of all manufacturing industry. Khair al-Din Hasib, *National Income of Iraq 1953–1961* (Beirut,1963), 99.

7. Khalid Ikram, *Economic Management in a Period of Transition* (Baltimore, 1980), 258–60.

8. Ibid., 36, 225. The annual growth of manufacturing in Egypt, according to this source, was close to 8 percent between 1955–1960. Its productivity growth was slightly higher than 3 percent between 1945–1954, and 2.9 between 1954–1962.

9. Talʾat al-Shaibani, "Dirasa fi-Iqtisadiyat al-Qutn al-Iraqi," *Federation of Industry Yearbook 1956–1957* (Baghdad: Ittihad al-sinaʾat), 30–68. Acreage in dunums put under cotton cultivation in the three countries:

Year	Iraq	Syria	Egypt
1947	34,289	77,340	2,106,978
1949	42,398	101,181	2,842,567
1951	45,109	868,000	3,050,380
1955	229,750	971,888	3,050,380
1956	232,727	1,088,964	2,776,833

For a comparison on the productivity of land for both staples and cotton among these countries, *see* Hashim Jawad, *Taqyim al-numow*, vol. 2, 16, which shows that Iraq had the lowest productivity level.

10. "No one can deny, for example, that before the merger, the Egyptian national bourgeoisie was stronger and more developed than the Syrian one. . . . In contrast to Syrian capitalism which is a recent and a more vigorous capital—a capital that is moving rapidly towards its final break from western capitalism—Egyptian capitalism was and still is closely integrated and therefore more dependent on western imperialism, especially American capitalism. . . . It was inevitable then that a merger between these two countries would end in constricting Syrian capitalist interests and would bring it back to the folds of western capitalism . . ." Aziz al-Hajj, "Mawqif thabit min qadiyat al-wihda al-arabiya," *Ittihad al-Shaʾb*, January 30, 1959. cf. Munir Saʾid, "Muqarana bayn al-Sinaʾa al-Suriyia wal-Iraqiyia," *Majalit al-sinaʾi* 1 (January, 1962), 15–42.

11. Hajj, "Mawqif thabit min qadiyat al-wihada al-arabiya," *Ittihad al-sha³b*, January 30, 1959.

12. *Ittihad al-sha³b*, December 14, 1959.

13. Elias Murqus, *al-Marxsiyah wa-l-masa³alah al-qawmiyah*, 182–83.

14. In February of 1963, Qasim was overthrown by another military coup, led and organized by the Ba³thists.

15. ͨArif flew to Damascus, on his own accord, to meet with Nasser on July 18, 1958. Batatu, *Social Classes*, 817.

16. The recruitment centers were closed down because they were run locally and, as a result, many of them came under the influence of the communists.

17. Three weeks after opening, 11,000 members registered in these centers. Batatu, *The Old Social Classes*, 848–49.

18. Hilal Naji, *al-Iqtisad al-³iraq fi-³amayn*, (Cairo, 1961), 11–12. Incidents of violent confrontations between the pan-Arab nationalists and the ICP militia in al-³azmaiyah district of Baghdad, in the upper Euphrates, Mosul, Najaf, and Karbala were reported by both parties. *See* also *Ittihad al-sha³b*, April 6, 1959. The most comprehensive narrative of the struggle between the Ba³th and the communists is recorded by Hanna Batatu, *The Social Classes*.

19. Naji, *al-iqtisad*, 12. In the election for the Lawyers Guild held in August 1958, the NDP, the ICP, and independents ran on the same ticket, thus assuring the isolation and the loss of the Arab nationalists. Fa³iq al-Samarra³i, a well-known Arab nationalist, lost the presidency to a communist. The remaining Arab nationalists were too small and insignificant a faction to participate in the meetings and the events of the Guild.

20. *Ittihad al-Sha³b*, April 4, 1959.

21. Batatu, *Social Classes*, 844–45.

22. Some accused members of the board were put on trial; others, such as Sa³dun Hamadi, the editor-in-chief, managed to escape. Naji, *Hukm Qasim*, 13.

23. On February 7, 1959, the Arab nationalists were removed from their governmental posts. Mohammad Kubbah and Siddiq Shanshal from the Istiqlal Party resigned. So did Staff Brigadier Naji Talib, the Minister of Social Affairs, and Dr. Abd-ul-Jabbar al-Jomard, the Minister of Foreign Affairs. Shaikh Ali Baba and Rikabi were removed from their respective positions. *Ittihad al-Sha³b*, February 8, 1959.

24. Quoted from a Lebanese newspaper, *al-Sahifah*, in Dann's, *Iraq*, 141.

25. The Kurdish Nationalist Party, which was founded in 1946, called for some form of a democratic Kurdish state, of Khaniqin, the province of Mosul, Arbil, Kirkuk and Sulymaniya, that would be federally linked to Iraq. The KDP had close connections to the ICP because of the latter's support of the inalienable rights of the Kurds within the framework of the Iraqi state.

188   THE MAKING OF IRAQ 1900–1963

26. Nasser was openly attacking the Arab communist parties, labeling them "agents of a foreign power," denouncing, in particular, the Iraqi communists "for attempting to pry Syria loose from the UAR and incorporate it in a 'communist Fertile Crescent.'" Batatu, *Social Classes*, 863. Also, the Ba'th by now was claiming that 'Abdul Karim Qasim was already under the influence of the communists, warning that the Communists had exploited the national revolution and made it deviate from its right path. It also accused them of staging terrorist attacks against the Arab nationalists and carrying out collective killings. The intention of the ICP in eliminating the Arab nationalists, according to them, was to destabilize the revolution and ultimately take it over. See the secret documents and other publications of the Ba'th on the 1959 crisis in Iraq in *Nidal al-Ba'th: watha'iq hizb al-Ba'th al-'arabi al-ishtiraki* (Beirut, 1964) vol. 4, 72–87.

27. In traditional Orientalist interpretation, such as the works of Majid Khadduri and Uriel Dann, social conflicts are reduced to irrational acts of violence rooted in a primordial culture, as the following quotation from Dann illustrates: "violence is part of the political scene in Iraq. It is an undercurrent which pervades the vast substrata of the people outside the sphere of power politics. Hundreds of souls can be easily mobilized on the flimsiest pretext. They constitute a permanently restive element ready to break into riots which more than once in recent years resulted in butchery." Uriel Dann, *Iraq Under Qassem: A Political History* (New York, 1969), 6; also *see* Khadduri, *Republican Iraq: A Study in Iraqi Politics since the Revolution of 1958* (Oxford, 1969).

28. Batatu, *Social Classes*, 866.

29. Ibid., 44. The Kashmulahs' as sheep traders were closely tied to the sheep-herding tribes in the region.

30. Warriner, *Land Reform*, 138; Batatu, *Social Classes*, 869–71.

31. For details, see Batatu, *Social Classes*, 882–89; and *Ittihad al-sha'b*, April 8, 9, 10, 12, 13, 16, 1959.

32. Dann, *Iraq*, 217. According to Dann, while the communists held two-thirds of the seats, the other one third of the General Federation of Peasant Societies seats were held by the NDP and their followers.

33. *Ittihad al-Sha'b*, April 16, 1959. The Congress for the Federation of Peasant Societies was held in Baghdad.

34. On the entrenchment of the communists at the popular level, *see* Batatu, *Social Classes*, especially chapter 45, "The Flow," 891–921.

35. The new members added to the cabinet were by and large social democratic elements. Hashim Jawad, an NDP sympathizer was given the Ministry of Foreign Affairs; Hasan al-Talabani, an ex-NDP and present KDP member became the minister of communication and public works; Tala'at al-Shaibani (NDP member), chosen for the ministry of development; Hussain Jamil (leading NDP) for ministry of Guidance, and Fu'ad 'Arif, a Kurd and KDP sympathizer became the minister without portfolio. *Ittihad al-sha'b*, February 8, 1959; and Dann, *Iraq Under Qussem*, 152.

36. Gabbay, *Communism and Agrarian Reform*, 127, Dann, *Iraq Under Qussem*.

37. The government would pay for confiscated lands the sum equivalent to the price of similar land, plus the estimated value of immovable property and trees. Compensations were to be paid in 3 percent government bonds, redeemable within a period of no more than 20 years. Gabbay, *Communism and Agrarian Reform*, 109.

38. Dan, *Iraq Under Qassem*, 63.

39. Further concessions were made to this group, such as the reinstatement of Settlement law 61 in 1961, which recognized the right to ownership of *lazma* lands already held by the clergy. Saʾdown Hamadi, *Nahwah islah ziraʾi ishtiraki* (Beirut: Dar al-Taliʾah, 1970), 26.

40. Gabbay, *Communism and Agrarian Reform*, 113.

41. Article 14 of the Law required the new owner to pay the value equivalent to the compensation paid for the said land as decided by the *lajnat al-taqdir* (Estimation Committee). Payments were to be paid over a period of 20 years. Abdul Salih ʿAlwan, *Dirasat fil-islah al-ziraʾi* (Baghdad, 1961), 237.

42. Of the 4 million poor peasants, for example, an estimated 1,425,000 were landless and the rest owned less than 4 dunums a family. *See* Talaʾat al-Shaibani, *Waqiʾ mulkiyat al-ziraʾiya fi-l-ʿiraq* (Baghdad, 1958), 35.

43. *Ittihad al-shaʾb*, July 28, 1958.

44. "At one point, ʿAmer ʿAbdallah, member of the Politburo, ʿAbdul Qadir Ismaʾil, the editor of Ittihad al-Shaʾb, and other leading Communists had signified to him [Qasim] their eagerness to take four ministerial portfolios, including the interior." Batatu, *Social Classes*, 899.

45. It is important to point out that in this period, the Communist Party was torn between two factions: those who opposed confrontation with the national government and wanted to maintain the older position of supporting Qasim as a national revolutionary figure and the national government as progressive; and those who opposed this conciliatory line and pushed towards a confrontation with the regime which was dismantling the popular movement. Mahmoud, *Inshiqaq al-hizb*, 15.

46. "Concessions should not be paid to those who raped state and peasant lands." *See* Khairi, *al-Hizb al-shuyiʾi*, 50; 120–21.

47. *Ittihad al-shaʾb*, April 15, 1959.

48. *Ittihad al-shaʾb*, May 18, 1959.

49. The Federation defined itself within the framework of the nationalist project, as a "professional peasant organization with the aims of safeguarding the Iraqi Republic and its democratic regime, raising the social and economic conditions of the peasantry and protecting their interests." The most important provision was section 7 which designated the General Federation the power to authorize the formation of peasant societies. Gabbay, *Communism and Agrarian Reform*, 129.

50. Ibid., 131.

51. A delegation sponsored by the NDP was sent to Baghdad to petition against the communists who were "allegedly using their power to prevent the licensing of non-communists societies." Violence between the delegation and the communists erupted in front of the Defense Ministry. cf. *al-Ahali*, June 8, 12, 1959. Also *al-Ahali*, August 4, 1959 which reported that the communist Kazim Farhud prevented the NDP delegation from entering the Federation building in Baghdad.

52. *al-Ahali*, June 15, 1959.

53. *Ittihad al-sha'b*, June 15, 17, 18, 1959.

54. Gabbay, *Communism and Agrarian Reform*, 131. Gabbay gives a conspiratorial analysis of the communists (as infiltrators etc.) and totally ignores their popular appeal among the peasantry, which he himself records in his own account.

55. Batatu, *The Old Social Classes*, 812. Appointed in 1959, he was relieved of his post in February 1960.

56. In any event, the policy of land leasing did not hasten the pace. Unlike the confiscation process, which was carried out swiftly, distribution continued to be "disappointingly" slow. From 1958 until the end of 1960, only 3 percent of the expropriated land was distributed. *See* ʿAlwan, *Dirasat fil-islah*, 227–29; Gabbay, *Communism and Agrarian Reform*, 115. The explanation usually given for the delays, technical and bureaucratic inefficiency, is only partially true. The slow process of distribution was also due to conflicting interests and policies within the governing bureaucracy, especially in regards to the long-term objective of the reform; for example, whether it should be founded on a peasant economy of petty production or collective farming. In his trial in the aftermath of the 1963 nationalist coup, Kubbeh attributed the delays in distribution during his tenure to deliberate procrastination of his ministry in order to keep the lands out of the hands of the rich landowners, since the existing land reform favored those who had land or access to capital over those who were poor and landless. Ibrahim Kubbeh, *Difaʿ Ibrahim Kubbeh amam mahkamit al-thawrah* (Beirut, 1969), 90. During his tenure, however, Ibrahim Kubbeh was accused by *al-Ahali* of delaying distribution of land for ideological reasons: as a Marxist, he allegedly favored state or collective farming. *See al-Ahali*, September 12, 1959. Also Zaki Khairi who denied these accusations held against the communists in *al-Hizb al-shuyuʿi*, 66.

57. Ibid.; *Ittihad al-Sh'ab*, April 28, 29, May 7, 10, 1959.

58. *Ittihad al-sha'b*, April 16, 18, 22, 1959.

59. *Itihad al-sha'b*, April 28, 1959.

60. Batatu, *Social Classes*, 900. The communists, however, claimed that on "May Day, a million citizens like a great river flooded al-Rashid Street," cf. *Ittihad al-sha'b*, May 5, 1959. The principal slogans raised in this march were "The ICP Participation in Government Is A National Demand" and the "ICP Representation in Government Will Consolidate Our National Democratic Republic."

61. The communists' public bid for power terrified both the Arab and Western world. The radio and the press in the UAR took this opportunity to attack Qasim as the "divider of Iraq" and an agent of the communists. Two radio stations, "Voice of Iraq" and "Radio of the Free Iraqi Republic," were set up in Syria to campaign against the communists. Dann, *Iraq under Qassem*, 188–89. *The New York Times* (April 29, 1959) reported on the director of the CIA, Allen Dulles, describing conditions in Iraq as "the most dangerous in the world today." The British at the same time proclaimed that they were selling arms to Iraq to boost the national government and enable Qasim to maintain his independence. Batatu, *Social Classes*, 899.

62. *Ittihad al-sha⁾b*, May 20, 1959, *see* also *al-Waqai⁾ al-ʿiraqiyah*, May 20, 1959.

63. Before the call for suspension of political parties, Qasim began his official public denunciation of political "partisanship" and "parties" (meaning the ICP) for their divisive politics which proved to be "of no benefit to the country at this time," suggesting in this "transitional period" the suspension of all political parties. Government of Iraq, *The Principles of the July 14 Revolution in the Speeches of Its Leader Abdul Karim Qasim*, 80.

64. This decision, contended the opposing faction within the NDP, was taken by Muhammad Hadid without consultation with other leading figures including the president, Chadirchi. In an interview with the author, Hussain Jamil claimed that Hadid was the real instigator of this whole political maneuver, asserting that Hadid was the political figure with the most influence on Qasim in this period.

65. *Ittihad al-sha⁾b*, May 23, 1959. Aziz al-Hajj, an ex-member of the Central Committee, related the retreat to pressures put on the party by Moscow. Aziz al-Hajj, *ma⁾ al-⁾awam: safahaat min tarikh al-harakah al-shuyu⁾iyah fi-l-⁾Iraq bayn 1958–1969* (Beirut, 1981), 58. Batatu's account concurs with ʿAziz al-Hajj's: "According to ʿAndan Jilmiran, the then member of the Mosul Local Committee, the Russians sent at this point to Bagdad George Tellu, a member of the Iraqi Politburo, who had been undergoing medical treatment in Moscow, with an urgent request to the Irai party to avoid provoking Qasim, and withdraw its bid to participate in the government. The Russians apparently had no wish to cut all their bridges with Nasir, or jeopardize their new policy of "peaceful coexistence," or wreck the chances of a visit to Washington which Khruschev contemplated. . . . " Batatu, *Social Classes*, 903.

66. The celebration of the first anniversary of the revolution ended in a bloody confrontation between the Turcomans and the Kurds resulting in the death of 79 people, mostly Turcomans. The evidence, while strongly suggesting the involvement of Kurdish communists belonging to the People's Resistance and Youth groups in the bloodshed, fails to implicate the leadership of the party. For a detailed description and analysis of the events, the best source available is Batatu, *Social Classes*, 921–46. Qasim, if not explicitly, then implicitly held the ICP responsible for the massacre ("can this be the acts of organizations which allege to be democratic?") and denounced the perpetrators as "without honor of conscience" and "baser than fascists." At the same time, the government-run television in Baghdad broadcast horrifying pictures of the massacre as a

spectacle of communist doing. Sluglett and Sluglett, *Iraq Since 1958: From Revolution to Dictatorship* (London: Routledge and Kegan Paul, 1987), 71.

67. *Al-Ahali*, August 5, 1959. The article reported that the "spirit of the workers in the trade unions was against raising productivity levels and for raising wages . . . " On August 9, 1959, *al-Ahali* called for the resignation of the trade union leadership and for free new elections. Also the response of *Ittihad al-sha⁾b* to the accusations in the issues of May 25 and June 2, 1959.

68. *Ittihad al-sha⁾b*, June 22, 1959 reports of attacks against their Youth Organizations and Trade Unions. Other issues in June, July, and August reported violent incidents against communist centers in Diwaniyahh, Samawah, Baghdad, Hindiyah, and others. *See* also issues of June 19 and 25, and those of July 10, 11, 12, and 13.

69. *Ittihad al-sha⁾b*, August–September issues of 1959.

70. *Ittihad al-sha⁾b*, September 3, 1959.

71. Batatu, The *Old Social Classes*, 923.

72. Ibid., 936.

73. Ibid., 938. Once the state recognized Sayigh's party as the official communist party, the old ICP changed its name to Ittihad al-Sha⁾b, rewrote its program and dropped its revolutionary line stating that the party "intends to help create the proper conditions for the eventual development towards socialism . . . the party intends to follow this line through democratic and peaceful means." *See, Ittihad al-sha⁾b*, February 3, 1959.

74. Hamadi, *Nahwa islah zira⁾i*, 25–28.

75. Ibid.; Khairi, "Masa⁾il fi-l-islah al-zira⁾i," in *al-Hizb al-shuyu⁾i wal-masa⁾lah al-zira⁾iyah*, 133; also *Ittihad al-sha⁾b*, April 8, 1959.

76. As reported by *Ittihad al-sha⁾b*, June 9, 1959, over 350,000 peasants were organized in societies. Ibrahim Kubbeh, *Difa⁾* (98–99) reports that in Samawah, peasant complaints about the landlords cutting off water supplies were ignored by the courts.

77. *Ittihad al-sha⁾b*, December 14, 1959. As recorded by Mahmoud in, *Inshiqaq al-Hizb*, the article was written by ⁽Amer ⁽Abdallah, the head of the right-wing coalition within the party. The title of the article was, "Hawl al-wad⁾ al-siyasi fil- ⁽Iraq" ("Regarding the Political Situation in Iraq"). It is during this period that the ultra-leftist elements within the party were purged. cf., 14–20.

78. Khairi, "Masa⁾il fi-l Islah al-Zira⁾i," *Ittihad al-Sha⁾b*, March 1, 1960. The articles that appeared in *Ittihad al-sha⁾b* in February and March were later reproduced under *al-Hizb al-shuyu⁾i wa-l-masa⁾alah al-falahiyah*.

79. *Ittihad al-sha⁾b*, March 3, 1960.

80. The retraction of the CP and its revival of the "United Front" with the "progressive" nationalist forces created a schism within the ranks of the Communist Party leading to a split in its ranks in the-mid 1960s. In this period, however, three of the leaders held responsible for the ultra-leftism of party were relieved of their duties. According to

Aziz al-Hajj, the right wing under the influence of Moscow, was victorious in this period. Aziz Al-Hajj, *Ma'a al-'awam*, 396.

81. *Ittihad al-sha'b*, August 16, 1960.

82. Naziha al-Dulaimi, "a card-carrying Communist" was appointed as the Minister of Municipalities on July 14, 1959 to "mollify the Communists" after dropping their bid for power, and was dismissed from her ministerial duties in November 1960. Batatu, *Social Classes*, 910; 944.

83. Since the formation of the Iraqi nation, the Iraqi Kurds were in perpetual revolt, calling for their right to autonomy and independence. From 1927 on, the Kurds were led by the Barazani tribe, headed by Mulla Mustafa al-Barazani. Kurdish revolts, were brutally crushed by the Iraqi army in 1930 and in 1946; the leaders of the revolt were driven into Iranian Kurdistan, and Barazani into exile in the Soviet Union.

84. After submitting its program, the Ministry of Interior insisted that the KDP drop "self government" in section six of the party platform which declared one of its objectives " to broaden the national rights of the Kurdish people on the basis of self-government within the unity of Iraq;" and also "the right to self-determination" in section twenty three of the program which originally stated that "the struggle of the Kurdish people in the various parts of Kurdistan for their liberation from the imperialist and reactionary yoke, and for their right to self-determination." The national government, in insisting on the removal of these terms and others from the KDP program, had the intention of restricting Kurdish national claims to cultural rights.

85. The Kurdish weekly, *Deh Nagi Kurd*, was suspended for 10 months and its editor fined for criticizing the authorities' handling of the Kirkuk riots. In November 1960, Ibrahim Ahmed, a KDP leader and publisher of the *Kha-bat*, was put on trial for "stirring up national dissension and instigating fanaticism." By April 1961, all publications of the KDP were suspended. *See* Dann, *Iraq*, 332–33.

86. According to Jawad, the KDP condemned the rebellion of the landowners and initially supported the measures taken against them. *See* Sa'ad Jawad, *Iraq and the Kurdish Question: 1958–1970* (London, 1981).

87. Even though in 1961, 'Amir 'Abdallah was discharged from the secretariat and Hussein al-Radi took over, the change in the leadership did not result in any changes in the political and strategic policies of the party. Cf. Mahmoud, *Inshiqaq al-Hizb*.

88. Jalal, *Role of Government*, 54.

89. Durrah, *al-Tatawwur al-sina'i*, 120. Also *see* chapter 3.

90. Batatu, *The Old Social Classes*, 276–82.

91. The first economic plan (1959–1962) drawn by the revolutionary government gave the highest allocation to public buildings and housing (48.7 percent), which was largely spent on the construction of Madinat al-thawra (the town of the revolution), a low-income housing project for the sarrifa dwellers of Baghdad and on other low housing projects for government employees. Industry was allocated only 9.8 percent (I.D.38.7

million) of the total budget, this did not include the funds required for the industrial projects under the Iraqi-Soviet agreement of 1959. The second plan (1961–1965) gave the industrial sector the highest allocation (29.9 percent). The objectives of these plans, the Ministry of Guidance maintained, were "to change radically the direction of economic planning of the previous regime . . . in a manner which can serve the interests of the Iraqi people" by using "oil revenues that have been previously wasted on matters of no interest to Iraq." Farhang, *The Role of Government in the Industrialization of Iraq*, 38–39.

92. Ibid., 103–5.

93. *al-Ahali*, February, 11 1960.

94. Production increased from 9,000 tons between 1958–1959 to 20,000 tons in the following year. Durrah, *al-Tatawwur al-sina'i*, 145; 122.

95. Ibid., 132.

96. Ibid., 133.

97. Ibid., 175.

98. Government of Iraq, *Statistical Report on the Active Companies in Iraq 1919–1969* (Baghdad: Government Press, 1969), 56.

99. Ibrahim Kubbeh, *Difa'*, 57–64.

100. Durrah, *al-Tatawwur al-sina'i*, 156

101. Naji, *al-Iqtisad al-'iraqi*, 212–17.

102. The amount of 750,000 Iraqi dinars for the importation of men's woolen cloth and the amount of 400,000 for women. Ittihad al-Sina'at, *Yearbook 1961–1962*, 55–56.

103. *Al-Ahali*, May 1, 3, 10, 1960 published the details of the conflict between the two factions over participation in government, which took place on February 12, 1959. Hadid wanted to remain in government while the opposition demanded resignation of all members of the NDP and called for the re-establishment of a National Front.

104. Batatu, *The Social Classes*, 956.

105. Interviews conducted with Muhamad Hadid, Hussain Jamil, and the historian Fadhil Hussain, April and March of 1983.

106. *al-Bayan*, September 14, 1961. The exception was Arak al-Zakam, sirkal who seemed to have acquired new agricultural wealth and had since 1958 played an important role as the NDP's leading member and later the president in the General Federation of Peasant Societies.

107. The second split was between al-Chadirchi and Hussain Jamil over Chadirchi's criticisms of the government's harassment of the communists involved in the Mosul revolt. See *al-Ahali*, March 12, 1961.

108. Majid ʿAbdul-Rida, *al-Qadiyah al-kurdiyah fil-ʾiraq* (Baghdad,1974), 110–15. After two years of fighting, the Iraqi army was still unable to crush the rebellion. Just to the contrary, the Kurdish rebels were able to inflict heavy losses on the Iraqi army. Besides the heavy military losses, the cost of the war was a drain on the Iraqi economy, another factor which helped to alienate the government from the Iraqi people.

109. *Al-Bayan*, July 2, 1962. Muhamad Hadid announced the suspension of the party due to the absence of political freedom, "Our party is unable to play a real political role any more. . . . the time has come for our party to suspend its political activities . . . until a solution to the political problem is found."

110. Waldemar Gallman, the American ambassador at the time, reported that in March 1958, Nuri al-Saʾid was pushing the United States. and Britain to pressure Kuwait into joining the Iraq-Jordan federation launched on February 12, 1958. The Federation was founded to offset the Egyptian-Syrian merger of February 1 and undermine mounting popular pressure in Jordan to join the United Arab Republic of Syria-Egypt-Yemen. For more details, *see* Waldemar Gallman, *Iraq Under General Nuri: My Recollection of Nuri al-Said, 1945–1958* (Baltimore, 1964), 141–59.

111. According to ʿAbdul Razzaq al-Hasani, King Ghazi was planning to occupy Kuwait in 1939 and was discouraged from acting out his plans by Naji Shawkat, the vice prime minister at the time, because it would anger the British, the "protectors" of Kuwait. Hasani, *Tarikh al-wizarat* (Beirut: Dar al-Kutub Press, 1974) vol. 5, 62.

112. Gallman, *Iraq Under General Nuri*, 148.

113. Iraq's offers to even lease the two islands from Kuwait were in vain. The border dispute and access to deep waterway continued to plague relations between Iraq and Kuwait throughout the 1970s and 1980s. It was a major contributing factor to the Gulf War of 1991.

114. The best informed work on the Baʾth regime and the opposition is, is Sluglett & Sluglett, *Iraq Since 1958: From Revolution to Dictatorship* (London: I. B. Tauris, 1987).

EPILOGUE

1. Different from the book, which centers around the formation of capital and classes, the epilogue considers the transformative character of modern power by using the Foucauldian formulation of the insertive and constitutive nature of modern power.

2. A strong argument for why Marx's critique of capitalism remains indispensable to a critical understanding of modernity in the colonized world, despite the relevance of French post-structural theories, is presented by another member of the *Subaltern Studies* collective, Dipesh Chakrabarty. *See* "Marx after Marxism: Subaltern Histories and the Question of Difference," *Polygraphy*, July 1993; and "The Death of History? Historical Consciousness and the Culture of Late Capitalism" in *Public Culture*, Spring 1992.

196   THE MAKING OF IRAQ 1900–1963

3. Chatterjee, *The Nation and its Fragments*, 6.

4. Ibid., 203.

5. Besides Chatterjee's, the other works that shed light on the nature of colonial/ post-colonial experience are Talal Asad, *Geneologies of Religion* (John Hopkins University Press, 1993); Gyan Prakash, "Writing Post-Orientalist Histories of the Third World" *Comparative Studies in History and Society*, April 1990; Ann Laura Stoler, "Rethinking Colonial Categories" in *Colonialism and Culture*, Nicholas Dirks, ed. (University of Michigan Press, 1992).

6. Ireland, *Iraq: A Study*, 148.

7. Ibid., *Iraq: A Study*, 82–83. The Iraq Code, as Ireland records (83), in "its provisions and in manner of its application seems to have made little distinction between India and Iraq. Section 8 explicitly stated the code of criminal procedure and other enactments for administration of criminal justice in British India shall have effect as if the occupied territories were a district in the Presidency of Bombay." The Code was later revised in response to the resistance against it being "Indian."

8. Alongside with the civil-criminal system of justice, the British continued to maintain the Shar'ia Muslim religious courts, which dealt with personal matters, as well as the Jewish and Christian spiritual courts for the Jewish and Christian communties.

9. Ireland, *Iraq: A Study*, 85.

10. Ibid., 89–90.

11. Ibid., 87–88.

12. For more information on the development of the air force as a disciplinary measure, *see* David Omissi, *Air Power and Colonial Control* (Manchester: St. Martins, 1990).

GLOSSARY

1. *"Tribal" hierarchy*
shayk-al-mashayikh	paramount chief
emir al-imara	prince or chief
Shaykh	chief
asha'ir	clans
fakhd/bayt	individual tribal household

2. *"Estates," classes, and other social categories*
fallahin/fallah	peasants/peasant
hushiya	armed retainer of chiefs
mullak	landowners/renters
sirkal/sirkal	"agent"; supervisor of cultivation; sub-lessee'
ra'iya	Ottoman subjects/common people
tujjar	merchants

3. *Taxation*
iltizam	tax-farming
multazim	tax-farmer
muhassil	salaried tax official
shartnama	annual land leased by an annual terminal agreement

4. *Ottoman administrative terms*
qa'immaqam	sub-governor of province
wali	Ottoman governor of a province
pasha	Ottoman title
wilaya	province

5. *Land holdings, access, and rights*

Dira	tribal domain
muqataʾat/muqataʾa	estates/estate
qitaʾh	smaller tract of land
saniya	royal domain
sahm/khait	small plots of land
lazma	customary prescriptive claim of the tribe to the land
miri/miri-sirf	state domain land
miri-lazma	state domain granted out on assignable tenure
mulk	private property
mulkiyah	land rent
naqshah/kasarah	land tenure with strong customary rights (rice cultivation)
taʾabah/mugharasah	land tenure with strong customary rights (date cultivation)
talʾiyah	non-taxable land
taswiyah	land settlement
waqf	religiously endowed land

BIBLIOGRAPHY

ARABIC

ᶜAbdul Jabir, Talib, 1960. *Rubᵓ qarn fi tarikh al-harakah al-ᵓumalliyah.* Baghdad: Matbaᵓit al-Shaᵓb.

ᶜAbdul Raᵓuf, Ismaᵓil, 1955. "Tatawwur sinaᵓat al-halj wa-atharuha fi-l-tijarah al-qutniyah." *Majalit al-ziraᵓa al-ᶜiraqiya* 10 (May–July): 314–18.

Abuel-Haj, Ribhi, 1957. "The Oil Industry: A Strategic Factor in the Economic Development of Iraq." New York: Columbia University, Ph.D. thesis.

ᶜAbul-Rida, Majid, 1974. *al-Qadiyah al-kurdiyah fil-ᶜiraq.* Baghdad: al-Tariq al-Jadid Press.

ᶜAflaq, Michel, 1959. *Fi sabil al-baᵓth.* Beirut: Manshurat al-talᵓiah.

———, 1959. *Choice of Texts from the Baᵓth Party Founder's Thought.* Italy: Cooperative Lavarators, 1977.

al-ᵓAlawan, ᶜAbdul Sahib, 1961. *Dirasat fil-islah al-ziraᵓi.* Baghdad: al-Tijariya Press.

———, 1961. "al-Taqadum al-fanni wa-l-takniki fi-ziraᵓat al-ᶜiraq." *al-Iqtisadi* 1 (July).

al-ᵓAtiyah, Wadi, 1954. *Tarikh al-Diwaniyah: qadiman wa-hadithan.* Najaf: Rafaᶜil al-Batti.

al-ᵓAzzawi, Abbas, 1956. *ᶜAshaᵓir al-Iraq.* 4 vols., Baghdad: al-Tijarah wal-tibaᵓah Press.

———, 1955. *Tarikh al-ᶜIraq bayn ihtilalyn.* Baghdad: al-Tijarah wal-tibaᵓah Press.

al-Bustani, Sulayman, 1908. *ᶜIbrah wa-Dhikrah: al-Dawlah al-Uthmaniyah qabla al-Dustur wa-baᵓdahu.* Cairo: al-Akhbar.

al-Chadirchi, Kamil, 1970. *Mudhakarat Kamil al-Chadirchi wa-tarikh al-hizb al-watani al-dimoqrati.* Beirut: Dar al-taliᵓah.

al-Dalli, Abdul Ghani, 1949. "al-Mashariᵓ al-sinaᵓiyah fi-l-ᵓiraq wa-musahamat al-masraf al-sinaᵓi." *Majalat ghurfit tijarit baghdad* 12 (January–February): 37–45.

al-Durrah, Sabah, 1958. *al-Tatawwur al-sinaᵓi fi-l-ᶜiraq, al-qitaᵓ al-khas.* Baghdad: al-Nujum Press.

200   THE MAKING OF IRAQ 1900–1963

————, 1969. "Hawl al-burjuwaziyah al-sina'iyeh fil-'iraq." *al-Thaqafah al-Jadidah* 2 (May): 193–99.

Fahmi, Ahmad, 1926. *Taqrir hawl al'iraq.* Baghdad, n.p.

al-Faydi, Sulayman, 1952. *Fi ghumrat al-Nidal.* Baghdad: al-Tijarah wal-tiba'ah.

————, 1946. *Usul al-taba'ah wa-ahkamuha fil-Basra.* Basra: Times Press.

al-Fayyad, Abdallah, 1957. *Mushkilat al-aradi fi-liwa-al-Muntafiq.* Baghdad: Matba'it al-adhami.

————, 1963. *al-Thawrah al-'iraqiyah al-kubra.* Baghdad: Matba'it al-irshad.

Fayyad, 'Amer Hussein, 1980. *Judhur al-fikr al-ishtiraki wal-taqadumi fil-'Iraq 1920–1934.* Beirut: Dar ibn rushd.

al-Fir'awn, F. al-Mizhir, 1949. *al-Qada' al-Asha'iri.* Baghdad: al-Najah Press.

————, 1952. *al-Haqa'iq al-nasi'ah fi-l-thawra al-'irqiyyah 1920.* Baghdad: al-Najah Press.

al-Hajj, 'Aziz, 1981. *Ma' al-'awam: safahat min tarikh al-harakah al-shuyu'iyah fi-l-'iraq bayn 1958–1969.* Beirut: al-mataba'i al-'arabiya lil-dirasah wal-nashr.

————, 1959. *Ayna yaqifawn wa-ayna yaqif al-'iraq.* Beirut: Dar al-farabi.

————, 1958. *Thawratuna fil-'iraq wa-qadhiyat al-wihdah.* Beirut: Dar al-farabi.

Hamadi, Sa'dun, 1970. *Nahwah islah zira'i ishtiraki.* Beirut: Dar al-tali'ah.

al-Hanafi, Jalal, 1966. *al-Sina'at wal hiraf al-baghdadiyah.* Baghdad: Dar al-jumhuriyah.

Hasan, Razaq Ibrahim, 1976. *Tarikh al-harakah al-'amilah fil-'iraq.* Beirut: Arab Institute for Research and Publication.

al-Hasani, 'Abd al-Razzaq, 1974. *Tarikh al-wizarat al-Iraqiyyah.* Beirut: Dar al-kutub, vols. 5–6, 7–8, 9–10.

Hasan, Muhammad Salman, 1965. *al-Tatatuwwur al-iqtisadi fil-'iraq: 1864–1956.* Beirut: al-Maktabah al-'asriyah.

al-Haydari, Ibrahim Fasih, 1869. *Kitab 'unwan al-majd fi-ahwal Baghdad wal-Basra wa-Najd.* Baghdad: Dar al-Bisri Press.

Hmaidi, Ja'afar 'Abbas, 1976. al-Tatawurat al-siyasiyah fi-l-'iraq 1941–1953. Najaf: Matba'it al-nu'man.

————, 1955. "al-Zuyut al-nabatiyah bayn himayit al-muntij wa-himayit al-mustahlik." *Majalit al-Tijarah* 18 (July): 17–19.

Hashim, Jawad, et al., 1971. *Taqyim al-numow al-iqtisadi fil-'iraq 1950–1970.* 2 vols. Baghdad: Manshurat wizarit al-takhtit.

Hilal, Naji, 1961. *Iqtisad al-'iraq fi-'amayn.* Cairo: al-sharikah al-'arabiyah li-tiba'ah wal-nashr.

————, 1962. *Adhwaᵓ ᶜala hukm ᶜAbdul Karim Qasim*. Cairo: Dar al-karnak.

al-Hilali, ᶜAbdul Razzaq, 1958. *al-Hijrah min al-rif ila al-madinah*. Baghdad: Matbaᶜit al-najah.

————, 1967. *Qisat al-ardh wal-fallah*. Beirut: Dar al-kashaf.

al-Husri, Satiᵓ, 1948. *Muhadarat fi-nushuᵓ alfikrah al-qawmiyah*. Beirut: Dar al-taliᵓah.

Hussein, Fadhil, 1963. *Tarikh al-Hizb al-watani al-dimoqrati*. Baghdad: al-Shaᶜb.

Ittihad al-Sinaᵓat, 1958. *Yearbook 1957–1958*. Baghdad: al-Rabetah Press.

al-Jadir, Adib, 1955. "Sinaᵓit al-ghazl wa-l-nasij," *Majalit al-ziraᵓah al-ᶜiraqiyah* 10 (May–July): 299–310.

Jamil, Hussein, 1983. *al-Hayat al-niyabiyah fil-ᶜiraq 1925–1946: Mauqif jamaᵓit al-ahali mihah*. Baghdad: Manshurat maktabit al-muthanah.

Jamil, Mudhafar Hussain, 1949. *Siyasit al-ᶜiraq al-kharijiyah*. Cairo: Nahdhah Press.

al-Jawahiri, ᶜImad Ahmed, 1978. *Tarikh mushkilat al-aradi fil-iraq: 1914–1932*. Baghdad: wizarit al-thaqafa wa-l-funun.

al-Khaffaji, ᶜIsam, 1983. *al-Dawlah wal-tatawwur al-raᵓsmali fil-ᶜiraq: 1968–1978*. Cairo: Dar al-mustaqbal al-ᶜarabi.

Khairi, Zaki, 1974. *al-Hizb al-shuyuᵓi wal-masᵓalah al-ziraiᵓyah*. Baghdad: al-Shaᵓb Press.

Khasbak, 1973. *al-Iraq al-shamali*. Baghdad: Matbaᵓit Shafiq.

al-Khayyat, Kamal Muhammad al-Saᶜid, 1970. *al-Tatawwur al-tarikhi li-hiyazit al-aradi*. Baghdad: n.p.

Kittanah, Saᵓid, 1953. "al-Tibgh fi-l-ᶜiraq," *Majallet al-ziraᵓah al-iraqiyah* 8 (July–August): 685–89.

Kubbeh, Muhammad Mahdi, 1962. *Mudhakarati fi samim al-ahdath 1918–1958*. Beirut: Dar al-taliᵓah.

Kubbeh, Ibrahim, 1969. *Difaᵓ Ibrahim Kubbeh amam mahkamit al-thawra*. Beirut: Dar al-Taliᵓah.

Mahmud, Muhammad, 1980. ᶜAhwal al-ᵓashaᵓir al-iraqiyya al-ᵓarabiyya wa alaqatuha bil-hukuma.ᵓ Baghdad, M.A. Thesis.

Mahmud, Najm, 1968. *al-Siraᵓ fil-hizb al shuyuᶜi-ᶜiraqi: qadhayah al-khilaf fil-harakah al-shuyuᶜiyah al-ᶜalamiyah*. Beirut: Dar Ibn Khaldoun.

Min wathaᵓiq al-hizb al-shuyuiᶜi al-ᶜiraqi, 1967. *Kitabat al-rafiq fahd*. Baghdad: al-Tariq al-jadid.

————, 1973. *Mawqifuna min al-masaᶜalah al-qawmiyah al-kurdiyah*. Baghdad: Matbaᶜit al-shaᶜb.

Murqus, Ilyas, 1970. *al-Marksiyah wal-mas'alah al-qawmiyah*. Beirut: Dar al-tali'ah.

———, 1964. *Tarikh al-ahzab al-shuyu'iyah fil-watan al-'arabi*. Beirut: Dar al-tali'ah.

al-Nadwani, 'Abdul Karim, 1961. *Tarikh al-'Amarah wa-'ashairuha*. Baghdad: Matba'it al-'ani.

Nidal al-ba'th; wathai'q hizb al-ba'th al-'arabi al-ishtiraki. Beirut: Manshurat dar al-tali'ah, 1964.

Nuwwar, 'Abdel 'Aziz, 1968. *Tarikh al-iraq al-hadith min nihayit hukm Dawud Pasha ila nihayit hukm Midhat Pasha*. Cairo: al-Kitab al-'arabi.

al-Ridha, Majid 'Abd, 1974. *al-qadiyah al-kurdiyah fil-'iraq*. Baghdad: Manshurat al-tariq al-jadid.

al-Sa'idi, Humud, 1974. *Dirasah 'an Asha'ir al-Iraq: al-Khazai'l*. Baghdad: Maktabat al-nahdhah.

Salim, Shakir, 1970. *al-Jabayish*. Baghdad: Matba'it al-'ani.

Sarkis, Ya'qub, 1955. *Mabahith 'iraqiyyah*. 3 vols. Baghdad: al-Tijara wa-l-tiba'a Co.

Sartawi, Hamdi Muhammad, 1953. "al-Tawasu' fi-intaj al-zayt fil-'iraq." *al-Tijarah* 16 (January): 52–56.

al-Shabibi, 1974. *Min wathai'q al-hizb al-shuyu'i: kitabat al-rafiq al-shabibi*. Baghdad: Matba'at al-sha'b.

al-Shaibani, Tal'at, 1958. *Waqi' mulkiyat al-zira'ah fil-'iraq*. Baghdad: al-Ahali Press.

al-Suwari, Hasan Muhammad, 1955. *al-Iqta' fil-Kut*. Baghdad: Asad Press.

al-Tahir, 'Abdel al-Jalil, 1972. *al-'Asha'ir al-iraqiyah*. Beirut: Matabi' Libnan.

al-'Umari, Sana, 1980. *Intaj wa-istihlak al-hintah f-il-'iraq*. Baghdad: Dar al-huriyah li-l-tiba'ah.

al-Wakil, Fu'ad Hussain, 1976. *Jama'it al-ahali fil-'iraq*. Baghdad: Dar al-Rashid press.

al-Wardi, 'Ali, 1965. *Dirasah li-tabi'at al-mujtama' al-'iraqi*. Baghdad: Matba'it al-'ani.

Zubair, Abdel Razzaq, 1969. '"al-Islah al-zira'i wa-mushkilat al-hijrah min al-rif ila-l-madinah, *al-Thaqafah al-jadidah*, vol. 5, 13–28.

ENGLISH

Abrahamian, Evrand, 1982. *Iran Between Two Revolutions*. Princeton, New Jersey: Princeton University Press.

'Aflaq, Michel, 1977. *Choice of Texts from the Ba'th Party Founder's Thought*. Florence: Cooperativa Lavaratori Officine Grafiche.

Akhtar, Tehmina, 1993. "Thinking the Nation: Historiography, Education, and the Minority Question in Egypt," (unpublished paper).

ᶜAli, Hasan Muhammad, 1955. *Land Reclamation and Settlement in Iraq*. Baghdad: Baghdad Printing Press.

Amin, Samir, 1978. *The Arab Nation*. London: Zed Press.

Arab Baᵓth Socialist Party, 1974. *Revolutionary Iraq 1968–1973: The Political Report Adopted by the Eighth Regional Congress of the Arab Baᵓth Socialist Party-Iraq*. Baghdad: n.p.

al-ᵓAtiyyah, Ghassan, 1973. *Iraq 1908–1921: A Socio-Political Study*. Beirut: The Arab Institute for Research.

Asad, Talal, 1993. *Geneologies of Religion: Discipline or Power in Christianity and Islam*. Baltimore: Johns Hopkins University Press.

———, 1986. "The Idea of an Anthropology of Islam." Center for Contemporary Arab Studies Georgetown University, Washington D.C., March 1986.

———, 1980. "Ideology, Class, and the Origin of the Islamic State," *Economy and Society* 9 (November): 450–73.

———, 1978. "Equality in Nomadic Social System?" *Critique of Anthropology* 3 (Spring): 57–65.

———, 1970. *The Kababish Arabs*. London: Hurst.

Batatu, Hanna, 1978. *The Old Social Classes and the Revolutionary Movement in Iraq*. Princeton: Princeton University Press.

Bell, Gertrude, 1920. *Review of the Civil Adminstration of Mesopotamia*. London: His Majesty's Stationary Office.

———, 1927. *The Letters of Gertrude Bell*. London: Benn.

Berque, J., 1955. *Structures Sociales du Haut-Atlas*. Paris: Presses Universitaires de France.

Blunt, Ann, 1879. *The Bedouin Tribes of the Euphrates*, vol. 2. London: Cass (1968 edition).

Brenner, Robert, 1977. "The Origins of Capitalist Development: A Critique of Neo-Smithian Marxism." *New Left Review* 104: 25–100.

———, 1985. "The Agrarian Roots of European Capitalism" in *The Brenner Debate: Agrarian Class Structure and Economic Development in Pre-industrial Europe*. eds. T. H. Aston and C. H. E. Philpin. New York: Cambridge University Press.

Bruinessen, Martin V., 1992. *Agha, Shaikh, and State: The Social and Political Structures of Kurdistan*. London: Zed Books Ltd.

Chakrabarty, Dipesh, 1993. "Marx after Marxism: Subatlern Histories and the Question of Difference." *Polygraphy* (July).

————, 1992. "The Death of History? Historical Consciousness and the Culture of Late Capitalism." *Public Culture* (Spring).

Chatterjee, Partha, 1993. *The Nation and Its Fragments: Colonial and Postcolonial Histories*. Princeton: Princeton University Press.

————, 1986. *Nationalist Thought and the Colonial World: A Derivative Discourse*. Minneapolis: University of Minnesota Press.

Claudin, Fernando, 1975. *The Communist Movement from Comintern to Cominform*. Middlesex: Penguin Books.

Cook, M. A., ed., 1970. *Studies in the Economic History of the Middle East from the Rise of Islam to the Present Day*. Oxford: Oxford University Press.

al-Dahiri, Abdul Wahab Matar, 1969. *Introduction of Technology into Traditional Society*. Baghdad: al-ʾAni Press.

Dann, Uriel, 1969. *Iraq Under Qassem: A Political History: 1958–1963*. London: Pall Mall.

Donner, F. M., 1981. *The Early Islamic Conquests*. Princeton: Princeton University Press.

Dowson, Ernest, 1932. *An Inquiry into Land Tenure and Related Questions in al-Iraq*. Letchworth: The Garden City Press.

Duri, A. A., 1987 (translated by Lawrence Conrad). *The Historical Formation of the Arab Nation*. London: Croom Helm.

Economist Intelligence Unit, 1980. *Iraq: a New Market in a Region of Turmoil*. London: Economist Publication.

Edmonds, C. J., 1957. *Kurds, Turks, and Arabs: Politics, Travel, and Research in North-Eastern Iraq, 1919–1925*. London: Oxford University Press.

Empson, C., 1933. *Economic Conditions of Iraq 1933–1935*. London: Great Britain, Colonial Office.

al-ʿEyd, Kahdim, 1979. *Oil Revenues and Accelerated Growth: Absorptive Capacity in Iraq*. New York: Praeger.

Fattah, Hala, 1986. "The Development of the Regional Market of Iraq and the Gulf 1800–1900." Los Angeles: UCLA, Ph.D. thesis.

Fernea, Robert, 1970. *Shaykh and Effendi: Changing Patterns of Authority Among El-Shabana*. Cambridge: Harvard University Press.

Fernea, R., and Roger Louis, Wm., eds., 1991. *The Iraqi Revolution of 1958: The Old Social Classes Revisited*. London: I. B. Tauris.

Gabbay, Rony, 1978. *Communism and the Agrarian Question*. London: Croom Helm.

Gallman, Waldemar, 1964. *Iraq Under General Nuri: My Recollection of Nuri al-Said, 1945–1958*. Baltimore: Johns Hopkins University Press.

Gellner and Micaud, eds., 1973. *Arabs and Berbers: from the Tribe to Nation in North Africa*. London: Duckworth.

Gellner, E., 1969. *Saints of the Atlas*. London: Weidenfeld and Nicolson.

Goodman, David, and Redclift, Michael, 1981. *From Peasant to Proletarian: Capitalist Development and Agrarian Transformation*. Oxford: Oxford University Press.

Government of Iraq, 1938. *The Agricultural and Industrial Bank Yearly Report 1937–1938*. Baghdad.

———, 1952. *The Agricultural and Livestock Census*. Baghdad.

———, 1954, 1960, 1962. *Reports on the Industrial Census of Iraq*. Baghdad.

———, 1958. *The Agricultural and Livestock Census of 1957–1958*, Baghdad.

———, 1960. *Land Reform in Three Years*. Baghdad.

———, 1964. *Land Reform in its Sixth Year*. Baghdad.

———, 1969. Report on Active Companies in Iraq 1919–1968. Baghdad.

Great Britain, Colonial Office, 1919. *Administrative Report of the Nasiriyah District for the Year 1919*. London.

———, 1921. *Report on the Administration of Iraq 1920–1921*. London.

———, 1922. *Report on the Administration of Iraq 1921–1922*. London.

———, 1924. *Report on The Administration of Iraq 1922–1923*. London.

———, 1926. *Report on the Administration of Iraq 1924–1925*. London.

———, 1927. *Report on the Administration of Iraq 1926–1927*. London.

———, 1929. *Report by his Majesty's Government to the Council of the League of Nations on the Administration of Iraq for the Year of 1928*. London.

———, 1930. *Report by His Majesty's Government to the Council of the League of Nations on the Administration of Iraq for the Year of 1929*. London.

———, 1931. *Special Report by His Majesty's Government to the League of Nations on the Progress of Iraq during 1920–1931*. London.

Great Britain, 1931. *Report by his Majesty's Government to the Council of the League of Nations on the Administration of Iraq, 1930*. London.

———, 1932. *Report on Iraq for the Period January to October, 1932*. London.

Haider, Salih, 1966. "Land Tenure in 19th Century Iraq," in *The Economic History of the Middle East: 1800–1914*, ed. C. Issawi. Chicago: Chicago University Press.

Haider, S., 1942. "Land Problems of Iraq." Unpublished Ph.D. thesis, London University.

Haj, Samira, 1991. "The Problems of 'Tribalism': The Case of 19th Century Iraqi History." *Social History*, vol. 16: 45–59.

Haldane, Aylmer L., 1922. *The Insurrection of Mesopotamia: 1920*. London: William Blackwood and Sons.

Hasan, Muhammad Salman, 1966. "The Growth and Structure of Iraq's Population, 1867–1947," in *The Economic History of the Middle East: 1800–1914*, ed. C. Issawi. Chicago: Chicago University Press.

————, 1970. "The Role of Foreign Trade in the Economic Development of Iraq, 1864–1964," in *Studies in the Economic History of the Middle East from the Rise of Islam until the Present Day*, ed. M. A. Cook. Oxford: Oxford University Press.

Hasib, Khair al-din, 1963. *The National Income of Iraq 1953–1961*. Beirut: Dar al-tali ʾah.

Ikram, Khalid, 1980. *Economic Management in a Period of Transition*. Baltimore: Johns Hopkins University Press.

International Bank for Reconstruction and Development, 1952. *The Economic Development of Iraq*. Baltimore: Johns Hopkins University Press.

Ireland, Philip Willard, 1937. *Iraq: a Political Development*. London: Jonathan Cape Ltd.

Isma ʿel, Tariq, 1976. *The Arab Left*. Syracuse: Syracuse University Press.

Issawi, Charles, 1988. *The Fertile Crescent, 1800–1914*. Oxford: Oxford University Press.

————, ed., 1966. *The Economic History of the Middle East: 1800–1914*. Chicago: Chicago University Press.

Iverson, Iverson, 1954. *Monetary Policy in Iraq*. Baghdad: National Bank of Iraq.

Jalal, Ferhang, 1972. *The Role of Government in the Industrialization of Iraq 1950–1965*. London: Frank Cass.

————. *Iraq and the Kurdish Question 1958–1970*. London: Ithaca Press.

Jwaideh, Albertine, 1963. "Midhat Pasha and the Land System of Lower Iraq," in Albert Hourani, ed., *St. Antony's Papers*, XVI. London: Chatto & Windus, 105–36.

————, 1965. "The Saniya Lands of Sultan Abdul Hamid II," in *Arabic and Islamic Studies*, ed. G. Makdisi. Cambridge: Harvard University Press.

————, 1984. "Aspects of Land Tenure and Social Change in Lower Iraq During the Late Ottoman Times," in *Land and Social Transformation in the Middle East*, ed. Tarif Khalidi. Beirut: American University of Beirut Press.

Karpat, Kemal, 1968. "The Land Regime, Social Structure, and Modernization in the Ottoman Empire," in William Polk & Richard Chambers, eds., *Beginnings of*

Modernization in the Middle East: the Ninteenth Century. Chicago: University of Chicago Press.

Kelidar, Abbas, ed., 1979. *The Integration of Modern Iraq.* London: Croom Helm.

Khadduri, Majid, 1951. *Independent Iraq: A Study in Iraqi Politics Since 1932.* Oxford: Oxford University Press.

————, 1969. *Republican Iraq: A Study in Iraqi Politics since the Revolution of 1958.* Oxford: Oxford University Press.

————, 1978. *Socialist Iraq: A Study in Iraqi Politics since 1968.* Washington: Middle East Institute.

Khalidi, Tarif, ed., 1984. *Land Tenure and Social Transformation in the Middle East.* Beirut: American University of Beirut Press.

al-Khalil, Samir, 1989. *Republic of Fear: The Politics of Modern Iraq.* Berkeley: University of California Press.

Lacoste, Yve, 1978. *Ibn Khaldun: the Birth of History and the Past of the Third World.* London: Verso.

Langley, Kathleen M., 1967. *The Industrialization of Iraq.* Cambridge: Harvard University Press.

Little, Arthur D., 1961. *A Plan for the Industrial Development in Iraq.* Cambridge: Arthur D. Little, Inc.

Longrigg, S. H., 1925. *Four Centuries of Modern Iraq.* London: Oxford University Press.

Makdisi, George, ed., 1965. *Arabic and Islamic Studies.* Cambridge: Harvard University Press.

Marr, Phebe, 1985. *The Modern History of Iraq.* Boulder: Westview Press.

al-Nasrawi, Abbas, 1967. *Financing Economic Development in Iraq: The Role of Oil in a Middle Eastern Country.* New York: Praeger.

Niblock, Tim, ed., 1982. *Iraq: The Contemporary State.* New York: St. Martin's Press.

Nieuwenhuis, Tom, 1982. *Politics and Society in Early Modern Iraq: Mamluk Pashas, Tribal Shaykhs and Local Rule between 1802 and 1831.* The Hague: Nijhoff.

Omissi, David, 1990. *Air Power and Colonial Control: Royal Airforce 1919–1939.* Manchester: Manchester University Press-St. Martin's.

Owen, Roger, 1981. *The Middle East in The World Economy: 1800–1900.* London: Methuen.

Penrose, E., and Penrose, E. F., 1978. *Iraq: International Relations and National Development.* London: Benn.

Prakash, Gyan, 1990. "Writing Post-Orientalist Histories of the Third World: Perspectives from Indian Historiograghy." *Comparative Studies of History and Society* (April).

Sa ᶜd, Jawad, 1981. *Iraq and the Kurdish Question*. London: Ithaca Press.

Salim, Shakir, 1962. *Marsh Dwellers of the Euphrates Delta*. London: University of London, Athlone Press.

Salter, Arthur, 1955. *The Development of Iraq: A Plan of Action*. Baghdad: Iraq Development Board.

Shaw, Stanford, 1975. "Nineteenth-Century Ottoman Tax Reforms." *International Journal of Middle East Studies*, vol. 6: 421–59.

Simmonds, S., 1953. *Economic and Commercial Conditions in Iraq*. London: Board of Trade.

Sluglett, Peter, 1976. *Britain in Iraq: 1914–1932*. London: Ithaca Press.

Sluglett, Marion Farouk, and Sluglett, Peter, 1987. *Iraq Since 1958: From Revolution to Dictatorship*. London: Routledge and Kegan Paul.

———, 1983. "The Transformation of Land Tenure and Rural Social Structure in Central and Southern Iraq: 1870–1958," in *International Journal of Middle East Studies*, 15: 491–505.

———, 1983. "Labor and National Liberation: the Trade Union Movement in Iraq, 1920–1958." *Arab Studies Quarterly*, vol. 5, no. 2 (1983): 139–54.

Stoler, Ann Laura, 1992. "Rethinking Colonial Categories: European Communities and the Boundaries of Rule," in *Colonialism and Culture*, Nicholas Dirks, ed. Ann Arbor: University of Michigan.

The 1968 Revolution in Iraq: Experience and Prospects: the political Report of the Eighth Congress of the Arab Ba ᵓ th Socialist Party in Iraq, January 1974. London: Ithaca Press, 1979.

Tibi, Bassam, 1981. *Arab Nationalism, a Critical Inquiry*. London: Macmillan Press.

———, 1986. "Islam and Modern European Ideology." *International Journal of Middle East Studies* 18: 15–29.

United Nations Technical Assistance Administration, 1953. "The Social Problems of Urbanization in Iraq." New York.

United Nations, 1958. *Yearbook of International Trade Statistics*. vol. 1. New York.

Warriner, Doreen, 1962. *Land Reform and Development in the Middle East*. Oxford: Oxford University Press.

Wilson, Wilson, 1931. *Mesopotamia 1917–1920: A Clash of Loyalties*, vols. 1 and 2. Oxford: Oxford University Press.

Zeine, Zeine, 1958. *The Emergence of Arab Nationalism*. New York: Caravan Books.

COLONIAL OFFICE REPORTS IN THE PUBLIC RECORD OFFICE (PRO)

FO371/6349; 6350; 6351; 6352; 7801; 7772 (1921–1922)

FO371/12304; 12305 (1927)

FO371/14521 (1930)

FO371/16037; 16049; 16050; 16051 (1932)

FO371/17858; 17869 (1934)

FO371/18945; 18953 (1935)

FO371/20015; 20013; (1936)

FO371/20795; 20800 (1937)

FO371/45302 (1944)

FO371/61595; 61589; 6166; 61690 (1947)

FO371/68447; 68450; 68451; 68467; 68479; 68481; 68452 (1948)

FO371/75130; 75127; 75128; 75130; 75127; 82422; 82462; 82505 (1949)

FO371/91629; 91631; 91632; 91634 (1951)

FO371/98734; 98759; 98784 (1952)

FO371/104664; 104668; 104694; 104732 (1953)

INDEX

ʿAbd al-Nur, Thabit, 45
ʿAbdallah ʿAmir, 116, 128
ʿAbdul Ilah, Regent of Iraq, 99, 100, 101, 103
ʿAflaq, Michel, 90, 91, 112, 117
agrarian land reform, 6, 121–23, 127
See also Iraqi Communist Party; National Democratic Party
Agrarian system, 1, 5, 38
  agrarian crisis, 12
  agrarian development, 10–11, 44
  Agricultural and Industrial Bank, 60
  agriculture, 5, 10, 11–12, 23, 36, 41, 42–53
  and tribes, 18
  commercialization of, 2, 32, 49
ʿAjiba wheat, 44
Albu Muhammad, 25
ʿAli, Hasan M., 33
ʿAmadiyah, 42
ʿAmarah, 20, 24–25, 26, 27, 28–29, 31, 34
  and 1920 revolt, 29–30
  and 1958 revolution, 6, 12, 127
  peasant uprising, 38
ʿAnaizeh, 17, 21
al-ʿAjil, Ahmad, 52
al-ʿAlwan, ʿAbdul Sahib, 51
al-Asfar, Najib, 45
al-ʿAtiyyah, Ghassan, 15
al-Baʾth, 89–92, 108, 109, 117, 138
  See also Pan-Arab Socialist Party
al-Bazzaz, ʿAbdul Rahman, 90
al-Chadirchi, Kamil, 86, 88, 133, 134
al-Gaylani, Rashid ʿAli, 99
al-Hajj, ʿAziz, 115–16

al-Husari, Satiʾ, 90
al-Khalil, Samir, 3
al-Pachachi, Hamdi, 45, 99, 103
al-Saʿid, Nuri, 71, 79, 80, 103
  break with Salih Jabr, 99, 183n.
  conflict with Palace, 99
  Constitutional Union Party, 104
  Kuwait and, 135
  premiership, 100, 106–7
  al-Zuhayr merchants of, 21
Algeria, colonization of, 13
Amin, Samir, 9
ARAMCO, 71
ʿArif, ʿAbdul Salam, 13, 108, 117, 118, 136
Azra Yaʿcub and Company, 58

Baghdad, 27, 41, 42, 48, 51, 57, 58, 92, 124
Baghdad Pact, 107–8
Bani Lam, 25
Banu Asad, 18
Basra, 9, 22, 27, 41, 42, 52, 57, 138
Batatu, Hanna, 3, 4, 15, 44, 118, 119
Bell, Gertrude, 42
Berbers and the "Kabyle Myth," 13, 14, 15
Brenner, Robert, 10, 151n., 158n.
British colonial rule, 5, 12, 27–32, 79, 82
  and agricultural policies of, 44–49 (*see also* tribes)
  and tribal shayks, 29–30, 84, 174n. 2
  government of, 28
  historiography, 14
  modernizing mission, 32, 81–82, 84, 174n. 1

British Cotton Growers Association, 45, 60

capital, in developing countries, 3–5
capitalism in Iraq, 1, 4, 9
Chalabi family, 60, 64
Chatterjee, Partha, 84–85, 143–47
class struggle, 80, 99–101
cotton, 45–47, 60, 63, 68
  cotton export, 168n.
  cultivation of, 168n., 172n.,186n. 9
customary rights, 19–20, 26

Dann, Uriel, 2–3, 120, 188n.
dates, 31, 48–49, 59–60
  date-packing industry, 18
  export of, 31
  production of, 23
Dayr al-Zur, 21
Development Board, 35–36, 37, 56, 72–74
  See also industry
Dobbs, Henry, 28, 29, 174n.
Dowson, Ernest, 48, 49

Egypt, 34, 114
  See also United Arab Republic
ethnic-religious differences, 2, 81
  Mosul revolt and, 119
Europeans, and colonialism, 14
exports of Iraq, 9, 31, 32, 37, 48–49

Fahd, 96, 97
Fatla tribe, 26
Fattah, Nuri, 58, 64
Federation of Industries, 62, 68, 74, 131, 177n.
Federation of Peasant Societies, 124, 125, 127
Fernea, Robert, 3
freehold land, 19
French Orientalists, 13
  and colonization, 13–14, 152nn. 10, 13

grain, 32
  cultivation of, 35
  exports of, 48–49, 161n., 166n.
Gramsci, Antonio, 85, 145
Gulf War, 138

Hadid, Muhammad, 86, 87, 118
  as Minister of Economy, 126
  break with National Democratic Party, 133–34 (see also al-Chadirchi)
  National Progressive Party and, 134–35
  on land reform, 122
Hasan, Mohammad Salman, 9, 43
Hindiyah, 26, 31
Hobsbawm, Eric, 143, 144
Hussein, Jamil, 86, 87

Ibrahim, Salah, 58, 63
iltizam, 18
India, 27, 146,147, 149
industry, 5, 55, 62, 74
  cement, 64–65
  Development Board and, 73–74
  domestic, 56–57, 131–32
  Federation of Industries, 62, 68, 74
  protectionism, 66, 67, 68, 132–33
  subsidiary agricultural, 59–61
  textiles, 58–59, 63, 68
  vegetable oil, 65–67
Industrial Bank, 62
International Bank for Reconstruction and Development (IBRD), 35, 36, 37, 67, 69–70
iqta', 11–12, 26, 34, 37, 38, 41, 46, 49, 50, 53, 55, 67, 70, 74
  commercialization of, 11
  peasant exploitation and, 35
  productivity levels of, 5, 9, 10, 28, 52, 55, 79, 84
Iran, 107, 138
Iraq-Iran war, 138
Iraq Petroleum Company (IPC), 36, 82, 100, 137

Iraqi Communist Party (ICP), 80, 82, 86,
    94, 103, 108, 109, 117, 118, 121,
    126–28, 136, 189n.
  and oil, 94
  and social unrest, 103
  and the national question, 97, 115–16
  and USSR, 93–94, 96
  bid for power, 125–26, 189n., 191n.
    61
  ideology of, 92–93
  on agrarian reform, 97–98, 122–24,
    128
  on colonial rule, 94, 95
Iraqi national bourgeoisie, 62–63, 113,
    115, 116, 117, 130–32
Iraqi nationalism, 6, 82–83, 84
  See also Iraqi nationalists
Iraqi nationalists, 114, 115, 117, 118
  See also National Democratic Party
irrigation, 35, 36
Issawi, Charles, 9
Istiqlal Party, 103, 108, 112, 175n.

Jabayish clans, 60
Jabr, Salih, 103, 104
Jamil, Fakhri, 46
Jamil, Hussein, 86, 87

Kazimiyah district, 58
Khadduri, Khadduri, 65, 131, 134
Khadduri, Majid, 2, 188n.
Khayyun al-Ubaid, 29
Khazaʿil confederation, 13, 26
kinship, 10, 18
Kirkuk, 126, 191–92n. 66
Kurdish Democratic Party, 119, 187–88n.,
    193n.
Kurdish nationalists, 119, 129, 134
  on merger with United Arab Republic,
    119
Kurdish revolt, 129–30, 136, 150
Kut, 26, 27, 28–29, 31, 34, 37
Kuwait Oil Company, 71

labor, 11, 46–47, 55
  division of, 10
  labor strikes, 100–1, 182n.
Land Code of 1858, 24, 25, 42
  See also Ottoman centralization
land reclamation, 73
Land Settlement of 1932, 32, 46, 48, 49, 50
land tenure, 1, 28, 42, 73
landholding, 34
Law for the Encouragement of Cultiva-
    tors to Use Pumps (1926), 47
Law for the Encouragement of Industry,
    61, 62
Law Number 80, 137
Law of the Settlement of Land Rights, 33
lazma, 18, 20, 51
Lazma Law Number 29, 50
  Law Number 51, 49–50
lazma rights, 42
Lenin, 92, 93, 178n.
Longrigg, Stephen, 28, 30

machinery, in agriculture, 51
mandate system, 5, 28, 33, 41
  agrarian policies, 44
  and parliamentary system, 33, 81,
    174n., 175n.
  termination of, 82
  See also British colonial rule
Marr, Phoebe, 2
Mesopotamia, 13, 14, 18, 24, 25, 27
Midhat Pasha, 25, 26
modernization theory, 1, 9
Mosul, 27, 41, 42, 44, 57
Mosul revolt, 119–20, 123, 125, 150
mulk, 19, 41
Muntafiq, 17, 19, 24, 28, 30, 34, 38, 106
Muntafiq confederation, 13, 21, 24, 28–
    29
Murqus, Ilyas, 93, 116

naqshah, 19, 20
Nasser, Gamal ʿAbdul, 107, 108, 112,
    117, 188n.

nation-state (Iraq), 5
    and national bourgeoisie, 85 (see also
        national bourgeoisie; National
        Democratic Party)
    as modernizing agent, 84
    formation of, 81–82
    post-colonial, 116
National Democratic Party (NDP), 82,
    87–89, 91, 103, 108, 109, 117, 120,
    124, 126–28, 134, 136
    and iqta˒, 86, 88
    doctrine of, 87–88
    factionalism, 133–34
    newspaper, 85–86
    on Arab unity, 97, 113
    on land reform, 88, 122
    political entrenchment, 120
    relations, with communists, 86
    to national bourgeoisie, 87, 130–33
National Revolution of 1958, 1, 2, 6, 79,
    109, 111, 136, 144–46, 149

oil, 1, 4, 36, 55, 80, 109, 114, 115
    development of, 70–74
    nationalization of, 137
    oil industry, 5, 55–56
    oil revenues, 5–6, 72 (table), 104, 137,
        162n. 99
    Oil Treaty of 1952, 70, 71, 74, 104
    social change and, 3–5
    See also Iraq Petroleum Company
oligarchic monarchy, 12, 32, 79, 108–9,
    114
    and agrarian crisis, 32–34
    and political crisis, 79–81
    and political opposition, 82–83
OPEC, 137, 138
Ottoman Iraq, 11–12, 24
    centralization policies of 11, 22–24,
        27, 158n.
    land policy, 20, 42
Owen, Roger, 4

Pan-Arab Socialist Party (al-Ba˒th), 82,
    83, 103, 117
    coup, 137

ideology, 89–91
    on Kurdish nationalism, 118–19
    on merger with United Arab Republic,
        112–13
pan-Arabism, 6, 83, 120, 133
    See also al- Ba˒th party
parliament, 32, 33, 146
'passive revolution,' 130
pastoralism, 12
peasantry, 1, 41, 43
    and Land Reform, 190n.
    exploitation of, 35
    Federation of Peasant Societies, 124,
        125, 127, 189–90n.
    flight of, 11, 38
    indebtedness of, 48, 166n.
    revolts of, 36, 162n. 101
    standard of living of, 69–70
Portsmouth Treaty, 102, 103, 105
Protectionism, 62, 65, 67, 131, 132, 138
pumps, 47–48
    investors in, 166n.

Qasim, ˒Abdul Karim, 108, 115, 117,
    118, 125 128, 134
    offense against Iraqi Communist Party,
        126–28, 191n. 63
    on Kuwait, 135–36
    on land reform, 121–22

Sabunji family, 43–44
Saddam Hussein, 137, 139, 148
Salter, Arthur, 70, 73
Shamiyah, 20, 26
Shammar, 17, 21, 52, 120
sharecroppers, 1, 10, 22, 26–27, 46, 52
Shari˒a, notions of, 14
Shatt al-˒Arab, 42
Shaykh ˒Abdallah al-Yasin, 29
Shaykh Muhammad al-Sayhud, 29
shaykhs, 3, 16, 19, 31
    claims to land, 30
    conflicts with tribesmen, 23–24, 163n.
        111
    of tribes, 20–21
Sluglett, Peter and Marion, 195n.

Stalin, 93, 94
Suez Canal, 9, 107
Suq al-Shuyukh, 20, 22, 26, 28, 29, 30, 34
    See also Muntafiq
Swaidi, Tawfiq, 101
Syria, 34

taʿabah rights, 19
tapu rights, 25, 42
tapu system, 26, 51
taswiya courts, 33
textiles, 51, 67
    mechanization of, 58–59, 63–64

tractors, 51
trade, European, 23
trade, expansion of, 9
transit trade, 10
Tribal Civil Dispute Regulation Act, 29, 30, 50, 81
tribal shaykhs, 29, 33, 82
    and 1932 Land Settlement, 33–34
    as landholders, 35–36, 37
    conflict with tribesmen, 37–39 (*see also* peasantry)
tribalism, 3, 13;
    historiography on, 13–16, 147–48, 152nn. 13, 17
    See also tribes; French Orientalists

tribes, lower Mesopotamia, 3, 13–18, 29
    agriculture and, 18
    central power and, 22
    conflict with, 25–27
    economic activities of, 12, 17–18, 21
    Ottoman centralization policy and, 23–24, 158n.
    property relations, 18–20
    regional markets and, 13, 20–22
    relations with towns, 22
    social organization of, 17, 20
    under British rule, 27–31, 33–34

United Arab Republic, 6, 117, 112, 114, 115, 136
United National Front, 80, 108, 111, 112
Uprising, of 1948 (al-wathba), 79, 100, 102–3
    of 1952 (intifadah), 105–6, 108
    of 1956, 107–8

Warriner, Doreen, 51
Wolfra Syndicate, 45, 46
World War I, 14
World War II, 47, 56, 57, 61, 63

Zubaid confederation, 13